A VOICE IN THE

DARKNESS

A Voice in the Darkness

Memoir of a Rwandan Genocide Survivor

Jeanne Celestine Lakin

with Paul J. Lakin

For my parents and all victims of genocide.

FOREWORD

In May 1994, while I was home in Pennsylvania celebrating my graduation from college, surrounded by close friends and a loving family, the most intense and horrific genocide in modern history was taking place in Rwanda, Africa. I remember reading a *New York Times* article about this genocide against the Tutsi people. It included pictures of inconceivable horrors being perpetrated against the children there on a mass scale. At that time, about six weeks into the killing campaign, it was estimated that nearly 800,000 Rwandans had already been murdered, a rate five times higher than during the Holocaust. And although I took a mental note of the vexing paradox between the personal safety and joy I was experiencing and the fear and sorrow those in this horrific conflict were experiencing, I could never have imagined that some of the children who were trapped in the chaos of this gruesome hell would one day become the survivors that would guide me into the deeper mysteries of God and the strength of human spirit.

It was Christmas 2004 when I first met Jeanne Celestine. It was like having a serendipitous encounter with a heavenly being in disguise. She and a friend were coming to stay with me. In preparation for their arrival, I found myself cleaning and preparing my house so completely that I began to chuckle and say out loud, "Why am I cleaning my house like this, as if the Queen of England is coming to stay?" And from somewhere deep inside of me, like a whisper from the Spirit of God, came a response to my heart, "Because members of My royal family are coming to stay with you." In that unique and holy moment, I finally understood the deeper meaning of scripture verses that call God the Father to the fatherless. The King of all kings is serious about being the father to those who are without.

Because God was opening my eyes to the ways of His kingdom, I paid great attention to all that Jeanne would share with me that weekend. At first, I couldn't believe how she could remain so poised and tenderhearted after all the atrocities she had witnessed, the suffering she'd endured, and the scars she carried with her. As the years passed and our relationship grew, I understood the secrets of her soul's extraordinary triumph over darkness.

The book you hold in your hands is one of the most moving testimonies concerning the depth of the human spirit. Jeanne not only gives a human face to the Rwandan genocide by telling her story, but also testifies to the power of how a little girl who depends on God can overcome the most overwhelming odds. Through Jeanne's willingness to share her incredibly painful and intimate story, she enables us to better grasp horrific historical events that are impossible to imagine. But Jeanne goes farther in her journey than simply being a witness to history, she teaches us true courage. As a child, she peered into the faces of hardened killers and displayed immense strength by protecting her little sisters. She was subjected to unthinkable abuse, but through it all she kept a piece of her spirit that now shines brighter than ever.

Jeanne's story reminds us that no matter how painful our experiences may be or how broken our lives and bodies become, there is a God who loves us, who can make beauty out of ashes, and can fashion a mosaic from the broken pieces of our lives. Thank you, Jeanne, for presenting the mosaic of your life to encourage us all to be courageous enough not to hide our brokenness, but to entrust the pieces to our Heavenly Maker for healing and redemptive use.

Having been orphaned as a child, Jeanne now devotes her life to giving a voice to the voiceless orphans and foster children in this world. She openly shared her inspirational story for the good of thousands, and it is my prayer that through this tremendous work, her story will be shared with millions in need of the deeper truths and healing that her story has to offer.

May all who read this book perceive the golden threads woven throughout this narrative of suffering to learn the secrets of how a human soul can possess true inner peace in the midst of utter chaos, remain good while being surrounded by pure evil, and shine as a light in the darkness. The words of French contemplative Francois Fenelon remind me of the type of spirit Jeanne embodies, "Inner peace exists not in the flesh but in the will. We can hold onto peace in the midst of the most violent suffering, as long as the will remains firm and submissive to God despite its abhorrence of the situation."

In May 1994, the cover of *Time Magazine* read, "There are No Devils Left in Hell," the Missionary said, "They are All in Rwanda." But as Jeanne Celestine's story has taught me, even in the darkest of places there inevitably remains those inextinguishable flickers of heaven hidden in a remnant of human souls destined not only to survive but to rise, and one day to testify of the truth for the sake of future generations.

"The light shines in the darkness, and the darkness has not overcome it." John 1:5

—**Kerry Hasenbalg**, Founding Executive Director, Congressional Coalition on Adoption Institute.

Author's Note

I n this memoir, I have narrated incidents and conversations to the best of my recollection. Originally, this book was in journal form. It was a raw image of the events, emotions, and recovery that swirled in me after my parents and relatives were murdered. It is my personal history. Where my thoughts and memories are incomplete, I have tried to present them as authentically as they occurred. Still, memory is far from perfect, and the thoughts and feelings expressed here are mine alone.

I use my legal name and the names of my brothers, sisters, parents, and husband, but many others have been changed to preserve their identity and to protect their privacy.

This book is not meant to be a history book or an explanation of genocide. There are no words to describe the depth of evil in the act of genocide. Its nature stirs both a sorrow and shame so deep in the human spirit that it cannot be fully defined.

Instead, this book is, in part, a tribute to my parents as they passed in a most horrible way and in the most terrible of conditions. They were not allowed a proper burial. There were no grieving faces aside from my own. Therefore, it is up to me to tell the world what kind of people they were: they were simple, thoughtful, kind, and loving. They only had about ten years to shape me into a decent human being, and I pray that they succeeded.

My little sisters, Teddy and Teta, were three years old at the time of the genocide against the Tutsis and were under my care for the three months that we hid in the bushes and miraculously avoided death. When they grew into early adulthood, I recounted the months surrounding the massacre to them, and they thanked me. They said that I kept them alive, but it is they who kept me alive. For my sake, I am grateful they did because I would have never seen the complete lesson pain had to teach me without them.

Introduction

There were around two dozen of us in line that day. The killers gathered us near the refugee camp by the Nyabarongo River. We were withered down to human shells, immersed in fear and suspended in time. A few feet from me, a group of lifeless bodies drifted down into the Nyabarongo River.

I felt like a stranger to this madness, but I wasn't: I had witnessed three months of mob murder, including the killings of my family and other innocent men, women, and children.

One by one, they dragged us out of the line to meet their machetes and clubs, and one by one the victims fell, Tutsis who had been marked for death by their physical features—men, women, and children younger than me.

The killers outnumbered us. Their blood- and sweat-stained clothes clung to their bodies as they took turns with their "duties."

"Remain still," warned one of the hardened men as he pushed an elderly woman to her knees, lifted his machete, and butchered her.

They called for more, and more bodies fell. Soon, the line in front of me evaporated, and it was my turn.

"Let's go!" barked the killer, pointing his machete at me, but I was so frozen, I couldn't even blink.

I narrowly avoided death that day, just as I had the previous three months of the genocide. Not long before this terrifying incident near the Nyabarongo River, I was a typical Rwandan girl, living happily and peacefully in the countryside with my cherished family. But now most of my family members were dead, and my fate was uncertain and dismal.

In 1994, my country, my world, and my family were decimated. An organized massacre was set in motion in April of 1994 by the Hutu extremist government. A propaganda campaign was established to dehumanize the Tutsis; militias were mobilized and trained. 500,000 machetes were imported. All that remained was the lighter to spark the fuse that burst into the mass annihilation of one million humans.

Even though many years have passed since this horror took place, my mind boggles when I reflect on the entirety of the killing campaign. The history, the signs, the mass graves, the screams that still echo in the archives of my memory—it was all so daunting that I had to write it down, partly to process the darkness I witnessed and partly to be a witness as a survivor. Today, I hope my testimony serves as a reminder and a warning to future generations of the damaging and potentially destructive effects of ethnic labeling and the harmful concepts that can be linked with race. Other historical, political, and economic issues were factors in the genocide against the Tutsis, but the most essential and sinister was the systematic stripping of our humanity. One day we were called Tutsis, an ethnic group and a branch of the human family. The next day we were "cockroaches," "snakes," and other pejorative names…no longer human.

This book is about my loss of innocence, the genocide against the Tutsis, the dehumanization of humans—but mostly it's about how I reconnected with the world after this immense trauma.

My name is Jeanne Celestine Lakin, and I am a survivor.

Chapter One

Before the bloodshed in Rwanda, my brothers and sisters might have said I was a reserved person, and that was likely true. For as long as I can recall, I preferred observing over speaking the thoughts in my mind. Although I enjoyed spending time with friends, I was also content being alone. As a young girl, I marveled at the way my mind slowed down time when I watched a butterfly dance from stem to flower or observed a cow blink just before it turned its head.

I was almost ten years old when the genocide descended on my country. It came suddenly, the way a storm moves over a hillside. And when it arrived, everything changed. I saw the change twist in me over the years. It silenced me, it consumed me; it taunted me in the middle of the night when I was alone and sleeping in a stranger's home, reminding me that my beloved parents were no longer here. That's when the silence inside me went from being something I once appreciated to a prison for my soul.

In the months before the killings, it was a different Rwanda. I lived in a comfortable home with a backyard view of the Virunga Mountains, featuring Mount Sabyinyo, Rwanda's oldest volcano and known to locals as "Old Man's Teeth" because its jagged summit resembles the worn teeth of an old man's gum line. In my mind, I can see the entryway of our farmhouse and the path that led to a handful of eucalyptus trees. Anchored past the eucalyptus stood a field of bamboo trees that appeared to spring up and reach for the clouds surrounding the mountain range. Behind our home, sunlight nurtured plots of fruitful land where my family harvested sweet potatoes, coffee beans, and plantains. My motherland was an impoverished but stunning tropical country called Rwanda, also known as "The Land of a Thousand Hills." Yet to me, it will always be the place where I was cared for and cursed, protected and hunted, where silence became oppressive, and where I reclaimed the voice I lost.

As a child, I could not have imagined the carnage to come. Death was unfamiliar to me; the only killing I saw was acted out on the television screen. We treated our surrounding neighbors as friends and part of our expanded family, never fathoming they would become killers.

The nearest houses to ours belonged to my uncles and grandparents. They owned herds of cattle that fed and rested under the warm sun just west of our compound, and beyond the cows stretched a plot of cassava and dozens of pine trees. If I looked in the opposite direction, I saw low-rolling hillsides with four more houses resting on top and scores more livestock, which also belonged to my uncles, all strung together along a private dirt trail. From this place, the wind carried the scent of burnt firewood and purifying jasmine flowers, which emphasized to me that I belonged exactly where I stood. Seven uncles, seven aunts, and many cousins were my immediate neighbors. That was my first community— a family commune within a village, all within a two-mile radius of my front door. So when I think of my birthplace, I am reminded of the people, the love, and security I lost.

My house was less than ten miles from the nearest city, Nyanza, which was also the old capital and once home to our kings and monarchs. My dad worked in Nyanza teaching business classes to the locals. He also owned a clothing store, selling traditional dresses and Western-style attire. Paved streets were scarce, as were streetlights and power lines. Life was quiet except for the occasional noisy motorcycle or bus winding its way down the dusty road that linked my relatives' houses. So noiseless was our hometown that I could hear our cattle bellowing in the meadow behind my house while I sat at our dining room table.

Before 1994, I chased crickets through the hills of our farmland and competed with my brothers at impersonating the sound of the brown-necked birds that lived in the bushes near our garden. It was I and my massive extended family, celebrating birthdays, baptisms, and marriages. I enjoyed family parties and afternoons in the pasture behind our house, kicking a soccer ball with my twin sister. Guests from miles away flooded our house carrying loaves of bread and traditional Rwandan dishes. My parents, especially my mother, were social and well-liked, and our house was never shy of visitors. I never once considered that one day our lives would be in jeopardy.

As a child, I did not know that our many guests were of various ethnicities, nor was I aware of any political conflict in Rwanda. All I experienced of life were from the books I read, movies I watched, my farming community, and the love and connectedness I felt with my parents, cousins, siblings, and playmates. We were protected with limited problems, living as kids should.

Without a lot of modern technology except for a television, VCR, and old radio, our dining area was our main place for entertainment. Our dinner table was not only a place to eat, it was also where I learned to share my ideas and feelings, to love and deal with the troubles of daily life. At least several times a week, my family huddled around our table to play amakalita, a Rwandan card game. What made the game fun wasn't always about winning, but that we children were separated into teams with Mom and Dad as captains. Sometimes I joined Mom's team, but most of the time I took a chair closer to Dad. The game grew exciting when one of my brothers tried sneaking a card under his rear end, which always led to him getting caught. After the cheater was named, Dad sternly looked at the culprit and we shared a laugh. Being together, smiling, joking, and caring, were the moments that formed my early childhood and who I am today.

Although I favored silence, I valued another family tradition called "sharing time," as Mom and Dad named it. Practically every night with few exceptions, Mom and Dad called us back to the table after dinner for a group conversation. During "sharing time," everyone spoke and mentioned at least one thing they were grateful for plus one difficulty of the day. Our shared stories were always about simple schoolyard failures or victories:

complaints such as so-and-so shoved me, so-and-so made fun of me; or victories, like I won a race, or I had the highest score on a math exam. I started out as millions of other kids do around the world, sometimes complaining about my teachers, but ultimately interested in having fun and pleasing my parents.

"Sharing time" brought us together to talk, and I always appreciated the comfort and strength that I received from my family when I talked about my challenge of the day. Whether it was game night, "sharing time," or dinner, my twin sister Jeannette was right beside me. Growing up with a twin sister was not at all boring. Jeannette and I were inseparable. Nearly every day, we played hide-and-seek or dress-up with our little brother Cyiza. For Cyiza, that meant involuntarily sacrificing himself as our fashion model. We couldn't help laughing as we dressed Cyiza in an oversized pink dress, Mom's high heels, and caked his face with blush and cherry lipstick. That was the price poor Cyiza had to pay for having sisters two years older than he was.

We were not identical twins but could pass for each other if we wanted to. Tall for our age, we were among the tallest in our class, and though we were about the same weight, Jeannette was tougher. She was so strong that she could bring a bully to his knees in an instant, and I saw her do it more than once. Back in the third grade, I did well at math, and my teacher advanced me to the fourth-grade level after the initial semester. My first period with the fourth-graders brought unwelcoming glares from my new classmates. That day, as I strolled home behind Jeannette, three boys gathered and teased me.

"Here is the smart one," they quipped as they whirled me around, taking turns nudging me. It was not long before I lost my balance, fell, and scraped my knee on the gravel path. The wound was minor, but when Jeannette saw the tears in my eyes and the blood trickling down my shin, she dashed after the boys like a mother lioness. The boys begged for calm as Jeannette slapped them, and after the dust cleared from their fight, Jeannette pulled me to my feet and we sauntered home arm in arm. "They won't bother you anymore," she said. That was my twin sibling, a sympathetic heart and a devoted sister. I admired her bravery for standing up for me and others. Through all our playing and quarrels, my sister always looked after me, and in turn, I cared for her.

Jeannette and I were not the only twin girls in the family. Fortunately for Cyiza, Mom gave birth to twin girls, Theresie and Therese, known by their nicknames Teta and Teddy, respectively. They were three years old at the time of the genocide, filled with energy and enthusiasm. Teddy never failed to amuse us and Teta was shy and serious. They both were full of questions. In my eyes, they were cute little girls with little button noses and plump cheeks. As she did with me and Jeannette, Mom often dressed them in matching outfits. Jeannette and I took them on piggyback rides to the nearby creek or through the cornfield behind our house. The girls were light and I occasionally carried both for entertainment. They clung to us, never leaving our sight, and at night they shuffled across our bedroom floor and cuddled with us. The girls loved me, and I thought of them as my little girls. Little did I realize how thoroughly I would take on a mother's role in the months to come.

In early 1994, my mom, Speciose Uwimana, was six months pregnant with her eleventh child. She had a reputation for charity in the community; she regularly donated grains, vegetables, buttermilk, soap and money to the locals. Also, she often brought us to the orphanage in Nyanza to visit and encourage the orphan children. I never imagined I would end up as an orphan.

Mom was strikingly beautiful and Dad was her greatest admirer. He once described the moment they first met, and rather than pointing out her sparkling eyes, he carried on about her fingers.

"I was taken with her hands, her slender fingers," he said in a subdued manner. I grinned, and although I did not know a thing about romance at that age, I knew love when I saw it, and they loved each other deeply.

To my parents, community and family were one in the same, and the people in our hometown respected and admired them. Possibly that is why Mom and Dad were so certain that our family would be protected during the genocide against the Tutsis.

5

As a young girl, there was no person I appreciated more than my father. With ten children, our household could change from serene to chaotic in a matter of moments. But through all the commotion, Dad was unfailingly composed. I always imagined he was engrossed in deep thought because he remained quiet unless he had something worthwhile to say.

Just as unique as his wisdom was his height; at six feet and seven inches tall, he was like a mountain. When I stood near him, my head reached just above his waist, which made me feel secure. He was thin boned and wore eyeglasses perched on his slender nose. I sought out Dad's knowledge so often that I shadowed him around the house, seeking his clear thinking on the hows and whys of my young life, often wondering about human nature as I saw it.

Dad called me "Umutoniwase," which means Daddy's girl or "Umutoni" for short. He supported my interest in school and pressed me from an early age to be a lawyer or a physician. On my ninth birthday, he presented me with a lab coat and a stethoscope, announcing, "You have to visualize what you want to be in this life. Live it." With my parents' support and values, I stood out in school, leading my class in scores every semester.

I remember the time Dad nurtured the potential lawyer in me. He stuck his head in my bedroom late in the evening and with a businesslike grin said, "Grab a notepad and pen; you are going to take down notes at a gacaca hearing tonight."

I collected the materials and headed to the living room, nearly stumbling over my own feet. Gacaca is an important event and central to Rwanda's community legal system. Because of Dad's reputation for honesty in our village, he was appointed as a legal mediator for citizens near and far. People who had conflicts over land borders or disagreements over business issues took their disputes to my father, hoping to find resolutions. If the disputes were not cleared up at this stage, they continued to local courts. To my surprise and delight, Dad called upon me to record the statements of the plaintiffs while he directed the hearing! I was honored that he gave me this responsibility and wanted to do the best I could.

When the Gacaca hearing began, the two men in conflict grew loud and animated, bickering and talking over each other and making it difficult for me to write down their conversation. I felt relieved when Dad drew the men back to the circumstances at hand, speaking carefully and calmly, which gave me a chance to catch up. When it was finally worked out, the men shook hands and then Dad's. They left, leaving the two of us alone.

I looked over my notes and realized I had missed a few statements.

But Dad smiled while reading over my notes. "Quite good, Umutoni; you will make a fine lawyer someday."

Like many people in Rwanda, my parents were Catholic, which was common after the Belgium colonization. Yet they were "moderate" concerning religion. If we missed a Sunday Mass, it was not the end of the world. But they attempted to take us to service every week. More than the religious teachings, my parents followed the Golden Rule: treat others as you want to be treated. But the most powerful spiritual message they taught us was compassion. After we saw Mom giving bread to the hungry in Nyanza, she explained her philosophy to us: "If God gave to you, you should provide to others." As it became apparent later in life, there is a close connection between poverty and the disorder and havoc violence inflicts.

Through my young eyes, my parents seemed flawless, and in my heart they remain my heroes. They had faults and moments of weakness as all people do, but the people in our village loved and respected them. The evidence of that is I am still alive. Many times in the days ahead, their influence and past good deeds spared my life and those of the twins.

When I reflect on the days before our extermination, my world was satisfying; you could even say I was a little spoiled. My family was together. There was no way to imagine the horror awaiting us. The coming genocide stripped my body and my spirit, transforming me forever. But even worse, it threatened to break up what I loved most in this world: my family.

Chapter Two

Three months before the violence, I learned about Rwanda's ethnic divide from a teacher at my school. Mr. Theodore, my math teacher, was a fair-minded, hearty man who wore thick black eyeglasses. I always responded to the enthusiastic way he taught our class, adding personal stories when he explained a math concept, like the story he recounted about splitting a candy bar to help us learn fractions.

This day, however, Mr. Theodore looked serious. In the morning, he called for our attention.

"Students! Take your things and come to the front. I have new seating arrangements; the classroom must be divided up by ethnic groups."

Going over his notes on the clipboard, he cleared his throat, finished writing, and then declared once more when he saw me and three others standing still: "Again, I need Tutsis on the left side, Hutu and Twa on the right."

Confused, I remained still with the other students. I wasn't so concerned about switching places as long as I stayed in the first row, my favorite place, where I could pay attention and still be close enough to my best friend Dora. I looked at the others standing with me but they stared at me for assistance. Then I looked over at Dora who was now on the Hutu side.

"What is wrong with you children?" the teacher yelled, scowling at us through his thick spectacles. "Are you foreigners, or are you some kind of aliens in our country?"

I was compelled to reply for the crowd. "Mr. Theodore, I don't know what I am, and I am sure the others don't know, either."

He grimaced as my eyes sank to the floor in shame. I felt stupid, like I had been asked a simple question that I should have known the answer to but didn't.

"Are you pretending that you're not a Tutsi?" he asked.

"I do not know," I replied.

"If the four of you do not acknowledge which group you belong to by tomorrow, then you don't have a place in my school."

He then sent the four of us to the Tutsi side and went on with the class. I'm not sure what the others had in mind, sitting on the Tutsi side, but besides feeling belittled, I wished that I was a Hutu. There is a hollow emotion that accompanies the identity of a minority, especially taking into account that my best friends were with the majority of the class on the Hutu side. I did not understand it at the time, but I had just had my first lesson of segregation in Rwanda's ethnic divide and it made me feel isolated and confused.

After school, I rushed home to learn about my ethnic group. Mom was in the kitchen with our maid peeling sweet potatoes. I greeted her with an embrace and proceeded right to the point.

"Mom, who am I? I mean, who are we?" Now it was Mom's turn to look perplexed. "Are we Tutsis, Twa, or Hutus?" I asked.

Mom placed the knife and partially skinned sweet potato on the table, took my hands, and looked into my eyes. "Who asked you such a question?"

I told her about the new seating arrangement at school, described Mr. Theodore's order, and pleaded for her to tell me. I examined Mom's face as I waited for an answer. She remained hushed, her gaze fixated on the table, while she carefully selected her words. Then answered, "You're a daughter of God, and should not trouble yourself with these matters."

"But Mr. Theodore demanded I tell him tomorrow or else I will be removed from the school."

"When your dad gets home, we will talk about this as a family," she said and hugged me.

Not satisfied, I gathered the issue must be serious and retreated to my bedroom to change. Later, I reenergized myself with the thought I might persuade Mom to tell me. I went back to the kitchen, determined to continue my "assignment," and managed to whittle down her resolve.

"You're a Tutsi," Mom said, finally conceding, and still peeling the sweet potatoes. "But that does not matter because God loves Tutsis, Hutus, and Twa alike," she insisted. Mom's words hit me like a punch in the stomach, and I was worried my friend Dora might reject me because I was not Hutu.

What I did not know until years later, was that classroom segregation arrangements were common. All over Rwanda at the time, schools were divided similarly. The aim was perceived by many as a structure for discrimination established by then-President Juvenal Habyarimana, who took command in a 1973 coup. Many in the Hutu-dominated government thought discrimination could balance the higher-education scholarships and civil servant jobs to match the population. Because Tutsis only made up about 14 percent of the population, the best jobs went to Hutus.

However, it was clear that the Habyarimana government sought to identify all of the Tutsi population in the event violence broke out. If that had been the end of it, we would have been blessed. Unfortunately, circumstances were about to worsen. Before this incident, I had never heard the labels adults gave each other or the tone of bitterness that ethnic titles could have, depending on who used them and the context.

In the coming weeks, I learned that our land managers and many of the smiling visitors in our home were Hutus. My teachers, friends at school, and fellow church members were mostly Hutu. In fact, over 80 percent of the population was Hutu. In my household, we avoided those classifications; I assumed these labels had become inappropriate over the years.

Even when I became aware of those labels, my young mind did not see the visible stereotypes that stood between us: the thin Tutsi nose, the wider Hutu nose; the tall, skinny Tutsis; the shorter and bulkier Hutus or Twa. I found this all baffling. Even though there was resentment around ethnic labels, people looked to get along, at least in my eyes. And because all Rwandans spoke the same Mother tongue, Kinyarwanda, and took part in the same culture and traditions, I assumed all people were neighbors and friends.

The following day at school, I sat on the Tutsi side. When Mr. Theodore walked in the classroom, he started to pace. With one hand gripping his broad chin and his head tipped toward the floor, he paused directly in front of the Hutu students.

"Aha! I see the best students in class are Tutsis," he said, glaring at the Hutu students. "They are smarter than you!"

I looked around the room to see if he was accurate. Sure enough, the top six students in our room, including me, were on the Tutsi side. I expected Mr. Theodore to be proud of the six of us, but an intense sense of unease bellowed from him and resonated around the classroom. We waited for Mr. Theodore to resume class, but he continued pacing back and forth among us, shaking his head, revealing his teeth through a stiff smirk. It looked as if he was making a significant discovery.

"This is unusual, isn't it?" he said, addressing no one in particular. I shifted in my seat, wondering what we had done to agitate him.

Mr. Theodore's pacing slowed as he stooped to pick up a yardstick propped up alongside his desk, laughed, and mumbled something. Mr. Theodore then swung the yardstick against the blackboard; the snap of the stick made us jump in our seats.

"Can't you see?" he shouted. "They are better than you!"

He waved his stick over the Hutu students. "Why is that?" he asked.

The students were too shaken to answer.

"They are few in numbers, but in their brains," he added, still shaking his head.

When we were dismissed for recess, I suspected something was up. Dora dashed by with a group of our Hutu classmates. I approached them, but they did not acknowledge me. When I asked what was wrong, they stared at me blankly. I then stepped closer to Dora and asked her if I had done something to upset her.

"No, you didn't," she replied, not looking at me as she answered.

On my way home, I stewed over the day's developments. It all originated from those ridiculous labels we placed on each other. I regretted that my Tutsi status meant isolation from my friends, but more disheartening events were on the horizon. And the next one, soon to follow, involved my brother Adam's departure.

Chapter Three

"He's gone! Adam is gone!"

The sound of Mom's voice rang with anxiety in the early dawn hour. I did not know where my oldest brother went or when he would come back, but the angst in Mom's voice told me he was in danger.

I wandered into the living area wearing my nightgown to hear the end of my parents' discussion. Dad said something about Uganda and the Rwandan Patriotic Front (RPF). I did not have a full sense of what was taking place, but over the course of the following weeks, I discovered Adam's departure from our home and country caused severe consequences for our family.

My early memories of Adam are positive, but because of our age gap—he was almost ten years older than me, nearly twenty at the time—we didn't spend much time together or talk that much with each other. But Adam was a big brother in the truest sense. The time he saved me from falling off the kitchen counter after a garden snake scared me senseless still makes me smile. He cradled me in his arms and reassured me I would not be the snake's dinner. But in the months leading up to the genocide, he barely joked. He looked discontented with his life. I am not certain what troubled him, but something ignited in my brother and prompted him to leave our family and go to another country.

One night, after our family card game, I searched for answers.

I asked Mom, but she didn't answer me. She simply shook her head and shut her eyes. Dad lifted me up and carried me to my bedroom. My parents remained quiet about Adam and silent about their personal battle with discrimination.

A few weeks after Adam disappeared, I spotted his friend at a store in Nyanza. He confirmed that Adam had joined the soldiers of the Rwandan Patriotic Front in Uganda.

Looking back to 1994, it is understandable why Adam chose to leave; Rwanda's history explains why. Rwanda's political instability and ethnic division stemmed from colonialism. In the 1900s, the Belgian colonials divided and labeled Rwanda's ethnic groups, and this introduced a race-centered social structure. Eventually, Tutsis became stereotypically synonymous with wealth and prosperity, whereas the other groups were perceived as poor. Because the Belgians worked with the Tutsi leadership when they first arrived, Tutsis were thought to be more prominent. After years of this relationship, jealousy and hatred took shape between the groups. Prior to Belgium's involvement, Rwanda functioned peacefully under a monarchical system. In 1959, the Tutsis called for independence from the Belgians and the right to self-govern. As a consequence, the Belgians swung their loyalty to the Hutus. This produced a bloody uprising, which displaced the monarchy. Over the following years, more than 100,000 Tutsis were killed in retaliation. By 1962, when the Belgians left Rwanda, the Hutu government was permanently in position. Tutsis were considered second-class citizens, facing persecution, prejudice, and death at the hands of Hutu extremists. The decades leading up to 1994 were an incubator of revenge. For thirty plus years, radical Hutus favored segregation, which flared up into violence against the Tutsis.

The Rwandan Patriotic Front my brother joined was a conglomeration of mostly Tutsi men and women who had either fled or been forced out of the country since the Hutu revolution of 1959. Many of them were born in exile and hoped to acclimate back into Rwandan society with fair opportunity regardless of their ethnicity. In the 1990s, the RPF was waiting in Uganda, working on a reconciliation agreement with Rwanda's president, Habyarimana, and other Hutu leaders in Rwanda.

But soon it was not only Adam that our family had to worry about.

About a week after Adam left, we found Mom distraught in the living room once more, but this time her concern focused on Dad. Mom informed us two policemen had arrested Dad at his business.

"They have a few questions for him," Mom explained as she placed a bowl of rice and greens on the dinner table.

The four of us, Aimable, Jeannette, Cyiza, and I, gathered around the table asking questions I never imagined.

"Why jail? What has Dad done?" I asked.

Jeannette, on the brink of tears, added, "Dad is not a criminal."

Picturing Dad shackled behind bars was agonizing, so the questions kept coming. Even the younger ones, Cyiza, Michael, and the little twins, recited their worries. Finally Mom set her fork down, cleared her throat, and reluctantly provided more information.

"They want to know where your brother is… and that is all! Now let's be quiet and eat."

The following day, we asked if we could visit Dad in prison, but Mom denied our request, explaining, "Your father doesn't want his children in a dirty jailhouse."

Jeannette and I stepped outside to kick the soccer ball around in an effort to take our minds off the situation. The sun sailed through the fluffy white clouds, birds chirped from the eucalyptus trees, cornstalks swayed in the wind. Despite all this beauty, my heart was heavy and my mind troubled. I lazily kicked the ball back and forth with Jeannette, squinting up at the golden sun, trying to make sense of it all. When I saw Mom in the kitchen for dinner, her face was tight with stress, but as soon as we embraced, she relaxed.

"Your Dad will be back shortly," she said with a faint smile. Even in her pain, she never lost sight of the discomfort we felt at our father's absence.

Just when I thought things couldn't get any grimmer, Dad strode through the front door. With a stubbly beard and a sweat-stained shirt, he came into the living area.

"Dad is back! Dad is back!" roared through the house. I was stuck somewhere between Dad's leg and Jeannette and Cyiza when Mom brushed us back and brought Dad to his favorite brown armchair in the living area. Mom served him tea and a bowl of beans, rice, and beef stew while the four of us surrounded him and spouted questions. After he told us how his colleagues were imprisoned with him, he softened and explained the arrest as a "political problem."

Jeannette asked a thoughtful question. "Dad, you told us only bad men go to jail. Did you do something you weren't supposed to?"

Dad glanced around the room, his sleepy eyes looked for an explanation. He looked at Jeannette and calmly shook his head.

That night, Jeannette and I knelt beside our beds and prayed. With my face buried in my hands, I thanked God for Dad's safe return.

Years after that, when talking to fellow survivors, I learned that these arrests were routine. Before the genocide against the Tutsis, men were interrogated in villages and districts across Rwanda. The purpose of the probe was to dig up information on families who supported the RPF and Paul Kagame in Uganda. My parents were not politically active, so I always questioned why there were numerous investigations at our home. We never learned if Dad discussed Adam's whereabouts with the police.

But later in life, I learned of a significant development that happened six months before Dad's imprisonment. In Tanzania, the RPF met with the Rwandan president to solidify a peace agreement called the Arusha Accords. This arrangement was meant to allow the RPF and Tutsis in exile to return to Rwanda peacefully. But many Hutu in Rwanda's government did not want a peace agreement and were actively working to disrupt it. One of the disrupters was a powerful Hutu colonel, Théoneste Bagosora, an architect of the genocide. Immediately after the peace treaty was signed, eyewitnesses said that Bagosora was overheard saying he was returning to Rwanda to prepare for the apocalypse. In April 1994, a UN officer and

Belgian colonel in Kigali, Luc Marshal, revealed that Bagosora told him that the only way to solve Rwanda's problems was to exterminate the Tutsis. Although the idea of a peace treaty looked encouraging to many, others in the Rwandan government used it as an opportunity to stir up anger among the Hutu population.

Months before the peace agreement was signed, the Rwandan government organized Hutu militias. The militias grew from Rwanda's Hutu population, made up of everyone from unemployed men to leaders in the community. From farmworkers to doctors, the Hutus citizens organized themselves into armed groups called the Interahamwe, which means "those who attack together." With the support of the Rwandan government, the Interahamwe were equipped with machetes, and locals organized meetings in which the paramilitary force gathered to incite anger and stoke fears. Once the killing force was prepared, the genocide strategists in the government waited for the opportune time to light the final fuse to ignite genocide against their Tutsi neighbors. All they needed was to give the Interahamwe a reason to start killing.

Unfortunately, my family would feel the effects sooner rather than later

Chapter Four

A few weeks passed since Dad's arrest, and our neighbors' attitudes grew colder. One day, Jeannette and I greeted our Hutu neighbor, Fatuma, but she looked troubled at our presence. As we walked by, she told us to enjoy our remaining days because we were soon running out of time. When we turned around, she added, "We will take everything you have."

We ran home to tell our parents about our neighbor's threat, but when we arrived, Mom was preoccupied with four armed men who cornered Dad at the door. After running to the back entrance, we joined our siblings by the living room window to watch their interaction. Cyiza worried aloud, "The men will put us all in prison," but Teddy innocently explained that "they only take bad children to jail."

We chuckled but understood the threat present. After a brief while, Mom returned to keep us company. Naturally, the questions started. She looked calm as she answered our questions and convinced us the men would leave Dad in peace. When Dad came through the door, I rushed to him and swung my arms around his waist. He stroked my back and promised all was okay.

Aimable, equally upset, then asked the critical question, "Are they here because we are Tutsis?"

Dad pulled him close, but Aimable wiggled away and said, "We should know, Dad, if they come back and you are not here." Mom and Dad then excused themselves to discuss the issue, and afterward gathered us around for the history lesson we were all dying to learn.

Mom started, "When I was young, something horrible happened in our country: one group of people attacked another and murdered many people."

She revealed that one night, the sound of gunfire woke her. After she stood up, men opened fire at her bedroom window.

"My family," she said, "fled in different directions. It was chaotic, but I made it to a river near my house." Tears collected around her eyes, but she continued.

"I was scared stiff in the dark of night... and when I was ready to leave, I noticed the right side of my body looked pale and wrinkled."

"Why?" interrupted Jeannette.

"I hoped no one would look near the riverbank, so I burrowed my body close to the water for days."

"How did you get away?" I asked, speaking for the first time.

"When the shooting stopped, I went back to my family. Thankfully, they were waiting for me...but the killers shot and maimed many people... even women and children. It was a painful time."

Out of consideration, we avoided speaking for a moment until she regained her composure. When I thought the moment was right, I asked Dad how people can tell if one is a Tutsi or Hutu. Dad reached for his wallet, removed a small card, and held it up for us to see.

"This is an identification card. It lists all our names and ages on it, and our ethnic group is printed here." He pointed to the creased lettering on the card that read, "Tutsi."

"My friend said Tutsis are tall and have narrow noses, and Hutus and Twas are the opposite," Aimable offered.

Dad explained how the colonials had characterized Tutsis as tall with longer noses and Hutus as shorter in stature with wide nostrils but emphasized the flaw in this generalization: Hutus and Tutsis had intermarried for generations, so it was difficult to identify a person by his or her physical characteristics. He highlighted the commonalities Rwandans share: our language, culture, and traditions. Dad also lamented the divisive politics of the time, but promised God's comfort for all Rwandans and stated that all people are equal under the Creator.

"Remember, children, God didn't divide us by race. There is only the human race. But sometimes people choose to split up when they should come together," he said, pulling Aimable and me close for a hug.

I went to bed that night reminiscing about Mom's story and thinking about what a challenge it must have been to experience a genocide. How unusual that my experience closely mirrors hers.

Not long after Dad's optimistic talk about Rwanda's ethnic troubles, disturbing news found its way to our doorstep. A lanky man traveled from Kigali to tell Mom grim news about her brother Emmanuel and his family.

The man shuffled into our living area, twisting his hands, and cleared his throat. "I am sorry, but I am here to give you bad news." Mom looked terrified. "I wish I didn't have to tell you this, but your brother and his family are dead."

We stood in shock as the man described the murders. He said he was on the telephone with Emmanuel when they came for him.

The intruders knocked on Uncle Emmanuel's door. Before he answered the door and set the phone down, he asked this man to tell his sister, my mother, if anything happened to him and his family.

"I heard screaming... then crying," the man said solemnly.

"Who were they?" asked Mom, her voice broken.

The man didn't know who the killers were but said they demanded money, and Emmanuel agreed to pay them. They then asked about his beautiful daughters and mocked him for being a Tutsi. That was when matters worsened. When the killers threatened to rape Emmanuel's daughters, he begged them not to hurt his children. Within seconds there was commotion, and the children ran for their lives.

At this point in the conversation, Mom buckled to the floor, sobbing, as the stranger finished.

"The men decided to kill Emmanuel and his wife first, then the girls, but Emmanuel pleaded with them to kill his daughters first so that they would not be raped, which is exactly what happened."

"What sort of person rapes and kills children?" Mom repeated, her voice strained.

The messenger left while we remained near Mom, rubbing her back. The following day, Mom called the radio broadcast station in Kigali to report the crime, but nothing came of it. Later, I remember my parents suggesting that the government was behind these early killings, but it could have been the Interahamwe. Kigali was changing, and it was because of the Arusha Accords, a peace agreement that placed six hundred Rwanda Patriotic Front soldiers in the city. The presence of Tutsi troops stirred up hostility among many leaders in the Hutu government and the Rwandan Armed Forces. To preserve the peace treaty, the United Nations deployed several thousand peacekeeping troops to Rwanda, mostly in Kigali. Despite the UN's presence, Kigali was a dangerous area for any Tutsi. The Interahamwe groups started the ethnic cleansing days before the government gave the signal. Human rights activists and foreigners left Rwanda with their families, believing violence was unavoidable.

The message was clear: it was no longer safe for a Tutsi in Rwanda. Dad and Mom talked to us about leaving the country. All we were waiting for was Mom to deliver the baby.

Mom slipped into a depressed state after learning about the death of her brother and his family. She slept more, ate little, and barely left the house. Jeannette and I served her meals in bed, reminding her that the baby in utero needed nutrition as well. In this dark time of Mom's life, my siblings and I cleaned our rooms and tidied up our messes without her asking or before she noticed. Sometimes, Mom sat on the couch staring off into the distance. Then one day, she came up with a plan to smuggle herself into Kigali, disguised as a schoolgirl, to respectably bury her brother and his family. While Dad understood her wishes, he discouraged Mom's unrealistic plan, reminding her that Kigali wasn't a safe place to travel and that she was on the verge of giving birth. She needed to rest at home.

Not long after that, on a quiet night, Mom went into labor. As it turned out, my siblings and I were at home alone that night. Dad had gone to meet with our uncles to discuss a plan to safely flee the country. Without an adult to help, Mom called my name in the middle of the night. I followed her voice to her bedroom, where she was on her knees holding her belly. "The baby is coming," she said as I stooped and touched her stomach.

For years, Mom had told us babies leave the body through the bellybutton, so I anxiously kept my eyes locked on her bellybutton, ready for the baby to come out from there. Feeling apprehensive, I asked if I should wake Jeannette, but she shook her head and grimaced in pain.

"Squeeze my hand but be strong; I will hold it tightly."

Mom then asked me to fetch towels and warm water. When I returned, sweat covered her face and she was breathing heavily. I carefully spread the clothes, wiped the sweat from her face, and held her hand as she exhaled heavily. I watched the arteries bulge in her neck while she gasped a few more times. Finally, she took a deep breath and gave one last push, and there he was, a baby boy.

Exhausted, she asked me to pick up the baby.

"Are you sure?" I asked.

Mom grinned. "Are you scared of this little boy? He won't bite, I promise." Mom directed me as I wiped away the slick fluid from his back and arms. "Make sure his throat is free of the umbilical cord," she instructed me.

"I guess I am in charge?" I asked.

"From here, you are in charge!" she replied.

After I pulled the cord away, I asked if the baby was okay.

"He should cry soon," Mom said, and shortly after he screamed and kicked his feet.

I looked down at my brother's face and then at Mom, who joked, "You just passed your first midwife exam."

The next day, the household rose to the chatter of my excited siblings. When Dad arrived later, Mom told him how I helped with the birth, and his face brightened with a smile. They insisted the baby was mine because of the support I showed Mom during the delivery. To recognize my performance, I was honored to give the baby a name. I named him Mucyo, which means sunrise or sunshine.

Unfortunately, we did not have a lot of time to celebrate the birth of Mucyo. Leading up to Easter, conditions were growing tenser in Rwanda. Hundreds of Hutus in our hometown joined the Interahamwe. When the sun set in our area, crowds of these new recruits gathered at meetings and then wandered the streets, shouting out, "Hutu Power!" My parents soon decided that trips to school were too dangerous for any Tutsi child, so we stopped attending classes and started homeschooling.

Just days before Easter, Dad told us at breakfast to be prepared to leave the country and flee to Burundi. He made it clear that we keep it a private matter. Mom was reluctant to travel with her newborn baby and still wanted a suitable funeral for her brother and his family before we left. It had been days since the man informed us about Uncle Emmanuel and his family's deaths, but Mom referred to them in the present tense as if they were still alive.

On April 3rd, we attended church service, and in the evening, our family and friends assembled in our living room to celebrate Easter Sunday. My friend Natalie came with her parents, which cheered me up since I had not seen her since we stopped attending school. As Natalie and I played in my room, I wanted to tell her about our plans to leave, but I remembered Dad had said to tell no one. I then asked Dad for approval to say goodbye to Natalie. At first Dad hesitated, but after several more appeals, he agreed. I pulled Natalie behind our house to let her in on our secret plan. Her family was also making arrangements to leave to go to Burundi, and her parents warned her not to tell anyone, too. We jumped for joy and clapped our hands together, hoping to attend the same school once we were relocated in Burundi.

That was the last time I saw Natalie and that was my last innocent childhood memory. The genocide was about to descend upon us and forever change our lives.

Chapter Five

In the days before the genocide, we were glued to our radio. Like most Rwandans, we listened to RTLM (Radio Television Libre des Milles Collines), a channel set up in 1993 by the Hutu power circle devoted to President Habyarimana. RTLM became a popular alternative to the official voice of the government, and one of its major objectives was to interfere with the Arusha Peace Agreement. They played Rwandan music and invited the public to call in to broadcasts rousing anti-Tutsi sentiment. The station was essentially a propaganda tool for genocide inciters. On the night of April 5th, we listened to the host appeal for Hutus to rise up against their Tutsi friends and neighbors, saying something to the effect that the "Tutsis are making us servants. We must take the first step. We must do away with them all, before they can get rid of us."

Distraught, Mom insisted we turn off the radio and not listen to this instigation. After a tense dinner as we were getting ready for bed, Dad told us the story of "Nyanshya na Baba," about Baba, a brother, and Nyanshya, his sister, who lost their parents and took care of each other even though they were young. I did not give any thought as to why Dad picked that particular story because he had many interesting stories to tell. Ironically, this story was a preview of my future, and looking back, I'm sure Dad had that possibility in mind.

The following day, Aimable and I listened to reports of killings on the radio, but Mom overheard and took the batteries out of the radio and stuffed them in her pocket.

"What if they come for us, Mom? We should at least know when to run away," Aimable argued. I agreed with him. As far as I was concerned, we had heard enough hatred from neighbors and the radio to know there was not much left for her to cover up.

Instead of arguing, Mom led us to her bedroom to pray. As we knelt beside her, she began, "Please God, bring peace to those killing today. Please soften their hearts and forgive them."

When she asked God to forgive the criminals, I opened my eyes and glared at her, catching her eye. Afterward, the sound of feet stomping on the floor drew us to the living room where Kalisa, my father's trusted Hutu guard, hurried through the house carrying a shovel. I wondered why he needed to work at a time like this, not realizing that the shovel was for his own protection.

Mom watched Kalisa leave and said, "It is time you learn the truth. There is a battle for control in our country. And the violence we are hearing about on the radio is the tool for gaining power."

She continued, "We didn't want to talk about this because you are too young to know about the conflicts in our country, but it is happening in front of you."

"Fatuma said they will take everything we have. If they want our house and things, we can give it to them. You and Dad can always buy more things," I said.

"I wish it was that simple," Mom replied, patting my shoulder. "Some of them want more than our possessions."

We spent another night in uncertainty waiting for Dad to return from work. We didn't know that the borders around the country had been blocked off by the Hutu government. Killing squads and regular citizens were policing villages all over the country. The genocide had begun.

The next morning, Dad entered the house, panting and absorbed in his thoughts. It was clear he was shaken by something.

We stopped eating breakfast and gathered around him. "Children, I have bad news. Please, listen to what I have to tell you." Dad told us the plane carrying President Habyarimana and the Burundi president had exploded over Kigali the previous night. He took off his glasses and placed them on the table.

"Oh Lord, did they survive?" Mom asked.

"Sadly, no one on that plane survived," Dad replied. Mom covered her mouth. "Unfortunately, what this means is we missed our chance to go to Burundi."

Aimable and I looked at each other in disbelief. "Dad, are we going to die?" Aimable asked.

Dad shook his head. Wiping the sweat from his forehead, he said, "We will be fine; now listen carefully. I am going to tell you how to get to a safe place." Dad continued, "I wish we had more time to tell you how much we love every one of you. You have made my life complete."

With a breaking voice, he reached for Mom's hand. "Your Mom has been the most caring woman. Thank you for the happiness and comfort you have brought us." Tears gathered in his eyes.

"Dad, you were about to tell us how to leave; now you are saying good-bye. Are we in danger?" I asked.

Dad wiped his tears, "We are. But we will make it. You have to be ready for what you are about to see."

This was the first time I did not have full faith in my father. He took a place in the corner of the sofa with us and described what he had witnessed on his way home from the town of Nyanza.

"There are bodies in the streets, and you will see them, but you must be strong. Do not stop to examine them. You must go on. Okay?"

Tears returned to his eyes. I had never witnessed my father cry before this day, which made the event seem unreal, more like a bad dream.

"The dead are people we know...Tutsis. Men and women. And...some are..." Dad choked. Trying to collect himself, he continued, "Some of the dead are children."

My face heated up as Dad explained the main roads were to be avoided and that Tutsis attempting to cross the borders were being killed on the spot.

"All borders are closed?" Mom interjected. "This is a nightmare," she muttered, shaking her head.

Dad then said our only hope was to remain in the country. Though I understood that he had a plan to protect us, I still felt defenseless, trapped in the type of nightmare you want to forget the second you wake up.

I coiled up in a ball on the sofa, waiting for Mom and Dad to soothe me, but only silence occupied our living room as we struggled to understand Dad's account. I fought to grasp how any human being could take up a machete and kill another breathing human. The afternoon hours that followed felt like minutes.

While Dad sat at the dining table, crafting a plan, Mom knelt beside him with her rosary held in her fingers, muttering Hail Marys to herself. Jeannette and I moved to the window to see if we could spot the killers coming. Even the young ones understood the strange activity around our house. The only one talking was Kalisa. He popped into the living room to give Dad updates on the destruction around our neighborhood.

Sunlight beamed over our garden as patches of smoke drifted from Tutsi homes. The weather was pleasant, but the knowledge of the slaughter taking place at the bottom of those smoke clouds made my stomach turn.

I walked over to Dad and Mom with the intention of telling them how much I appreciated them, but I did not want to seem like I was saying good-bye. Instead, I embraced them. Right then, screams from nearby victims rang out. Dad stood and ordered us in a group for a last meeting before we abandoned our house.

"The militias have lists. And it will only be a matter of time before they are here. They know every Tutsi's name and they are coming for us," Dad said.

He told Jeannette to take the boys, Byiringiro and Kayishima, who were a little over a year, to Ms. Judith, a Hutu and longtime family friend. Jeannette looked traumatized when Dad detailed the safest road to take.

"Dad, are you sure? They are killing Tutsis. Why would Judith defend us or not kill us herself?" Jeannette asked.

Dad guaranteed her that Judith's family would shelter them.

"Children, we will all gather here in a few days," Dad added.

"But, Dad, why isn't Jeanne coming with me?" Jeannette cried.

"My girls, I love you. I wish I didn't have to separate you, but you will be back together soon. It will not be long, I promise. Your Mom and I will check on you after things calm down in the country. Please, girls, be strong, and most importantly, follow my directions and take care of the young ones."

The screams from outside intensified. There was no more time for conversation. Suddenly, Kalisa ran through the doorway. He yelled that houses nearby were on fire, and Tutsis seeking refuge at the Hutu neighbors were being killed. Jeannette left the house with the little boys.

"Jeanne, you, Teddy and Teta will go to Aunt Josephine and Uncle Gustave's house. Your Uncle Gustave is a Hutu and will protect you until this is over."

Next, Dad called on Aimable. "Aimable, you will take Michael and Cyiza. Leave your bags, children, because if anybody sees your suitcases, they will think you are running away and hurt you. If anyone questions where you are headed, please tell them you are on your way to visit your Hutu relatives. Is that clear?"

We agreed, and with those final words, my family set off in several directions. Who would have known that was the last time I would see some of them alive?

Following Dad's instructions, I began to make my way with Teddy and Teta to Aunt Josephine and Uncle Gustave's house.

Chapter Six

Outside, the village was consumed in chaos. Crowds of families, hoping for protection at my Uncle's house, shrieked as neighbors directed the killers to Tutsis in hiding. We ducked out of sight and into a nearby forest that led to Aunt Josephine's house.

After trekking through some thick bush, we came upon a connecting path. We cowered in the shrubs when a man shouted to check the bushes. It was a strange thought under the circumstances, but as we squatted behind the thick shrubs, it reminded me of playing hide-and-seek with Jeannette. When the shouts stopped, we moved on.

There was still plenty of daylight left by the time we reached Aunt Josephine's house. We had left our house before dinner, so we were all hungry by the time I knocked on the door.

Aunt Josephine met us at the door looking disheveled. Her hair was a mess, her mouth drooped open, and her eyes ran through us. I recalled that same expression of confusion on Mom's face after she learned of her brother's death. Even though Aunt Josephine appeared disturbed, I trusted she would keep us safe. Josephine was Mom's younger sister, and they shared a special relationship since they lived closer to each other than their other siblings. Mom even introduced Aunt Josephine to her husband and hosted their wedding. But today, Aunt Josephine did not behave as she usually did. When we showed up, she didn't embrace us or seem pleased to see us. Without a word, she directed us past the sitting area, through the kitchen, and into a corridor in the back end of the house. There we ran into our cousins, two boys, who, unlike their mom, were excited to see us. They hugged us and wanted to know how long we planned to stay so we could play with them.

After a brief chat with our cousins, Aunt Josephine asked that we stay in a small room outside the main house. Entering the room, a wave of muggy air ran over my face. When I leaned in through the entrance, I saw a dozen adults jam-packed into the area. Some of them held children; others twisted their hands and looked off into the distance. I was disappointed; I had assumed we'd have a room to ourselves, but then predicted that Aunt Josephine would return later to show us to our special guest room.

I nudged through the crowd of people with Teddy and Teta behind me and settled in a corner.

The twins sat cross-legged on the floor as I stood over them, looking at the stunned faces around me and worrying about what the night might hold for us. I spotted a boy around my age staring at me from across the room. We traded a gaze, and I wondered what he expected. Maybe he was brave, or perhaps he was like me, panicked that his childhood was slipping away. The only thing I was certain of was my responsibility for the little girls huddled at my feet, although I was not prepared for nor wanted such a duty at my age.

Up to that day, I had always regarded Uncle Gustave as a peaceful and gracious uncle. In Rwandan culture, it's common for children to get spanked. I knew Uncle Gustave never used that punishment on us or his boys, so I viewed him as a fair-minded father. This was possibly why so many Tutsi men depended on him to hide their spouses and children. Although he was Hutu, I couldn't imagine him supporting the killers or their ideology. And besides, his wife was a Tutsi.

After a few hours in the room, I felt suffocated. There may have been close to twenty of us in that tiny room. Everyone stood shoulder to shoulder, and the stuffy air made my limbs heavy and tired. There was no room to move, and people stepped on each other. As the night ticked on, the children became irritable, mainly complaining about the hot temperature and their hunger.

Later in the night, I asked Aunt Josephine to feed the young children in the room. That was when Uncle Gustave entered, bearing a machete. He moaned, shook his head, and then asked everyone to leave. He wasn't hostile or brash, but he was adamant.

"People, please. You can't stay here any longer," he said again and again. "I can't be responsible for you all. Please, go; please, go," he urged us.

At first, no one had the courage to move on. Some protested, "They will kill us...there is nowhere to go." Their worried faces made me nauseous.

"Good people don't die," Teddy said to the crowd, and I asked her to stay quiet.

Uncle Gustave stood by the door until the people filed out. When the room was empty, I reached out to hug Uncle Gustave. When he didn't return my hug, I stepped back.

"You children have to go also," he said.

My mind spun as my heart raced. "Uncle, did you forget? It's me, Jeanne, Teddy and Teta."

"I know who you are," he replied, turned, and left the doorway.

In disbelief, I watched him leave and then wandered over to the girls and asked them to stand up.

Leaving the room, I looked for Aunt Josephine, praying that she would convince Uncle Gustave to let us at least stay the night. But Aunt Josephine's eyes never rose from the ground. Confused, my wobbly legs carried me past the gateway. Uncle Gustave closed the gate behind us.

As we crossed the road, a man nearby begged for his life. "Please, I have money, please stop. I will give you everything I have." Then the man's voice silenced to the thump of machete blades on his body.

After seeing a handful of women running from two men armed with machetes on a hillside not too far from Aunt Josephine's home, I wasted no more time. I pulled the twins into the weeds and bushes that bordered the path. Down the road, in the distance, another Tutsi man wearing a bright yellow shirt was surrounded by militia. *What an unlucky color to wear as you're*

31

being chased, I thought, considering the twins' vivid white sweaters as they illuminated against the bushes.

We were outside less than an hour when a mix of male and female screams bellowed out from near the road. I had a clear view of them as the killers circled around them. I trembled as I watched the victims fall. First the men, then the women. The killers were quick, a few swings each. Confusion clouded my mind as I questioned what the world had turned into. I remembered Bible stories like the Apocalypse, and in that moment, that was the only explanation for the madness around me.

A few hours later, it was too dark to go back to our house but I was petrified to take the main road. With few options, I thought of the cornfield behind Aunt Josephine's house. *The stalks might conceal us from the killers,* I thought. Looking at Teddy and Teta's bright sweaters and remembering the poor man in the yellow shirt, I leaned toward Teddy.

"Let me hold your sweater," I said as I tossed it in the bushes and then went for Teta's.

"No!" bawled Teta as I pinned her arms against her body.

"That's my sweater," they each cried.

"We'll come back for them, I swear. The colors will draw attention from the bad men."

"That's mine," Teta persisted and turned to pick it up. I ran back and picked her up.

Even though I whispered to the girls, they continued to speak in their natural, often high-pitched voices. They were simply too young to understand the madness around us.

After removing Teta's sweater, the three of us snuck alongside the road and into the cornfield. The cornstalks cracked and swooshed as we pushed our way to a point far from the road and a safe distance from Aunt Josephine's house. The rain-soaked soil made it easier to uproot a few stalks and lay them flat on the ground. But the soggy environment was uncomfortable for all of us. Soon I discovered the twins reacted and responded to how I acted. If I acted nervous and annoyed, they became unsettled, broke down, and cried. So I did my best to show confidence and contentment.

After I failed to make them understand why we had to hide, I told the girls that we were on a camping challenge. We had to sleep outside for the night, and if they didn't cry or complain, they would receive a candy in the morning. But the girls weren't impressed.

They whined into the night, their agitated voices taking turns.

"I want to go home," one said.

"I want Mommy and Daddy," the other replied.

"I don't want to play the camping game," the first responded.

I had compassion for the twins, but like any other person, I had a tipping point. "Girls, please be quiet. We'll see Mom and Dad in the morning, okay?"

"No!" they cried in unison.

Finally, in the darkness of night, relief filled me when their exhausted voices hushed. Lying flat on the wet stalks, I pulled their shivering bodies close to mine. Within minutes, they were asleep.

Chapter Seven

We were close enough to the roadblock by Aunt Josephine's house to hear the militia search and question people. After nightfall, the militiamen guarding the barricade retired and silence fell upon us. I took a brief rest and woke to the sound of movement nearby. Terrified, I imagined the noise was coming from the Interahamwe searching the field. Fortunately, the late-night intruders were my brothers: Michael, Cyiza, and Aimable. Like us, they had sought refuge at Aunt Josephine's. When they came across the blockade, they ducked into the cornfield. The six of us managed to sleep for part of the night. At dawn, I was the first to wake up, sitting up on my heels to watch the sunrise. Around me, birds chirped peaceful songs, as if pleading for calm for the day. As the morning breeze evaporated, the sun lifted in the sky and our hiding place shrank.

The sunlight in the cornfield revealed how exposed we were, and we could easily see the bodies throughout nearby fields. After everyone was awake, Aimable and I discussed a plan and quickly agreed to return home. We talked about how those killed the day before were easily caught because they may have looked like they were running from the killers. Therefore, we decided to walk down the trail like normal children with nothing to fear. We headed out, passing bodies on the road and the killers near Aunt Josephine's home.

Not even a mile into the trip, I spotted two groups of men. A small group of three was walking toward the larger group, which was farthest from us. The larger group fanned out across a field looking for victims.

They sang and scoured the area, "Wash away the Tutsi. Let's purify our land," they sang.

Aimable, without turning his head, whispered, "They are coming toward us. Act normal and don't run."

We all whispered back with a "yes," but the closer the group came, the more I wanted to run. However, Aimable was right; there was no way we could outrun them with the younger ones at our side. Even if we didn't have the young ones with us, it was probably impossible to escape such a large group.

By this time, the smaller group pointed at us and began cutting off our path. "Children! Come here!" one of them yelled as adrenaline pumped through my body.

"Don't run...we won't harm you," said another, as if he somehow heard my thoughts.

With every step, my thoughts quickened: *we're going to die, we're going to die. We should have stayed in the cornfield.*

I swallowed hard, and in an instant they stood before us. The first man to approach us crouched down and looked at the faces of my younger brothers. He rested his machete across his blood-speckled pants and searched us for Tutsi features. The other two circled around, staring hard at my younger brothers. I screamed on the inside, *Leave them alone. Please, God! Be with us!*

One of the men crowded Aimable. "These children. Look at these children...if they do not have cockroaches for parents, then I am a blind man. Are you a Tutsi, boy?"

"...No," Aimable stammered.

"Why are you here? And where are your parents?" One of the other men asked.

"...Uh...we...," Aimable stammered on, "We are coming...coming from our Hutu Uncle's house."

The man stared into Aimable's eyes and grinned, "Is that his name, Hutu Uncle? You know, I think your Uncle looks like you." He stepped toward me but continued talking to Aimable. "Long cockroach bones…like these," the man then grabbed my forearm and held it to Aimable's face.

Aimable remained quiet, so the man clutched my shoulder. A burning sensation flushed through my face and muscles tightened throughout my body. *This is it,* I thought. *I am going to die.*

He grabbed my arm, pinned it against a nearby tree and said, "I should shorten this long boned Tutsi." Urine trickled down my leg as I tried to speak, but my vocal cords were stiff. Aimable again stammered something about our Hutu Uncle. And finally, I forced out a word.

"Kayonza," I said barely loud enough to hear. "…Kayonza," I said a little louder. "Our father's name is Kayonza…He is a well-known Hutu in our village." The man looked to his companions. Of course, I didn't even know a person named Kayonza. I remembered the name from one of Dad's folktales, but I stuck with the story.

The man released my shoulder and stepped back. "You're lying, little girl…I think you're cockroaches…but what can I do until I talk to your Uncle?"

"We aren't roach…cockroach!" one of the twins replied. I cringed at her declaration, but by this time, the larger group had started a commotion, yelling and waving for the smaller group's attention. Down the trail, the large group had circled around a handful of Tutsi men, yelling, "Tutsi snakes! Tutsi snakes!" The men questioning us dashed toward the commotion. Once they joined, the killers proceeded to kick and beat the Tutsis with clubs. Seeing our opportunity, we rushed off the trail and into the bushes. The intensity of the screams from the Tutsi men gave me goosebumps. By the time the victims' cries were silenced, we were safely walking in the bushes to a nearby forest.

Going over the incident in my mind, I regretted lying to the killers. Looking back, I know it was absurd to feel remorseful for lying to save our lives, but our parents raised us to be honest, especially to adults. Little did I know this was the first of many lies I'd have to tell to overcome death.

But for now, I was more focused on finding a safe haven and taking care of the twins.

"WHY IS EVERYONE crying?" Teddy asked, incapable of making sense of the screams drifting into the forest.

I left the question unanswered, so Teddy turned to ask Teta, who was eager to answer. "They are ...are sad because they slept outside."

I gave them a slight smile. Even though our world had gone mad, their innocence brightened me up, and a break from my cloudy thoughts was exactly what I needed at that moment. After surviving the killers on the road, the six of us hiked into a nearby forest, using its cover to rest and discuss a strategy to get home. Aimable and I differed over who should look after the girls. I wanted to switch and look after the older boys while he argued that Dad had arranged for the girls to stay with me. When the twins caught on to our dispute, they burst into tears, and I quickly agreed to continue as their guardian. By the end of our conversation, we decided it was best to break into two groups, as Dad had originally planned for us. This time, Aimable opted to go where Dad had sent Jeannette and I would return home with the twins hoping to find Mom and Dad there. After the boys left, the girls and I rested a bit longer while I contemplated the chances Aunt Josephine would take us back. After more thought, it seemed more reasonable to find Mom and Dad. *Once they learned that things didn't work out with Aunt Josephine, they may arrange for us to stay with another Hutu they trusted.*

We advanced through prickly bushes and dense wilderness. As we delved deep into the wilderness, the thorny branches were inescapable and left their mark on the twins, who whimpered and pointed at the blood trickling down their shins. After frequent stops and plenty of coaxing, we neared the edge of our village, where carnage had taken place on the hills near our house. Bodies were scattered along the hills like fallen leaves under a tree. I attempted to distract the twins' attention away from the dead, but it was hopeless; some of the dead were just feet away.

"Why is she sleeping outside?" one of the twins asked as we passed a young woman's body.

"She's resting...let's be quiet," I replied.

We progressed alongside our coffee field until I froze in my tracks at the sight of a man lying still at the base of a tree. I walked beside him and noticed his green shirt was sliced open, revealing the wounds in his back. He was the first victim I saw close up. The deepest wound stretched a few inches near his hairline and stopped at his nose. His flesh was turned upward revealing bones, and some of the blood that seeped from his face had dried in his hair and ear. I can't recall what I said to the girls; I just pulled them forward toward the edge of our coffee plants.

As we passed the final trees, we came within a stone's throw of our house. Standing in what would be our backyard was an armed man facing our house. The man immediately looked familiar, but I couldn't be sure until I saw his face. He turned, and I was relieved when I saw it was Kalisa, our house guard.

"Kalisa!" shouted the twins and tried to run to him; I reached for their arms to stop them. After our experience with Aunt Josephine and Uncle Gustave, I wasn't sure whom to trust, but Kalisa wasn't just our house guard; in our eyes, he was a family member despite his identity.

The girls bounced with excitement as I tried to calm them. After several steps closer, I noticed Kalisa was attempting to quietly tell me something. He was mouthing a message, and he gestured toward the ground. I assumed he was signaling us to duck down, but I took one more step toward him anyway. That's when a commotion stirred in our house, and I understood Kalisa wanted us to hide from the men in our home. I snatched the twins by their wrists and yanked them into one of our bushy banana plants and cupped my palm around the girls' mouths to silence them. But I was too slow. A man shouted, "Three baby cockroaches are in the garden." Whoever saw us rallied the others and they agreed to track us.

The girls pulled at my fingers and attempted to talk against my palms.

"I will let you hold Mucyo if you're quiet," I whispered. "Be quiet, okay?"

The girls smiled against my palms at the mention of Mucyo. I had saved the promise of seeing Baby Mucyo all day, knowing the girls would do anything for a chance to hold him. The bush swayed as someone passed by. I held my breath. To my relief, the man moving the bush was Kalisa.

The killers fanned out across the field and encouraged each other to, "Kill those little snakes." As their voices swelled, I fought the urge to stand and beg for our lives. Kalisa must have anticipated my angst because he whispered to stay calm as he pretended to search our bush while misdirecting the others. After a little longer, a man came back and described our clothes to Kalisa, lamenting that baby cockroaches were still alive in his village. Without moving, I gave the girls a look that said we were in danger and not to move; they obeyed.

We lay still until the men gave up and went back into our house.

"Get up!" said Kalisa. "Get up and go…and never come back here."

I stood and helped the twins out of the bush. "Where will we go? I came here because I did not know where else to go."

"I don't know," he said sadly. "There is no place safe for Tutsis right now. Just go!"

I wanted to ask him if he had seen or spoken with our parents, but he rushed us away. All the while, I worried Mom and Dad might have been inside our house. *If they were inside, their chances of survival were slim.* The only confidence I had was in Hutus like Kalisa. He spared our lives, and I am forever grateful to him.

We departed; however, this was not the last time we returned home looking to find safety and Mom and Dad. But our immediate goal was to find a hiding place.

BETWEEN MY PARENTS' and Aunt Josephine's house is a vast area of rural land. It was mostly untraveled if you stayed off the main trail that connected houses on the hillsides. Nyanza sat to the east of our house, but it was another dangerous area for Tutsis because of the military presence and high prevalence of Interahamwe groups. Without any immediate alternative, we hiked a good distance into the forest and reached a narrow river, settling into a temporary hiding place. Towering plants with soft branches covered in almond-shaped leaves grew plentifully along the river's edges and were useful as a makeshift shelter for us.

I wandered around to familiarize myself with our new environment. In my mind, I visualized our distance to the closest houses and estimated how much time we'd have to run if someone snapped through the nearby bushes. I decided to make our hideout a little more comfortable, so I weaved long, whip-like branches together to make a crude bed.

The girls finally found a flash of pleasure thanks to berries I had discovered near the river. Sitting cross-legged, I watched them devour the tiny berries. Teta even choked, packing a handful into her mouth at once. After the girls finished, I went back to the river's edge and gathered several more handfuls for myself. I also packed more in my pockets for later that night. Although some of the berries were sour, it was a relief to have a source of food. When I returned, the twins laughed and rolled about, lost in the moment as only toddlers can. It was encouraging to watch them be children again. Once more, it helped ease the pressure off me.

When the girls were bored of playing, I walked them upriver to scoop a few handfuls of water. I had never drunk river water and I recalled being warned by my parents not to drink water from a pond. But we had no other options. Despite its brown color, the water cooled my dry throat. I then took turns holding the girls over the bank of the river so they could quench their thirst, too.

When the sun descended, I collected more berries and entered our fort for the night. Throughout the day, the twins seemed content sitting in the bush but when they realized they had to sleep there, they resisted. After a good while, they came to terms with their bed for the night and lay down beside me. When the twins nestled against my torso, shivering, I regretted leaving their white sweaters behind. My skirt and long-sleeved shirt were all we had for warmth. The three of us rolled and turned throughout the night. The sound of the water, the breeze against the leaves, and the insects' noises disturbed us all night long. I lay awake with the anxiety of sleeping in the middle of the wilderness weighing on my mind.

In the morning, I brought the girls back to the river to wash their faces and drink, then gathered more berries. We spent the early day tossing rocks in the river. As we continued to throw them, an occasional whiff of smoke caught my attention. When we returned to our bush, the odor was stronger. Within a few minutes, a veil of smoke rose above the trees. I guessed the fire was near the path connected to the nearby houses. Hesitant to abandon our new bush, we sat by the river and finished our berries until the high pitch of whistles caused me to stand in angst. Hoping whoever blew the whistle would stop, I remained fixated on the trees where the smoke had floated from, placing my index finger over my lips to silence the twins. But the whistler blew louder, clearer, and the bushes upriver swayed and snapped. A squad of Interahamwe slashed their way through the thickets attempting to flush out hiding Tutsis with the smoke. They quickly saw us, and the men cut the bushes faster, while others jumped over shrubs and ran toward us.

Aware that I couldn't escape these men on foot, I looked at the rushing river and then back. The girls would never have agreed to jump into the river, so instead of preparing them, I picked up one of the girls and swung the other on my back. "Hang on tightly," I ordered, backed up a few steps and took a jogging leap into the river. The chilly water must have startled the girls because they slapped the back of my head and scratched my neck. With the twins sobbing, I managed to keep the three of us afloat, and the current helped to propel us along. A few of the men hurried alongside the riverbank.

One of them cursed at us and threatened that if we kept swimming, he would kill us slowly, but I swam on. They pursued us but the shrubs along the riverbank slowed them down. When the current eased, I floated to the opposite bank and looked upriver. The men had given up and marched back to where the fire had been set.

Later, as I twisted water out of the twins' dresses, I smirked. Outmaneuvering the men left me with a sense of conquest, an emotion I dwelled on for most of the day. In the evening, we found another bush farther downriver and away from the burned portion of the forest.

Unfortunately, there were no berries or edible plants nearby, and our stomachs grumbled throughout the night.

The next day, we resorted to eating flowers and even the tall grass abundant in the area. Though we had three close calls with killers, hunger overpowered my fear and propelled me to take another chance that someone would help us.

Chapter Eight

As I scavenged for edible plants the following day, I thought a lot about Uncle Gustave's father, Fideli, a wise and cordial man. I was confident he'd feed us and hoped he would have news about Mom and Dad, or at the least help me find them. As we prepared to leave our hideout, I removed my shirt and wrapped it as a harness to support one of the twins on my back while I took the other in my arms. To reach Fideli's house, we passed another river and a paved road, managing to avoid Interahamwe's barricades that was set up nearby. The area was more densely populated with homes and compounds, all in close proximity to each other.

The village bustled with activity when we snuck through Fideli's gate and knocked on his door. He was armed with a machete when he opened his door, but welcomed us with the compassion and kindness that I expected. Surprised and saddened over our dirty clothes, he asked if anyone else traveled with us. I assured him it was only the three of us. Hoping he would offer us a meal, I described the past few days. He ushered us into his kitchen and handed us pieces of cassava and beans, and cups of water. Although it was a small gesture, it meant the world to me. Other than Kalisa, Fideli was only the second Hutu to show us compassion. Thankful, we accompanied him through his house to a back room. Inside stood five women and a couple of men, with the children huddled together under a table that was in the middle of the room. We squeezed below the table with the other children.

As we settled under the table, violence erupted outside Fideli's home. Firearms periodically popped off rounds as screams arose and then quieted. Several explosions erupted, along with more guns discharging and then another outpouring of screams from the wounded. With every blast, my body jumped and my heart thumped. When bullets tore at the dirt near Fideli's house, I looked at the faces of the adults. They all looked scared and confused. The sounds of murder lingered for hours. Minutes seemed like hours and hours seemed like days.

As nightfall came, I dozed, but sleep was out of the question. The space was so crowded that once people settled, no one wanted to move. Apart from Teddy and Teta, the room was silent in terror, yet the girls continued a series of grievances:

"I am still hungry."

"It's hard to breathe."

"It's too hot."

"He stepped on my leg."

"Please, quiet those spoiled kids," others said. "They will get us killed."

That night, some left the room to seek sanctuary elsewhere and created space for others. I slouched against a girl around my age. I didn't speak to her, nor did I say much to the others in the room. We sat in a trance, staring at the walls as the night slipped by.

At dawn, Dad's oldest brother, our Uncle Edward, arrived at Fideli's house. He was accompanied by two other men who were all soaked in rainwater. After a hushed conversation with Fideli in the hall, Uncle Edward entered the room, wringing his hands and staring at the floor. I waited for him to settle down and then pressed my way past the others near the door where he stood.

"Uncle, what is it? What's wrong?" I asked.

Uncle Edward remained silent, clearly distraught.

"Please, Uncle. You are worrying me."

"It is better you do not know," he said, still wringing his hands in angst.

"Uncle, please!" The feeling that he knew something horrible had happened caused tears to form in my eyes. "Is our family okay?" I asked.

He raised his palm to his head, then placed them over his mouth. He wiped the rain from his forehead, and said, "I have seen…" He stopped, closed his eyes, and clung to my arms.

"I have seen your Mom's dead body. They killed her."

With those words, my world shattered. Uncle Edward explained that he had been with my Dad and other Tutsi men and women on a nearby mountain the day before. They fought for their lives as Interahamwe and government soldiers shot at them from the bottom of the mountain. Then his face flattened and his voice lowered as he explained his departure from the mountain. He described how women and children ran in all direction and some hid in a banana plantation nearby. This was where Mom and a multitude of others were running when they were killed. He hastily looked over her body but later realized our three-week-old little brother, Mucyo, might still be alive wrapped in mom's swaddle band, known as "ingobyi" in Kinyarwanda. For the first time in my life, Uncle Edward bent down and hugged me tightly as I sobbed against his stomach. He had never been an affectionate man but in that moment, he knew I needed to be hugged.

Some people in the room noticed our exchange and offered condolences as I searched for a place in a corner, away from the twins, to release my tears.

At some point, Uncle Edward came over and hugged me again. He told me he was returning to the banana farm and would tell my dad, if he saw him, that the twins and I were safe. I thanked him and he reminded me to do my best to take care of the girls. Uncle Edward had a wife and five children of his own, all in their late twenties and early thirties. I couldn't bear to ask him about his family. I was afraid to learn the sad truth.

After drying my tears, Fideli walked in the room to update us on the threats outside. He warned us that his neighbors were suspicious because many women and children came in and out of his house. We had used his only bathroom, a squat toilet located outside his home, and that was how they knew we were there. When his neighbors pounded on his door with machetes in their hands, Fideli told us to avoid using the bathroom outside. And to avoid putting everybody in danger, the children were instructed to urinate on the floor.

Uncle Edward gave me just enough hope to consider searching the banana plantation for Baby Mucyo. I prepared a plan to keep Baby Mucyo alive in case I found him. Dealing with Teddy and Teta was tiresome, and I accepted it would be challenging, if not impossible, to care for an infant in this environment. But I had to try. If I recovered him, I planned to take him to Aunt Josephine's house and place a note in his pocket explaining that this child belonged to Josephine's deceased sister, our mom. I had it thought out: *I would knock on the door and then run once someone answered. No matter how hardened their hearts had grown, they could not allow an infant to die on their doorstep,* I assured myself.

At this point, Uncle Edward had been gone for several hours. Fideli entered the room for the last time. He told us his neighbors were taking part in the slaughter and accused him of hiding Tutsis in his house. They threatened that he better be rid of us by the time they searched his home or he should be prepared to clean up our remains. Fideli, with a saddened expression, asked the women and children to leave.

We allowed his words to sink in, and some attempted to delay the inevitable. I stood and took the twins out of the house. There was a window of silence outside so it seemed like my best opportunity to get out, and I could no longer delay my quest for Baby Mucyo. Fideli led us out, and I thanked him for his protection. He modestly bowed his head.

Fideli was among a minority of moderate Hutus who, despite the arduous conditions and the threat to their lives, risked their own safety to protect others. He did not give up his humanity.

Then my search for Baby Mucyo began in earnest.

LESS THAN FOUR miles from Fideli's residence stood the farm where Uncle Edward had spotted Mom's body. I was familiar with the area, as my Grandpa's and Uncle's houses were close by. We crawled up a steep ridge neighboring our family's eucalyptus forest and trudged along a stream, all the while feeling anxious at the sight of dead Tutsis in the area. I worried for my own sanity at the psychological damage I thought I would experience after witnessing Mom's remains. Still, I soldiered on as my private conflict persisted, trying to convince myself at times to abandon the idea of rescuing my infant brother altogether.

I resisted my angst and focused on my baby brother's face full of life again, knowing Mom would want me to protect him. This thought brought up my most recent memories of Mom, how strong she was when Dad was in jail and her willingness to help others. I recalled our last night at home together as she stood over my bed, covering me in my blanket and soothing me with her reassuring smile. My mind drifted to the night I helped her deliver Baby Mucyo, and the appreciative and proud way her face glowed afterward. Mom and Dad had declared Mucyo my boy. At that moment, I let the idea of him as my baby sink in a little longer. This reminder was the biggest push I needed to carry on with my plan to save him.

We rounded the mountain where Dad, Uncle Edward, and the others had struggled for their lives the night before and reached our family's vast forest. There were dozens of pine trees that blocked us from the sight of the Interahamwe on the mountain. I proceeded, wandering between trees and pausing at any sound. Distracted, the twins stopped and looked at a family of birds and wildflowers. We eventually made it out of the forest, feeling exposed as we entered a clearing.

After passing through shrubs, I caught sight of a man lying face down. I asked Teddy and Teta to linger behind me as I moved closer to look over the body and immediately recognized the man's khaki pants and long-sleeved, dark-blue shirt. Upon stepping closer, I confirmed the dead man was our Uncle Edward. Blood pooled around his skull and mixed with the soil and grass to form a murky puddle. His murderers had cracked his head open between two enormous boulders that lay beside him. I stood over him, chilled, and questioned who could viciously murder a man so old.

It seemed like I stood over him for a long time, but I couldn't be certain because of how shaken I was to see him lying there dead after talking with him just hours before.

"Come on, girls," I finally spoke. "Come this way, but don't look over here."

I lingered in front of Uncle Edward's body, obstructing their view as they strolled down the pathway, but Teddy promptly recognized him.

"Uncle Edward! Uncle Edward!" she announced.

"No, girls… Uncle Edward is napping. Let him be," I said, pushing them along.

"Why is he asleep in the mud?" Teta asked.

"I am not sure," I answered.

"We can wake him up so he can sleep in his bed," she insisted.

Unsure of how to counter, I replied, "Uncle Edward can't wake up right now. He is safe, and I am sure he is ok there."

We finally moved on and into our Grandpa's cornfield, a place where lots of pleasant childhood memories had formed.

As we rested, we ate raw corn and peas. We listened for the Interahamwe, hearing screams carried through the farms. We quietly sat in the garden and waited. After an hour or so, there was complete silence, and then I stood and checked the area. Finding it clear, we left the farm and moved toward the banana plantation where Uncle Edward said Mom and Baby Mucyo were. As we approached the center of the banana farm, it grew tougher for the twins to pass through, as bundles of banana stalks lying on the soil made it difficult for them to navigate. Every time an obstacle stood in their path, I picked them up and carried them over it.

We advanced, but the more we walked, the bloodier the banana farm became. Besides Uncle Edward's body, there were at least ten others, mostly women and children. It was clear the victims were scrambling for their lives by the way they divided themselves. There was no way to shield Teddy and Teta from seeing the horror. It was spread in the open, right before their eyes. I grimaced and looked away, but the twins were inquisitive about these dead people and wanted to look at each one of them. They had many questions. I did not have explanations and ignoring them wasn't enough. The plain answer was, "They are dead," but then I would have to explain what death was. What I came up with was, "Girls, all these people are out here because their houses are no longer safe." Then they asked, "Why do they have blood everywhere?" Again, without a good explanation, I ignored the questions and insisted we go on.

The farther we traveled, the more dead bodies we discovered. Worrying that the twins would be mentally scarred for life after viewing dismembered children and their mother's lifeless body, I led them back to the area where we had eaten our meal of corn and peas near Grandpa's garden.

I sat the twins down near a section of clustered trees and promised to return with Baby Mucyo. At first, they refused and demanded to come with me, but I insisted they would hold Mucyo and play games with him when I returned. Their large brown eyes gleamed as they agreed to stay.

"We can play with Baby Mucyo all day?" Teta asked.

"Yes, all day, I promise. Just don't move, okay?" To make sure they understood not to move out of the bush, I asked again, "You want to hold your brother, right?" They nodded and smiled once more. "If you leave from this spot, I won't allow you to hold Baby Mucyo, do you understand?" While sucking on their little fingers, they nodded their heads in acknowledgment.

I sprinted back to the banana farm and searched the group of women and children. Mom wasn't among them, nor did I hear a baby cry. As I went on down the trail, there were more bodies; I couldn't even estimate how many. Flies buzzed everywhere. I walked back and forth down the path, delicately stepping over the dead as I examined their bodies and skin. Mom was light skinned, so I looked at the victims' arms first, hoping to escape staring straight into their faces.

I continued on, then recognized a woman dressed in a yellow blouse. It was the same type Mom had worn when we fled the house. I stood over her, cautiously inspecting her skin and clothes. It was my beautiful Mom. I studied her wrist to see if she had on her gold watch, which she did. The side view of her face showed against the dark soil, which made her look to be in a peaceful sleep. I stooped and stretched across her body to pick up Baby Mucyo, who was covered in a swaddle band, or a satchel, on her back. The satchel was steeped in blood. Inside were the remnants of Baby Mucyo.

I stumbled back to my knees as the banana trees spun around me. I closed my eyes. A shooting pain pierced the side of my abdomen, and it felt as though someone was choking me. With my eyes filled with tears, I gently caressed my mom's shoulder and mumbled with a trembling voice, *I love you. You were the sweetest, most loving mother. I will miss you with all my heart. I will watch over the twins and work to keep them innocent, and I will always try to make you proud.*

I pulled Mom's traditional wrap out from under her and covered their bodies as best as I could.

I love you, Baby Mucyo. It was a privilege to help bring you into this world. You are now an angel in heaven, and I promise we will meet again.

I stared up between the banana leaves at the cloudless sky and pleaded to God. *Please welcome them into paradise so they both sleep in peace.*

I gradually stood up and wandered back toward the area where I had left the twins. I came upon them lingering in the same place, still sucking their stubby fingers.

"Where is Baby Mucyo?" they asked. I searched for the most suitable answer and decided there was not an appropriate response to this question.

We came together at the foot of the banana farm in the bush where we rested for the remainder of the day. When night fell, we left the bush, but the twins continued to ask about Mucyo. Finally, I squatted down in front of them so they could make out my face.

"He is in a safe place," I said, "and eventually you will see him, but not today."

Teta folded her tiny arms around her torso and demanded, "Why not today? You promised," she cried.

I was emotionally and physically exhausted. I wanted to find a hiding spot where we could remain longer than a few days. I thought of several bushes where we could set up our new hiding place. For protection, the bush had to be isolated and thick, an area that would be a lot of trouble for the Interahamwe to get through. After thinking for a while, I chose an area near a neighbor's farm, trusting that at some point I could get the twins their next meal. The houses near these farms were about a half-hour hike, so I decided it might be safe.

And so began our life hiding in the bushes.

Chapter Nine

We changed our location, moving from one bush to the next. In the following days, nightmares about Mom and Mucyo often roused me in the middle of the night, causing my heart to thump. What protected me was the tireless reminder that the rest of my family was alive someplace, and one day, the three of us would be reunited with Dad, my siblings, and our other relatives.

I wondered if Dad knew about Mom and Mucyo, and questioned how my siblings might deal with their deaths. But mostly I worried how Dad would get along without Mom. He loved her profoundly and as far as I knew, they were soul mates. If Dad did not know this terrible news, I feared the prospect of telling him about it. I even imagined keeping it a secret to protect him.

As the days ticked by, I improved our bush home. The twins watched in bewilderment as I yanked bushes away at the roots and stacked branches with lush, smooth leaves for us to sleep on. As toddlers do so well, they asked more questions.

"When are we leaving here?" one questioned.

Before I could respond, the other would usually comment. "We have been here for a long time."

"Girls, it is not safe at our house," I responded, "but I swear, I will get us out of here as soon as it is safe."

"Let's go and check if it is safe," suggested Teta.

"It's safe. Can we check now?" replied Teddy.

I warned them of the people screaming in the hills, plains, and ridges, and the suffering people they saw throughout the day.

"There are mean people out there who want to hurt us," I added, "and as long as you hear screaming, it is not safe. When they stop, we will go home."

On one occasion, Teta said something that struck me. "The bad guys only kill bad children and ...and... bad people," she announced.

"Jeanne, we have been good," added Teddy.

I was taken aback by their remarks. It grieved me to hear them talk this way, but I could not convey the truth of what was taking place. In moments like these, I would divert their attention to different subjects. I even created a few games to play. One game comprised of collecting a dozen rocks and branches. Once I had the supplies, I spread the pebbles and branches out and passed them each a stick.

"Now, let's see what we can make," I suggested. I took up a stick, drew a rectangle and an upside-down V in the soil. I placed pebbles in the middle of the rectangle. "A schoolhouse," I remarked, as I finished and waited for their reaction. Somehow, thankfully, this game entertained them for hours.

With the twins absorbed in the games, I took advantage of the quiet. Despite the turmoil outside our bush shelter, I realized there was a soothing aspect to nature. It was as if there was a magnetic pull toward plant life, maybe it was a way to see the vastness of God. I needed God at that time. Once, a group of tiny gray-and-white birds landed on the branches of the bush where we hid. They picked at the bugs and cocked their heads toward me. For a moment, the sun illuminated the leaves and the birds' songs made my mind relax.

But with the twins, quiet time did not last long. "Take us home!" they shrilled until their voices weakened. I tried not to react to their comments and grievances, as most of the time I was absorbed in my thoughts or carefully listening to what was taking place outside our bush dwelling.

For days, the Hutus burned bushes to flush us out. With this latest challenge of the Interahamwe tactics, it was time for me to implement new techniques to teach the girls to survive. One of these was a game I called, "The No Speaking Game." Whoever remained the quietest once I placed three fingers up received extra berries to eat or was carried on my back longer than the other. The twins were pleased with these rewards, especially because they were their ideas. To indicate an end to the challenge, I lowered my fingers and smiled.

By this point, we cherished food beyond measure. With our nutrition deficiencies, we all lacked the strength to travel long distances. Some days, I barely had enough strength to find food nearby; other times, and on a few silent nights, I found the determination to venture to farms near our hiding places. Sometimes I brought back a few guava and avocados that had fallen off the trees, which sustained us for a day or two. On a good day, we had two tiny meals.

There were times when we had nothing to eat for days. Other days I would leave the twins in the bushes, taking a risk by knocking on the doors of nearby Hutu farmers. One night, I was so desperate for food, I knocked on a door. I couldn't recall the name of the Hutu family who lived there, only that my parents helped them with school fees for their children. Their response was somewhere between indifference and sympathy, but they didn't seem to be remorseful until I brought up the death of my mother. Still, they ordered me on my way and requested that I should not come back to their home. "We don't want you to die here, you understand?" Without any food, I returned to the bushes.

By my best estimation, we had been living in the bushes for over a month and a half. Most days, the rocks, sticks, and leaves weren't sufficient to keep the twins busy. They'd recall that they once occupied a nice home, slept in warm beds, ate cooked meals, and had parents who loved them. They blamed me for living in the bushes, for taking them away from Mom and Dad. The situation was confusing to them. They even decided that I had kidnapped them, assuming it was my decision to live in the bushes.

Because many Tutsis were murdered at this point, the militias once again focused their efforts on the forests and bushes. One morning, I awoke to the sound of radio static. On the opposite side of our bush was a crowd of Interahamwe listening to a broadcast and scouting the area. Instructions blared out of the radio as the killers walked their dogs, searching for Tutsis near the creeks and the bushes. The voice over the radio emphasized the need to search the dense forests.

"Look under rocks, in the bushes, because Tutsis are no different than snakes. And remember, a baby of a snake is no different from its parents," a Hutu man with the radio repeated what the announcer said for the others.

They set fire to a stretch of forests and flushed out a few Tutsis. The smoke drifted to our bush and stung our eyes. I kept my three fingers up to signal to the twins and they understood we were playing the "No Speaking Game" for a long time. The girls were impressively quiet, though their eyes watered. The killers continued to burn up more of the area, chanting their dreadful songs, "Yay, tubagandagure…Yay, tubatsembatsembe," which translates as, "let's murder them" and "let's exterminate them." For hours, I prayed they wouldn't notice us. Finally, later in the evening there was silence. I had faith the killers had moved on from the area. We got up, stretched and drank stream water, then returned to our bush home.

The following day, the Interahamwe burned their way to us again, and it was time for us to move to a different hiding space. I didn't want to hurry into this choice for our safety. But the twins fell ill the same day the Interahamwe burned a section of the forest within earshot of our bush. I crouched over the girls as they dry heaved and unsteadily rose to relieve their diarrhea. I didn't know what was causing their sickness, only that their symptoms were flu-like. Whatever it was, their coughing and groaning could signal the killers. The twins looked too weak to travel, so we waited until later.

In the evening, I took off my shirt and fastened one of the twins to my back, looping my shirt under her armpits and across her trunk. With the other twin cradled in my arms, we traveled along the creek to a more secure area of the forest. Inhaling the night wind brought the taste of scorched trees into my mouth as we descended into a bush set far back along the stream. We moved away from houses and trails to an area that was compact with high plants and vines winding around them in every direction. The plants were like slippery ropes and hard to snap through to reach the thicket. There was just enough light to see swarms of beetles scurrying away as I worked our way in. Tiny gnats swarmed out of the bush as we took possession. I pulled the shivering twins onto my chest as I lay flat in the unfamiliar bush, praying there were no snakes living with the insects.

For days, the twins remained in rough shape. I remember my grandma giving children herbal medicine, but I never paid attention when she gathered those herbs, so I did not know what to give them.

On the fourth day with no assistance, Teddy started to feel better and fed on seeds I had set aside. Teta, however, seemed to get sicker. Her skin looked pale; she choked up whatever was left in her stomach, and her forehead felt hotter even though she continued to shiver. I suspected she had caught malaria from mosquitoes. From accounts I had been told, malaria was a serious illness.

"Jeanne, let's take Teta to the hospital," suggested Teddy. Before I answered, Teta nodded her head, agreeing with her twin sister.

"Okay, we will when it is safe," I replied.

Early in the morning, the killers brought dogs with them to help in their efforts. The rowdy dogs howled and drowned out Teta's gagging and coughing. Luckily, the Interahamwe missed us. We remained in the deep bush for three more days. When the sun lowered on us, I took the twins back to the forest near Aunt Josephine's home. Other than vomiting, Teta was also getting better.

It was a calm night when we made it back to Aunt Josephine's property. The guards at the roadblocks had moved farther down the trail, but the odor from a mass grave at the old barricade was overwhelming and stung my nose.

We settled into a bush neighboring the cornfield we hid in the first night of the genocide. I was pleased to see the twins in pleasant spirits, fiddling with the white, yellow, and pink petals of the blossoms that grew in our bush. By this point, I was highly skilled at plucking out a shrub to live in. Sweat trickled off my face as the girls laughed and traded flowers. When I removed the interior of the shrub, I crawled over to the cornfield and plucked a few ears of corn. I snatched a handful of kernels off the ear and gave them to the girls, who grinned as they ate. I tried a few and enjoyed the sweetness.

That night, I rested better knowing the Interahamwe had moved their blockade and those hunting wouldn't be burning this area for the night. We spent two days in relative calm, and Teta was now feeling like her old self. I slipped out again to gather corn. I also snatched a handful of yellow flowers to go with the white flowers the twins played with.

After I fed them, we spent hours playing silly games. One game I had learned from my cousins, called Nyama, instantly became the twins' new favorite. "Nyama" means meat in Kinyarwanda language, and the premise of the game is straightforward. When it is your turn, you call out a name of an animal. If the animal is the type people eat, for instance, a cow or a chicken, the other players say "nyama." If you answer "nyama" when the animal referred to isn't the sort eaten by people, you get a point deducted. For about an hour, we whispered our way through the game. I grinned as the twins argued as they played it.

"Bird," Teddy declared. As I smiled, Teta looked puzzled.

"People don't eat birds," Teta looked at me. I advised her to ask Teddy about it. I watched as Teddy tried to make sense of her claim.

"I don't eat birds, but maybe other people do."

I could see they were bright little girls. As they were occupied with the game, each wanted me to find out why the other one was right or wrong. I learned not to take sides. My parents had always refrained from choosing sides when Jeannette and I had disagreements, and so I did the same with my twin sisters.

While the twins remained busy with the game, my mind drifted to the noise outside. I listened to the cries. Back then, I knew nothing of rape, until one cloudless afternoon.

Chapter Ten

I couldn't see the men, but I heard them—two distinct voices. At first they were grunting, and then the voices grew deeper, and then a third voice joined them. I will never forget the sound of the woman's cry, which in Kinyarwanda suggested that something was being taken forcibly from her. The woman was referring to her young daughter, but the men weren't trying to take her baby in that sense. Her translated words meant, "Please don't rape my child."

The men raped the baby and then the mother. They yelled and used ethnic slurs—"snake" and "cockroach." Then they murdered them. Although I did not see any of the people involved, the sounds and the woman's cry have lingered with me to this day. All I was left with was an unusual feeling connected with the word rape. It no longer meant to take forcefully; it now meant to degrade and contaminate, to humiliate someone to the highest imaginable degree.

After some time, while hiding out in the bush near Aunt Josephine, I ran up against a new sort of grief. Perhaps it was Mom's death, surviving in horrid conditions, or being separated from the rest of my family for so long. Most likely, it was a combination of all three. I sank into a state of self-mourning. With no one to share my experience with, I projected the sadness onto myself and bathed in my pain. After spending days thinking about how many ways I was hurt, I stared at Aunt Josephine's house and wondered what they were doing. After concluding their lives had to be immeasurably better, I decided to present the twins to them. Since I hadn't looked in a mirror in nearly two months, I assumed I looked like the twins, filthy and fragile. I imagined Aunt Josephine and Uncle Gustave might have mercy on us when they saw our condition. I thought that perhaps after telling them about Mom, they'd bring us in and look after us.

The twins and I got up and headed to their house. We knocked a few times and were greeted by Uncle Gustave, who looked at us like foreigners.

"Who gave you permission to enter my home?"

"Uncle, it's me. I have Teddy and Teta with me."

"And who gave you permission to be here?"

"Can you help us, Uncle? We are hungry."

"I don't want you to die here so please leave my house." He pointed his machete to the exit.

"Please let us stay at least for the night. We are hungry," I begged.

"Jeanne, do you understand me? Go! Go immediately!

The twins moved behind me and tugged at my clothes. I wiped tears off my face as we retreated back into our bush home.

MAINTAINING PATIENCE WAS the largest difficulty in the second month. Every day produced a new struggle to stay alive. Our bodies changed, but we never adapted to the point where we forgot how well we had lived before the massacre. Those difficult days reminded me of the ease and freedom our parents provided at home. My perseverance was being tested as never before: tested by the combination of lice and mosquitos feeding on my skin, the dehydration, growling stomach cramps, and having to lie still on a stack of itchy branches. We had dealt with the rain before, so at first it wasn't unbearable, but now it poured as if the skies wept for the dead. We were soaked, and the twins and I shivered. I collected banana leaves to cover us. At dusk, with the twins snuggled against my body, I braced the flimsy umbrella leaves above our heads, but the rain poured off and still found its way through. At some point, my arms gave up and I spread the leaves across our bodies. The last three rainy days were unbearable. On the fourth day of constant rain, we left the bush at night and fell asleep against a nearby tree with the banana leaves draped over our heads. By the next day, my endurance was gone. After having no luck pleading our case to two Hutu families whom I remembered my parents had supported financially, I was left with two possibilities: Ms. Judith, whom Dad arranged for my twin and our young brothers to hide with, or another Hutu couple named Mariya and Mugabo. This couple had attended all our family events and celebrations. Mugabo and his wife had worked for my parents for years, and both of them had a rich, active connection to my parents. After reflecting on it all evening, I decided that going to Ms. Judith risked Jeannette and my brothers' protection. Mariya and Mugabo were the better option.

I hoped Mariya and Mugabo would be more receptive than Uncle Gustave, especially when they caught sight of us soaked, muddy, and weak. Maybe they will allow us to stay until the storm stops. *Possibly even offer us a cooked meal,* I thought.

The rain continued. In the evening we emerged, crawled to the blockade, past the piles of corpses, and began down the narrow trail that led to Mariya and Mugabo's home. All was progressing easily for the first half of the journey until our trail connected with a wider dirt path. I pulled the girls behind a shrub when a motorcycle startled me. Once we could no longer hear the loud engine, we proceeded on our journey. A few minutes later, we saw Interahamwe militiamen. They looked drained as they sauntered around. Each carried a beer bottle in one hand, and a machete or "ubuhiri," which is a wooden tool that looks like a baseball bat, in the other. Most of them were staggering as they drank their beer. We watched as they slowly walked away, then carried on with our hike. After another mile, Teta ran out of strength and begged to be carried. After rejecting her first few requests, I picked her up, hoping to keep her quiet. When Teddy noticed Teta relaxed in my arms, she jumped in front of us and raised her arms high in the air, requesting a break as well.

With both girls now resting their heads on me, I walked through a valley and up a hill, passing another abandoned checkpoint where many victims lay. One body was spread out in the midst of the trail. The young victim was on his back with his eyes wide open, his face stiff in a final statement of horror. His insides had spilled onto the soil, which prompted me to recoil, but my eye caught another mutilated corpse, possibly a teenage girl. It was difficult to tell. I felt repulsed. I stared straight ahead as we walked by the others. The twins' tighter grips on my body told me they were scared of what they had witnessed, but they didn't say a word. Then my eyes lifted. A couple of wild dogs, feasting on the body of a dead boy, ran out to growl at us. The girls seized my neck even tighter. I continued to the other side of the path to avoid provoking the dogs. But one particular black-snouted dog was more hostile, and it snarled as it followed us. I kept moving slowly, hoping it would realize that I was neither afraid nor a threat. Because of its small size, it didn't intimidate me as much as the other big dogs, although it tried its best. The twins were concerned the dog might bite us, but I was more worried that the howling would draw attention and alarm the Interahamwe. After about a third of a mile, the dog surprised me. It stopped barking and trotted beside us. Still, the girls didn't trust our new companion and kept their eyes locked on it with their grips firmly on me.

Later that night, we arrived at Mariya and Mugabo's house. Our new friend stood watching us as we headed for the door. I set the girls down and glanced over to discover the dog trotting off down the path. It took a few knocks to awaken the family. Mugabo spoke from behind the door.

"Who is it?"

"Jeanne," I mumbled back through the flimsy door.

"Jeanne?"

"Celestin's daughter," I said louder.

The squeaky door opened halfway and Mugabo poked his head out from behind it.

He cleared his throat and looked us over, clucking his tongue. "My Lord, can't you girls see we are sleeping? Please do us a favor and leave our house. We don't need dead children around our house."

"We need to get out of the storm for a few hours," I replied, bumping the twins towards him, hoping he could make out their wet, dingy clothes and gloomy expressions. "Please, only two hours."

He opened the door and soon his wife accompanied him, cupping a glowing lantern in her hands. When she lifted the light to us and saw our state, she advocated for us.

"Shame on you, Mugabo. For all Celestin and Speciose have done for us, we can keep their daughters out of the pouring rain for a few minutes."

Mugabo reminded her that the Interahamwe had been by their home five times that day to see if they hid any Tutsis.

"Five times," he pronounced.

They went back and forth for a little longer, but soon Mugabo agreed to allow us to stay. He cautioned his wife to be prepared to see us killed if the Interahamwe came again.

"And they will make me do it," he whined, as he followed us into the living area.

"Should I remind you the meat our neighbor gave us may have belonged to Celestin's herd?" She rebuffed. "They will eat and then leave," she announced as she steered us to their rug and draped a heavy cotton blanket around us. It took my body time to warm up but when I finally did, the sensation was overwhelming. I pulled the blanket higher on my head. Mariya went in the other room, returning with three plates of food. Before she could pull her hands away, the twins dove in. Mariya looked at them with sadness and a bit of disgust as they shoved hot sweet potatoes in their mouths and spewed them out simultaneously, only pausing a couple of moments before they attempted again. Mariya held the forks for the girls, but they never raised their heads.

"Slow down, girls," I suggested, and took the forks from Mariya's outstretched hand. I waited until Mariya stepped back into the room to take my first bite of the sweet potato, which fell apart in my mouth. I sighed deeply through my nose, narrowed my eyes, and gulped. My body warmed even further. I fought to eat the beef from our herd. Odds were I had probably fed and bonded with this cow now on my dinner plate, but, I devoured every morsel. The girls begged for a second portion. I sat back and held my stomach, which hurt, likely because I hadn't had a cooked meal in weeks.

If I hadn't been so desperate for a good night's rest, I would've eaten the food, enjoyed the warmth of the blanket for a while, thanked them, walked out, and spent the night in the bushes. But I was psychologically and physically exhausted, so I begged them to let us stay for the rest of the night. This arrangement created a brush with death. After Mariya pleaded our position to Mugabo, he agreed to allow us to stay the night as long as we left before dawn. "We will be out around 4:30 a.m," I reassured them. Mariya gave us a red comforter and folded it in on top of the heavy cotton blanket, which was bundled securely around us. The twins slept in their typical position against my body. Within minutes, the lantern was out.

For the first time in weeks, I was inside a home and had a warm meal. I was satisfied, but I couldn't stop my thoughts from racing. Every time I shut my eyes, I visualized killers lunging at me with their machetes high in the air. Mom and Baby Mucyo's lifeless images flickered in my mind as if I were watching a horror movie. I wiped my tears and made an effort to remember more pleasant times, but my mind kept flying.

After struggling for a long time, the thoughts stopped and I drifted off. Within moments I sat upright, panting as sweat collected on my brow, palms, and nose. It was pitch black. Another nightmare had woken me, and I must've been shouting in my sleep because I found Mariya looking at me.

"Why are you yelling?" she asked as she stooped beside me. "This village is quiet. We don't want to disturb our neighbors. That could mean bad news for you three," she cautioned and rubbed my head. She slipped away, and I went back to sleep. What seemed like only moments later, I saw Mariya beside me again, though this time she was shaking me.

"Wake up. Wake up," she said anxiously. "They are outside. Wake up, Jeanne!"

I mumbled an apology for screaming again, but I wasn't certain if I was still dreaming. Confused, I rose up and saw Mugabo standing by the entrance holding a lantern as if somebody was coming towards the door. It was that moment I realized this was not another dream.

"They are almost here. Get these girls up and go," Mariya urged as she bent over and shook one of the twins.

Blood filled my muscles, and in an instant my eyes were wide open. I placed my hand on hers and spoke as if someone was communicating through me.

"The girls are too slow and we won't get far before they catch us. Let me place them in bed with your children. They will mix in." I surprised myself because I had never before told an adult what to do, but I didn't have time to figure out another plan.

"No!" Mugabo replied. "They look nothing like us. You want them to die here?"

Once more, feeling a peculiar certainty I had never known, I replied with a steady tone.

"They won't! Please, if not for us, or my parents, do it for God."

Without waiting for an answer, I picked up one of the twins and hurried into their children's bedroom. When I came back for the other twin, Mugabo and Mariya followed me into the bedroom. They looked as panicked as I was.

"We will keep the twins until the militia leave. But when they are gone, you come back for them. Understand?"

"Yes," I replied as I pulled the quilt up to the twins' shoulders. I caressed their cheeks and begged God to keep them concealed and sheltered under these covers. I noticed the couple's eyes on me as I swung around to pass through the living room. As I exited, I looked to the sides of the house and then straight ahead to where the dog had disappeared earlier. Four flashlights beamed bright in front of me. It was the Interahamwe, and they were seconds from catching me. *Carry me like the wind, God*, I whispered to myself as I walked around to the front side of Mugabo's home.

As I turned the corner of the house, a man shouted, "Who is that?" By the time the last word escaped his lips, I had hurried down the slope behind the house. As the men scrambled off in different directions, I rushed over the knee-high grass like a frightened gazelle. Everything wound up inside of me. The darkness in front of me even decreased. The soil tore underneath my sandals as I sailed over a sweet potato patch. Once I was a considerable distance from Mugabo's house, I slid to a halt and tumbled onto my back.

My knees and middle were covered, so I burrowed my body deeper in the foot-high bushes and ripped a few vines out by the root to cover my torso and face. I eased my arms beside me and froze. My heart was still pounding in my chest when I heard the man once more. "She went this way, into the field below." One of them reported the colors of my clothes. He stopped close to my hiding space. I resisted the impulse to jump up and run away again. Out of the corner of my eye, I noticed the flicker of his flashlight. *God, why did they have to stop here? Please, make them go away,* I prayed.

The men roamed about the field, discussing how far I could have gotten. One of them regretted not having his dog with him to help find me. Then he stepped backward. I heard the plants move about as he shifted around. His back was now visible out of the corner of my eye. I prayed harder, braced my body and held my breath. He took a swing out of frustration and another step toward me.

"Come out, snake!" he roared into the darkness. "I will send you away with one stroke of my machete. But if you make us hunt for you, work hard to find you, the pain will be one hundred times worse." He took another step and was now directly over me. He shuffled his feet and I felt his weight crush my forearm. *Is this it, God? Is this my time to die?* What transpired next could've been the trauma of separation, I don't know, but as I prayed hard and earnestly from my heart, peace came over my body. I looked toward the stars above me. At first they shone far away, but as I continued to pray, they became brighter and clearer. The stars were descending toward me, the radiant light now openly in front of me, blazing bright on my face. I heard a voice in my head say, *"You are safe, Jeanne."* Seconds later, the man lifted his boot off my forearm and walked away. The killers scoured the area longer and drifted away. Finally, they gave up. One of them yelled out as they marched off up the slope, "You may not die tonight, but you will die soon."

I remained embedded in the plants much longer than I needed to, then stood up and brushed the dirt and leaves off my clothes. I strolled up the slope. That sense of peace had left me, and uneasiness arose once more when I thought about the twins. I cringed at the thought of the killers searching Mugabo's house. I rushed up the hill. When I arrived, it was quiet. I softly thumped on the door. When no one answered, I knocked again, louder this time. Finally, Mariya greeted me and showed me in. I relaxed when I saw the twins sleeping where I had left them.

I stooped down. "Time to wake up, girls," I whispered. The twins were unaffected by my voice, so I brought in a cloth dipped in cold water and wiped it across their faces.

"We don't want to leave," they begged.

"We have to. Bad guys will come back," I replied.

"That's okay," Teddy murmured, "We are good girls."

"Yes, you are," I added, helping them get up. I accompanied them hand in hand through the living room. Mariya and Mugabo stood in the doorway, looking relieved to see us go.

"Thank you," I said as we walked out. Mariya locked the door behind us. We trudged down the pathway near the river, looking for a place to hide. After walking a safe distance away from the blockade we had passed earlier, we gathered together. I pulled the twins' shivering bodies tighter against my body. Minutes later, I heard a dog yelping in the distance and wondered if it was our companion from earlier.

Once again, I was thankful that our lives were spared. I wish this was the closest to death we would come, but the days ahead carried me even closer to the end and put the twins in greater danger.

Chapter Eleven

The militia continued to burn the bushes and dense forests to locate Tutsis. It was obvious that soon we would be exposed. For hours, I thought of ways to satisfy the so-called Hutu nose criteria. I let the twins play with twigs and my mind wandered. At first, an idea of flaring our nostrils wide came to mind. But then I imagined standing in the presence of the Interahamwe with our nostrils flared out, and I acknowledged it might put us in danger if they caught us attempting to imitate their looks. I looked at the seeds, which rolled around in the palm of my dirty hands, and I wedged them in my nostrils. Minutes later, I declared in my head, *"I am a Hutu."* I repeated, *"I am a Hutu!"* as I adjusted the seeds in my stretched nostrils. Finally, I said it out loud, "I am Hutu," while glancing at the twins. They wore puzzled expressions as rainfall pooled around their feet.

"I am Hutu," I practiced again, this time smiling at the twins and watching their confusion turn to amusement.

"What happened to your nose?" laughed Teddy.

"What is a Hutu?" Teta asked. I thought of her question, but all I could think of was, *they are people like us with slightly different features.*

"I am playing a new game today; you girls want to play?" They looked pleased and nodded. A few feet from our hiding place was another tree with thin stems covered with solid, lighter green seeds similar to the ones in my nostrils. I crawled out of the bush and harvested a handful. I placed the seeds on my lap and peeled off their outer layers. I remember before the genocide my twin sister and I played with these seeds, substituting them for marbles. We called them "intobo." As I organized the seeds, the twins had their eyes fixed on me and asked if they could eat some. As far as I could remember, the seeds were poisonous if swallowed.

"Please let us try one and see if it tastes sweet," begged Teta.

"These seeds are not edible. They will make you sick," I replied.

"No, that won't make us sick. You let us eat them yesterday," added Teddy.

I tried to explain that the seeds they ate the day before were not the same as the ones in my hands, but I realized I wasn't winning the argument, so I used my usual weapon, silence.

Despite how hard I tried to sell this game, the twins hesitated to join in. It was obvious they were baffled as to why we had to play this one. My simple explanation was, "This is funny and fun!" I smiled, trying to sound excited. "To play this game, you have to push these round seeds up your nose. This way, see, but don't force them too far; they could get stuck," I cautioned. Luckily, after pleading for a while the twins played along. I helped them insert the seeds and demonstrated how to breathe through their mouths. I sat back and looked as the twins grimaced and attempted to remove the uncomfortable seeds, rapidly losing interest. I attempted to regain their attention, advertising "I am a Hutu" as the greatest game I have ever played and stressing that we will always wear the seeds before we leave our bush. Over and over again, I emphasized the single phrase they had to memorize, "I am a Hutu."

We practiced throughout the daylight hours. In the evening we were all starving, so I left our bush to gather some berries and more rainwater to drink. Conveniently, there was a tree nearby with concave-shaped leaves that the rainwater gathered into, like a small cup. I carefully plucked up as many as I could without spilling the water and brought them back to the twins, who gulped the liquid and enjoyed a handful of berries.

In the morning, while again stressing the importance of keeping the seeds in our nose, I explained to the girls the possibility of being in the open and getting a break from hiding in the bush. The twins appeared to like the idea of venturing out. We inserted the seeds in our nostrils and practiced saying, "I am a Hutu," before leaving our bush. I prayed for our protection and that the militia we were likely to run into would automatically assume we resembled Hutus, letting us go on without any questions.

THERE WERE MANY occasions as a child when I recited prayers without thinking twice, but in our present state, I thought of my prayers differently; prayers were now a system to relax my body and unite me with something other than our world and brighter than our grim situation. Besides the twins, prayers were all I had. I was deprived of all on the surface so it caused me to go inside, to sink into the planes of my heart. When I prayed, the dark images that troubled my mind quieted. But the questions of who I was and who I would be after this massacre remained. I also wondered if there was going to be a way of life after this carnage.

I finished my prayer and then the twins and I walked around. Now that we had some sort of camouflage, it was time to venture out and experiment with our new Hutu identity in the open. However, my heart pounded as I realized we were taking a dangerous risk by being out in the open in daylight for the first time.

Our first trip was to Ms. Judith's home. I prayed Judith's family still housed my twin sister and my little brothers. Before we wandered far, I made sure the twins remembered that we were still playing "I am a Hutu game." With seeds pressed into their nostrils, they advanced through the thick brush, their bony arms tight alongside their bodies.

Along the path, the rumble of thunder bellowed from the ash-colored clouds above. The twins clung to my legs when a blast of lightning flared through the sky. I picked them up. At this stage, they had lost a lot of weight so it wasn't as difficult as it had been to carry them. Our initial stop was an area called Mukigarama where many dead were strewn about. I saw the militia guarding the barricade but wasn't sure if they had seen us, so we turned in a different direction. We had not gotten far when we heard the whistle and they called us over. Panicked, I placed the twins on the ground and walked to where the men assembled. The twins pulled me backward when they saw bloody machetes and wooden clubs, but I whispered to them not to worry as I dragged them forward with me. I tried to hold my head high and said to myself, "*I am a Hutu.*" The smell of blood on their clothes and their body odor made me feel sick to my stomach.

After they checked us over for Tutsi features, I explained that we were visiting our Hutu friend, Ms. Judith. They told us to sit down while they waited for their leader to determine what to do with us. I prayed while the leader glanced at us and then at his men. After some shouting, the leader of the group returned to his group a few steps away from us. They whispered something to each other and then returned to us. I watched every step the leader took. *God, please protect us*, I whispered.

"Is he going to hit us?" Teddy asked.

"No, he won't hurt us. We are Hutu," I replied.

"Jeanne, I am scared," Teta said while pulling on my arm.

"We will be fine," I reassured them. I was afraid but I had to appear calm and confident for the girls. Finally, the leader stood right next to us. My heart pounded. Sweat dripped in my palms, on my forehead and my back. I stared directly in his eyes, trying to appear confident and unafraid.

"Everyone seems to think you are Tutsis," he said, scratching his head.

Hoping he noticed my wide nose, I answered, "No. We are Hutus, headed to a Hutu family friend."

He took one more look at me, and then looked at his men.

"Let them go," he ordered.

"Get out of here!" one of the men yelled out.

Without looking back, we walked slowly at first. When we were out of the men's sight, I urged the twins to walk faster. We reached Ms. Judith's house, which stood on the summit of a tall hill. Ms. Judith, like our family, had extended family with their own homes around the area. I knew one of her sons, John, a man in his thirties who was strong and always wore a wide smile that displayed all his front teeth.

The twins and I descended a hill as we approached Ms. Judith's house, coming face to face with John. He was walking toward his mother's home with a small group of men. A wet fog hovered, causing my skin to feel moist. Knowing we couldn't escape the men, we proceeded toward them and were greeted by four offended stares. John looked shocked to see us. I weakly asked him if he planned on killing us. John stood silently for a few seconds, and then talked about my parents respectfully. He echoed what many others had suggested, that my parents were kind people, and he couldn't have our blood on his hands. The men accepted John's words as a signal to let us pass. We then proceeded to his mom's house.

Before the genocide, Ms. Judith struck me as a gentle person. I prayed she had not changed. When she answered the door and looked at us, she offered a faint smile but was obviously surprised to see us.

"Why would you girls come here?" she said, shutting the door behind her and moving closer to us as if she had company inside which she wanted to hide us from.

"My twin. I was hoping to visit her for a few minutes," I stammered.

She turned to look over her shoulder.

"You need to lower your voice; I have guests who are not aware that I am hiding your siblings. All you need to know is that they are safe for now," she whispered.

A burden lifted when she spoke her last words; for the first time in weeks, my chapped lips stretched into a full smile. She explained that my siblings stayed under her bed all day and she fed them when she was able. After she explained all this, her anxiety grew more obvious, and I realized staying at her doorstep could place my siblings in greater danger. I thanked her and walked away. When I had gotten a few steps away, she called me back.

"Have you seen your father?" she whispered.

I turned back towards her and told her I hadn't seen him since the genocide started.

"Your father was here just a short while ago," she responded.

"Is he looking for us?" I gasped. She was quiet and looked serious. "Is he injured?" I asked.

Her eyes fixed on the ground in front of her.

"Is he okay?" I asked once more, but this time I did not control my voice.

"He is hurt," she replied, "but alive."

"What happened?"

"When he knocked on my door to check on your siblings, he was holding the side of his head. It might have been a machete or bullet wound," she guessed with a sense of pity.

"Which way did he go?" I asked breathlessly.

"Over there, toward the banana field and cornfield behind my house. You can catch him if you hurry."

Without another word, I rushed the twins away and hauled them behind me toward the banana field. Hearing Dad was alive gave me a rush of strength. I imagined his embrace and this thought filled my body with warmth. As we hurried, the twins couldn't keep up with my pace. I sat them down in a small bush and begged them to remain there until I came back.

"I am going to get Dad," I said.

They smiled and agreed to remain in the bush. I then ran as if my body was as light as a leaf in the breeze, floating over the terrain. I made it into the dense area of the banana farm, frantically calling out, "Dad! Dad! Where are you?" For a moment, everything seemed to stand still. I continued to rush through the field only stopping every several minutes to cry out, "Dad, can you hear me? It's me, Jeanne!"

Sweat trickled down my face; I stopped to catch my breath again. Frustrated, I hurried back to the top of Ms. Judith's hill where I could see the fields and the plain below. The fog still hovered in the air and at the top of the neighboring hills. I ran from one field to the other. I then took a different route into a field and sensed I was now visible to people on the opposite hill, but my focus was finding my father, even if I was putting myself in danger. I imagined what life would be like to hide in the bushes with Dad, and a sense of safety and protection filled my heart. Realizing there was a possibility of finding him brought an incredible joy in my heart and a big smile to my face. I sprinted down the trail, and then I was startled by a shout coming from the top of the hill on the opposite side. It was the high-pitched voice of a Hutu man urging others to come and help. After I made it a little farther down the path, I heard the voice very clear, and I will never forget the words he yelled out, "Dore nyamuremurere. Dore nyamuremurere!" which translates in my native language to, "There is the tall person!" "There is the tall person!"

Immediately, I thought of my six-foot, seven-inch-tall Dad. The man asking for help yelled it again with importance, "Nimutangatange" "Nyamuremure nimutangatange," meaning "Circle the area. Get the tall man!" I continued to run down the trail until an opening revealed the man yelling to find the tall one. There were now at least five men racing down the opposite slope toward the tall man.

I eventually spotted the "tall man" they were after. More Interahamwe ran up the slope toward him, all converging on the "tall man" from multiple angles. I kept my eyes on this Tutsi man who was being hunted. I whispered as if he could hear me, *"Bend down, you have to stoop down."* I slowly moved and pressed on to see if he would slip away. When I moved closer, I saw the "tall man" was holding the side of his head. For a minute, I resolved not to think about what Ms. Judith had told me. *No, it couldn't be Dad.* When I noticed the "tall man" was wearing a dark gold jacket, the same color Dad wore when we left our house the first day of the genocide, I felt something I could not describe. I stood still, my eyes fixed on the men with machetes and clubs. A daze overcame me, and I was no longer thinking about hiding myself. The men came closer. I could see the "tall man" was my daddy. His long, deliberate strides showed his exhaustion. *"Please, Dad, stoop down. Bend down so they won't see you,"* I cried inside.

The faster the men moved toward Dad, the colder my whole body became. *"God, spare him. I swear, I will bring people to you and praise you, please. Save my Dad!"* I narrowed my eyes as tears flowed down my face. I saw the first blade come down on him, then another blow, and another. Dad buckled. More men joined in, taking turns swinging their machetes and clubs. He was soon lying on the ground. I fell down to the dirt and pressed my fists into my eyes. *"Why, God, why did you want me to see that? How could you let this happen to my daddy?"* An indescribable pain seized my body as I pulled

73

myself up and watched the men drag my father's body in the middle of the road. Through it all, Dad was quiet. He never begged for mercy, he didn't even attempt to fight them, although I wished he had.

I stared helplessly as they beat his limp body a few last times. After a while, denial took over my thoughts: *Maybe Dad was only wounded. Maybe he's still breathing. I could find him, take him water, and nurse him back to health.* Then the flash of the scene I had just witnessed displayed in my mind like a movie. I came to the realization that there was no way he would have survived that group of men and numerous blows. I can't recall how long I remained there, but I finally cleared my blurry eyes. I recall wishing I had a grenade or a gun. I would have fired at those animals.

A weighty quietness filled my mind. I stared blankly at the tree branches lying on the soil in front of me.

Earlier, I noticed Hutu children carrying stacks of firewood on their heads. These Hutu children passed by barricades freely. Like those children, I thought about us collecting tree branches and carrying them on our heads to cover our faces and make it seem like we had a Hutu family to go to.

I went back to where I had left the twins. They had not moved, and as I expected, they flooded me with questions about Dad and why I returned without him. Without words to explain the horror I had just experienced, I persuaded them to wear their seeds in their nostrils and carry a few twigs on their heads. The twins then followed me down the same dirt trail where I had watched Dad's attack. I peeped through the sticks I carried to see where Dad was dragged. My heart skipped when I noticed blood splattered in the dirt. When I saw Dad's black shoe in the center of the path, I dropped my sticks. "Stay here, girls," I said quietly. I picked his shoe and held it tightly against my chest. Tears welled up as I took a few more steps and found Dad's jacket. I picked it up and inspected it. Somehow there wasn't a speck of blood on it. I assumed the killers removed it before they started hitting him. I held the jacket to my nose and breathed in the vague scent of his citrus cologne. I thought hard about continuing forward. After staring at the ditch where I assumed his body had been discarded, I determined that my mind couldn't handle seeing another loved one's corpse. I cleared my tears and went back to the twins. They immediately scolded me for taking a coat that didn't belong to me. When I explained that it was Dad's and that he left it for us, they responded with more questions. Each of their questions tore at my heart a little more.

At nightfall, we stumbled back to our hiding area. When we arrived inside the bush, I forced the seeds out of my nostrils and toppled onto my back. That night I didn't hold the twins against my body. Instead, I wrapped Dad's coat around them so that I could cradle my body in my own arms.

Chapter Twelve

It was early June. The air still smelled of death and fire. The nights were warmer and the days more humid. We settled back in our favorite tall bush near Aunt Josephine's house. After many nights and days in this bush, it had become familiar to us. The twins and I came to accept it as our new home. Apart from this bush being closer to Aunt Josephine, we could see the remains of what used to be our house. I am not sure why but seeing our old neighborhood in the distance brought some comfort and hope that maybe someday, we would return home. Perhaps we could start a new life. There were many good childhood memories connected with that house which warmed my heart.

However, one early morning the militia scorched nearby bushes and it was time to move again. We inserted the seeds in our noses and recited the same words about our new Hutu identities. When we reached a nearby forest, I collected bundles of branches for us to carry. The girls placed their bundles of tree limbs on their heads and the three of us headed out. We scavenged for food and water, relying on our makeshift Hutu noses and tree branches to disguise us. For hours we wandered about. We watched the militias and the Interahamwe burn more bushes and rummage around, hunting for Tutsis to kill. Fortunately, no one stopped us. Without a specific destination in mind, we walked all day from one forest to the next. Being in the open was liberating. The twins' faces lit up as they walked up and down the hills, picking their own seeds to eat.

When the twins were tired of walking, I had them sit down. I took our small firewood bundles and scattered them all over the forest, picking up the limbs again one by one. I did this leisurely, so that if any Hutus spotted us they would assume we were Hutu children gathering wood for our stove.

For the next few days, collecting small firewood became our daily routine. We walked even longer distances, taking advantage of this limited freedom and collected a variety of seeds to eat. We even stole fresh corn and sweet potatoes from nearby farms. When night fell, we slept in whatever bush was nearby. We were always out again bright and early to take up the same routine again.

One day, we ventured near an Interahamwe killing squad. We quietly listened as they sang their killing songs, "Eh yay tubagandagure, Eh yay tubatsembatsembe," which translates as, "let's murder them" and "let's exterminate them." I avoided eye contact with the group as I signaled the twins, who were busy chasing after grasshoppers, to pick up the branches. We bent down and gathered whatever branches and twigs were near us.

After the group passed, I trembled. I wiped the sweat off my nose and thanked God for saving us once again. We then wandered toward more remote areas with dense forests. We arrived at our new bush, and three of us were exhausted. Once I cleared the area, the twins quickly laid down. In a matter of minutes, they were fast asleep.

Leaving the twins to nap, I meandered around the meadow and discovered dozens of orange butterflies hovering about the tall green foliage. Crickets sang and grasshoppers hopped. The meadow stretched out for a distance and was coated with knee-high blue and purple wildflowers. The flowers and tall leafy stems swayed to the lively wind. I spotted a family of small gray birds gliding back and forth, exposing their white-tipped feathers.

I returned to our bush and lay on my back. As I lay awake, I realized there was something about nature that revealed God's presence despite all the chaos around us.

Afraid that our bush would be burned, the next day we hiked to the forest adjacent to where Dad was murdered. I carefully listened as two men who looked like farmers discussed an "unpleasant" new policy they had heard about on the radio. "To forgive Tutsi women and Tutsi girls is absurd," one of the men shouted with anger. "How could our government agree to this?" They cursed the government's representatives for making such a mistake.

"We are now forgiven, for what? For being Tutsis? What is there to forgive about being born a Tutsi?" I wondered.

The men added, "They are now free and are safe to come out of hiding." They cursed, "Tutsi snakes and cockroaches." They went on about how Tutsi lives are useless and how all should be done away with.

Despite the uncertainty about this "women forgiveness policy," I went back to our bush that night feeling confident that we might make it through the slaughter after all. It made sense. *After so much devastation and killing, why wouldn't we receive protection? It sounded like the government was finally coming to its senses.* That night we feasted on a few avocados. With renewed spirits, we played "Guess the Animal," a game that involved producing animal sounds and guessing which animal it was. The twins giggled when I expanded my cheeks and let out a long "moo," catching my breath and reproducing the sound again. The twins continued to giggle and lick avocado flesh from their dusty fingers.

At nightfall, I rested a little better hoping what the farmers had said was true. The next day at sunrise, Hutu boys rushed through the farmland and deep into the bush to spread the same report we heard from the farmers the day before. "All Tutsi women are free! Come out of your hiding place. Bring your daughters! You may come back to your homes without violence!" The boys repeated this claim throughout the day. In the afternoon, another crowd came with a slightly altered message, "Government report: At midnight, all Tutsi women are free to come out of hiding!" The messengers repeated the declaration, running through valleys, up hills, and along the streams.

By the following day, I had heard the news about this new policy repeated numerous times. As darkness descended on us again, a flicker of confidence prompted me to reflect on Jeannette and my brothers; I could even imagine us rebuilding our house and returning to life as a family. I prayed the news was accurate. I remembered the peace I felt in Mugabo's field, the night the killer stepped on my forearm and light burned bright from the sky. I wanted to feel that same sensation of peace and safety. So, I recited the prayers I had said that night. It didn't last as long, nor did it feel as soothing as I had experienced in that field. My mind was conflicted. On one hand, I wanted to believe the messengers; on the other, I would have to disregard the intermittent cries of death I had heard the day before and the mass graves surrounding us. If the government was indeed protecting women and girls, I wanted verification from a government figure. I wanted a statement from an official who possessed authority in the village. That would be the only way I could feel assured about coming into the open as a Tutsi.

The only person who could verify the accuracy of this new policy was the mayor, Mr. Ndoli.

When the sunlight woke us up in the morning, I gathered our props, the sticks and nose seeds, and the three of us traveled to Mayor Ndoli's house. We took the main roads but walked around the checkpoints just to play it safe. Strangely, on this day, the roads were as quiet as the forest. About a mile from our house, I took to the forest behind our farms that led to the church near the mayor's home. As we advanced over the hillsides surrounding our home and relatives' homes, one of the girls made a remark that gripped my attention. With her eyes settled on the hills next to our house, Teta said, "Look, people forgot their clothes." I stood still and stared at the assorted colors of clothes peppered throughout the hills. Unlike the twins, I knew the clothes were still worn by the victims. There must've been a few hundred bodies strewn about the landscape.

When we made it to the small church, it was apparent that it was a stage for a mass killing. The side of the building had massive holes exposing the corpses inside, which were bunched together in piles. Many of the victims looked fresh, their eyes protruding out of their sockets, tongues swollen and popped out, and swelled skin. The stench and sight caused me

79

to choke. I dropped the branches and held my sleeves over my mouth. The twins also gagged, and I directed them away from the sight.

After the genocide, I learned that churches were common locations for mass murders because Tutsis assumed they would be protected in the House of God. However, the reverse was true. There were hundreds of men, women, and children dead on the church floor. Some of the homes surrounding Mayor Ndoli's were deserted. Broken water jars, cooking pots, and fragments of old clothing littered the lawns and path. It was easy to tell which houses had belonged to Tutsis, as they were reduced to piles of smoldering wood or completely destroyed.

We arrived at Mayor Ndoli's house. I readied my unsteady hands and knocked. Someone answered the door and I immediately asked for the Mayor. A few minutes later, the mayor showed up in the doorway. His plump face seemed troubled by our presence. Looking like three stranded puppies, we stared at him for some time before he spoke.

"Are you Celestin's girls?" he asked as he covered his mouth with a handkerchief. I nodded with a yes. "What do you need?"

He stood with one fist on his waistband while I repeated what I knew of the government's new policy. When I finished, he folded his handkerchief, placed it in the pocket of his smoothly pressed dress shirt, and said, "Let me explain something to you, kid. It is dreadful what has taken place the last few months. Believe me, we are doing all we can to prevent the killings." He then puffed out his cheeks.

He asked me a few more questions, mostly about where we had been hiding and about my parents. I trusted him so I told him everything, including that my parents were now in heaven, which the girls denied since I still had not told them. The longer I talked, the more I could see he was anxious to get rid of us. He kept glancing back over his shoulder as if he had business to tend to inside. Toward the end of our conversation, he told me the government would make due on its pledge. When I asked him what we should do until then, his response was direct: "Go back to your house," he said, "there's no reason to continue sleeping in the forests." He promised us that the Interahamwe would not harm us and that peace would soon be reached.

"But our house has been destroyed," I replied, hoping he might give us a place to stay until our home was repaired. To that, he stressed that it was not a matter for today. "Your home will be restored soon, child. You are safe now. So, go on!"

One of the twins tugged on my shirt and timidly asked if he could feed us. The visit was a success and I didn't want to push our luck. We left the mayor's home and started back down the path that led to our home.

With the good news confirmed by the most powerful man I knew in our village, I felt hopeful; we even squeezed the seeds out of our nostrils. We had abandoned our sticks near the church and hadn't felt it was necessary to collect more now that we had the protection of the mayor, or so I thought.

With the mayor's promise to fix our home and the newly enforced government policy in place, I wanted to survey the damage of our home and see if any of our belongings remained.

WE CONFIDENTLY WALKED the main road but then took a narrow trail, hoping to avoid our Hutu neighbor Fatuma and her son Bahati. But when we emerged from the pathway just past her home, she had already discovered us. She shouted, calling us over. As we turned towards her, she called her son, who stood in the middle of the road almost as if he was waiting for us. Catching her breath, she let out a gruff-sounding laugh and said, "Let me take a look at you," as she stabbed my temple with her index finger. "That Tutsi forehead!" She then stood back, motioning for Bahati to do his business.

But I held my arms high, hoping to stop him. Given seconds to speak, I frantically told them about our visit with the mayor, erasing the smirk off Fatuma's face. I knew Fatuma didn't have to believe me, but when I hinted at what might happen to her if she didn't, she looked distressed.

"Listen to the radio. Tutsi women and girls are free. If you hurt us, you will be killed," I confidently added.

"Shut up," her son shouted. My legs wobbled while he looked to his mother, who still glared at us. "How could the mayor betray his people? This can't be true," he added, shaking his head. I persuaded him that it was true. Then he jerked Dad's jacket from underneath my arm, tossed it at my feet, and swung his blade down upon it violently. With anger, he repeated hitting the coat until it was cut in numerous pieces. All the while he was doing this, I felt my arms get heavy and my chest swelled with anguish. The scene caused me to see Dad's death again in my mind, and my lips trembled as tears formed in my eyes.

When he finished, he scooped up parts of the jacket with the tip of the blade and flung them into the bushes. Instinctively, I tried to retrieve them but he shouted, "Leave it!" With one hand on his waist, he raised his machete and said, "All of this is our property!" pointing at various farmlands that had belonged to my family and other Tutsis in the area.

I stared at the strips of Dad's coat that now hung in the branches. Just then I heard a recognizable voice calling out from down the trail. It was our Kalisa. Fatuma and her son enthusiastically repeated our account with distrust to Kalisa. After some awkward silence, Kalisa assured them he would get the truth and led us down the road toward our house. When we were alone, Kalisa reminded us how dangerous it was to be near our neighborhood. I told him about the messages I had heard the day before and what the mayor had said.

Kalisa shook his head and explained, "It is a tactic to capture the remaining Tutsis. The Interahamwe believe there are some Tutsis women and little kids left in the bushes, and they are frustrated." I felt frustrated for believing the mayor. "These reports are meant to bring the Tutsi women to the same place, so they can be killed." He spoke softly as he squinted looking off in the horizon. "Listen, I can't protect you. The Interahamwe have been randomly searching moderate Hutu's homes. They will murder me if I'm caught with you." Kalisa lifted my hands, looked directly into my eyes and said quietly, "Take your sisters behind your house and once it is dark, leave this area. Just beyond your house is a killing squad, Jeanne, so wait for nightfall. Understand?"

I agreed and led the twins through our thick cornfield. We rushed, peeking back at the road where Kalisa said the killers were. We crouched behind a tall bush that shielded us from the road. I scooped up a few raw sweet potatoes and corn for us to eat. I struggled to clean the soil off the sweet potatoes with my shirt. Peeling the first potato with my teeth, I handed it to the twins, who took turns taking bites and passing it back and forth. The twins had been quiet since we left the mayor's house. They appeared to have somehow figured out the surrounding threats. Inside, I smiled as I did not have to remind them about the "No Speaking Game". They gnawed at the sweet potato and stared at the dirt.

After a few more hours, I heard noise coming from the plants nearby. Occasionally birds or lizards rattled bushes, startling us. This time, though, the object appeared to be bigger and slower. The surrounding bushes began to shake, and then stopped. With the three of us looking at the bushes as they bent again, out from it stepped a young boy. But my worried, fixed expression changed to a smile when I realized the young boy was our cousin, Joshua. He stood there surprised, holding a sweet potato in his hands, his mouth dangling wide. Without a sound, I motioned him over. He joined us as the twins watched every move he made.

Joshua was about six years old and was the youngest boy in his family. It had been months since I saw him or any of his siblings. As he sat there in his dirty-brown corduroy slacks and short-sleeved t-shirt, I made an effort to recall our last encounter. It may have been Easter for all I could remember. One of my favorite memories of Joshua was watching him dance; his broad smile and enormous brown eyes seemed to grow larger when he swayed to the sounds of drums. Even for a young boy, he possessed a smooth rhythm and always was the focus of attention when the music began. Now Joshua wore a narrow face and intense stare as we whispered greetings to each other. We talked about how we had survived, and it was comforting to know someone understood our troubles. He talked about how he hated the wet weather, and when I asked about his parents, his voice grew shaky.

Unsure whether it was trauma or anxiety, Joshua's body twitched. Like me, it was obvious Joshua was in a constant state of fear, and the terror in his eyes made it clear that he was always ready to run. He spoke faster than usual. "Mom and Dad and my little sister are hurt. I still visit them sometimes to see if they may wake up, but it frightens me." Uncertain if it was worth explaining to a young child that his family will never wake up, I leaned forward and embraced his skinny torso. In exchange, I whispered in his ears what I knew about my family. He didn't reply. He used his teeth to strip his sweet potato. The twins giggled and pointed out that he had soil in his mouth. He smiled back at them. Once he finished peeling the potato, he passed it to Teddy. I felt consoled seeing that life in the wild hadn't hardened Joshua's beautiful heart. He remained a gentle, considerate boy. After we finished eating the potatoes, Joshua asked if he could stay with us "after they stopped hurting people."

"You will live with us," I assured him with a smile. I even told him about my brothers and sisters, who I hoped were still alive. He had legitimate concerns about being taken care of by me and the others, but I promised him it would all work out. I then picked small, dried stems from his hair, which had apparently been there for days.

"You are like a kid brother to me, so don't worry about where you will stay after this chaos. We will be okay."

Joshua smiled and hugged me. He then excitedly told us about his strategy to stay alive.

"When the men see me, I run away as fast as I can, and then when I know I have lost them, I hide," he remarked with a proud smile. "Sometimes, they get angry because they can't find me, and they stomp the ground with their feet," he said as he let out a muffled giggle. The twins and I smiled with Joshua, but in my heart I knew what he was saying was disturbing and dangerous.

"You don't have to run anymore. You will live with us by the river until the killing stops. It has to happen sometime...in a couple of days," I said, trying to sound inspiring.

After a while longer, I told Joshua about some cassava roots we grew in our garden and suggested we could pack some in our pockets for the walk to the river.

We settled in our cassava farm several hundred feet away. We dug up fresh cassava roots that we all enjoyed. When we were all satisfied, Joshua talked about his older brothers and sisters and how he missed them. As the sun descended, the killing party must've broken into smaller groups. Some of them sounded like they were coming towards our cassava field, accompanied by snarling dogs. I pulled the twins into a tall plant and asked Joshua to stay with us. He followed me, but then he stopped, trying to see where the voices were coming from.

"Come on, Joshua," I whispered, "we'll be fine."

But Joshua was bouncing on his heels, not looking at me. "I can hear them," he anxiously whispered.

"I know," I said, "but they don't know we are here; come on! Please, stay with us, Joshua," I pleaded, looking in his eyes this time. He continued to bounce and looked around desperately. Without a warning, he dashed across the cassava field. "No! No, Joshua!" I said one last time.

Within a few breaths, I heard the killers alert others of the boy in the field and chased after him. Like the way they attacked Dad, their voices sounded from every corner. The men yelled familiar words, "Nimutangatange, nimutangatange!" which meant circle around or surround him.

My mind scrambled, *Run, Joshua, Run!* But soon I heard Joshua cry out, "Don't! Please don't hurt me!" mixed with yelping dogs and yelling men. His final cries were to his deceased father, asking him to rescue him. When his voice went silent, I knew they had finished him.

That night, the killers rounded up all the unsuspecting Tutsi women and children who were expecting the government's protection. For several hours, the nighttime sky rang with the outcry of female victims. I noticed the screams seemed to reveal various sentiments in their tone; some screams gave off the pitch of sheer outrage, while other screams carried the feel of disbelief mixed with horror. Most disturbing were the apathetic-sounding noises. After a while, the shouts sounded as if the casualties were already unconscious, and the vocal cords were working involuntarily. Hours after the screams stopped, in the pitch dark, we wandered through the farmland and near a swamp, where we spent a night.

When the sun came up in the morning, the twins had many welts from mosquito bites all over their bodies. Beyond the marsh was a barren slope and then a trail that descended into a eucalyptus forest that shone with the light filtering through the towering trees. It was in this desolate space that we made a home for a few days. Over the course of the following days, we wandered in this vast territory in pursuit of berries and pond water. It may have been Joshua's death that was a heart-wrenching reminder of how lucky we had been so far. *If they could do away with a tiny boy without question, how fortunate I had been to talk our way out of being killed.* And, unfortunately, that would not be the last time.

Chapter Thirteen

To kill time, the girls and I inserted our seeds, picked up small bundles of firewood, and moved out of our bush. We walked for miles, so when the girls became tired and demanded that I carry them, we abandoned our small bundles. Many mornings, we were drenched and our dirty clothes clamped onto our boney bodies. With the exception of the seeds widening our nostrils, we looked exactly like three displaced Tutsi children who had been residing in the bushes for months. When I looked up the trail with those thoughts in mind, it was obvious some men were assessing us. Steadily walking towards us was a group of Interahamwe. I continued onward with an image of Joshua's face in my mind. Afraid and shaken inside, I placed the twins down. Before we came face to face with this group, I gripped the twins by their hands. I cleared my throat and leveled my hunched back before we crossed paths. I repeated to myself, "*I am a Hutu and I belong here!*" The twins were terrified, their eyes fixed on the men's weapons. I dragged them forward as they pulled away from my grip. "Girls, we are Hutu and we will be fine," I reminded them.

Finally we were standing before them. With blood on their clothes and weapons in their hands, it felt as if their spirits had left them and they were now controlled by the devil. "Good morning," I said with an unnatural smile.

In hostile silence, the crowd closed off the trail and formed a half circle around us.

One of the leaders stepped forward. He was wearing a headdress with two horns attached to it, supposedly giving off an impression that he was a deadly wild animal. All I could do at that point was hope they weren't drawing the connection that was painfully evident, which was we were soaked, filthy, and in the middle of the forest because we were hiding. As I stared at their numerous killing tools, I wondered which one they would use to kill us and how painful it would feel. Before the man spoke, I begged God once more to protect us.

"What do you think, men? Are these three the children of our enemies? They look like the enemies to me, prowling near swamps like nasty little snakes."

A few of the men agreed as he stared at me.

"Where do you live?" he asked, walking around me and looking me up and down.

"Nyabisindu," I replied.

"Ha! Nyabisindu!" He smirked and scratched his head. "That is the home of kings and rulers! You must be a Tutsi then?" Without delay, he looked to the side of the flank and called for a young man to step forward. "Come here and deal with these snakes." My heart pounded and sweat dripped down my spine. *God, please protect us. Please cover us with your arms*, I prayed. A scrawny boy wearing an oversized, yellowish shirt, armed with a machete muddled his way through the rest of the flank, eventually standing before me. "Go ahead, they are little," said the leader, nudging the young boy's shoulder into the center of my chest.

I bounced back as I took notice of his blade again. The twins cried. *Oh God, we are about to be killed*, I screamed inside. Within moments, my muscles became tense, and I noticed an unusual energy. Deliberately, I shook my head, and with a manner of offense I announced, "What is wrong with you? What is wrong with you, Hutus?" I kept my eyes on the leader and gave him a glare. "You are about to cut down your fellow Hutus."

The men became quiet, and a sense of uneasiness filled the air. The scrawny boy's brow perspired as he angled his head toward the man who had given him permission to kill us. After a few more sighs, the leader's face went icy.

The twins continued to sob, so I picked them up, one in my right hand and the other in my left. After some of the killers mocked us, I had another chance to plead our case.

"Put the children down," demanded the leader, poking a bloody wooden club against my forehead, and affirming there was no way I had a Hutu's forehead.

"Our Dad is a loyal supporter of the mayor. He is at our home, and if I were you," I hesitated and added firmly, "I would not make the mistake of hurting us!"

Once more, my remarks seemed to shake them.

"We were with the mayor a few days ago. He is a family friend, and if you like, I will take you to him," I said, my fist pressed against my pelvis, my fake Hutu nose proudly flaunted, and my eyes screaming as if I was telling the truth.

As I stared into the eyes of the leader, the boy had taken a step backward. I decided that was my chance to escort the girls past the skeptical men. I never looked over my shoulder, but one of the men reminded me that a lie like that would not last long. "If we discover you're a Tutsi, I will split you into small pieces and serve you to the dogs," he warned.

I don't know if I looked confident during my conversation with the mob of Interahamwe, but as we stepped away, my eye twitched and my stomach coiled in knots. We found our next bush and we rested.

THE THREE OF us looked thinner. My bones pressed against my flesh. I couldn't say how much I weighed before the genocide, only that I was lean and healthy. Now, my clothes hung off my body, my skin had become pale, and my lips were cracked. Aside from soaking our faces in the stream nearby, we had not had a shower for over two months. Lice had forced their way into our hair, skin, and made themselves at home in our dirty clothes.

I spent my days thinking about how to stay alive and my nights about those I lost. It saddened me that prayers weren't said for Dad, as I at least prayed for Mom and Mucyo. As we roamed the forest, I convinced myself that Dad needed prayers: an improvised funeral to honor his kind spirit and generous heart. For closure, I needed to give him a final farewell. When the sun sank lower in the sky, we walked for hours until we approached the rear side of the hill where Dad's body had been dragged. I hadn't told the twins why, but I had asked them to carry wildflowers we collected along the way. I'm not certain what I was thinking, but I didn't press the seeds in my nose, nor did I bother carrying decoy firewood. Perhaps my thoughts were too bound up in the dread of seeing the condition of Dad's body. As we circled the hill, dodging as many roadblocks as possible, I reasoned that it would be best to pray at the place I had found Dad's jacket instead.

But when we drew near the other side of the summit, the sound of a motorcycle muffler rang through the forest. As the motorcycle came closer, I realized it was the mayor. He pulled up a few feet in front of us, turned off the engine, and kicked the stand out. Resting on the bike, he raised his forearm to his eyebrow to clear sweat and then squinted at us as he had done the last time we saw him. He was still amazed we had ridden out so many days in the wild and indicated that frequently in our discussion. I didn't want our meeting to go to waste, so I asked him if he knew of a place we could stay, again wishing he would volunteer his home to us. He rubbed his chin as if he was examining the trees for a solution. What he asked next I found strange, but the chance of him helping us was my first priority.

"Are they both girls?" he asked, pointing his index finger toward the twins.

"Of course they are girls. We are all girls," I clumsily answered, wondering what he wanted.

"Show me," he demanded, glancing back over the trail.

Confused, I asked, "Show you what?"

"You know what I'm proposing," he added, his eyeballs fixed on my skirt.

90

I unassertively told him my parents had said no one should see or touch our private parts. The mayor shook his head.

"So be it," he replied, as he swung back on his bike.

"Stop," I said, and unenthusiastically lifted my skirt and dropped my underpants to my knees. Embarrassed after several moments, I picked my underwear up and let down my skirt.

"Okay, now the others," he said, glancing at the twins again.

Teddy, suspecting what was coming, instantly protested.

"I don't want to be naked!" she said and stepped backward as I came for her. I struggled with her and then showed the mayor her privates and then Teta's. They were both upset with me, but considering our lives were on the line, it seemed unimportant to show this man our privates. After that, it was done. He cleared his throat and told us about part of a village near a checkpoint on the opposite side of the hill. He described how to get there and assured us we would be safe there.

"Things are difficult for the Tutsis right now. But I promise you will be protected at this place. Now, go!"

With that promise, he took off on his motorbike down the narrow trail. As we passed through the forest to reach the village, I had suspicions about the mayor's advice. But part of me wanted to trust him again. *There had to be order at some point. Maybe this is the beginning of real peace,* I hoped. Perhaps my inexperienced young mind caused me to be naïve, or it could have been that I was frantically yearning to find peace.

The mayor had already directed us to our home where many killers congregated, and now he was sending us to a Hutu- and Twa-populated section of the village. After a while, I concluded that if he wished to kill us, he would've done it himself. He had two opportunities to murder us, and he still sounded dignified, even though I felt strangely humiliated by his petition to show our private parts. With nothing but uncertainty ahead of us, I delayed the graveside prayers for Dad and followed the mayor's directions toward this "peaceful" part of the village, as he defined it.

Chapter Fourteen

I didn't realize at that time how close we were to surviving the genocide. To my best recollection, it was mid-June when I followed the mayor's recommendation for the second time. July 1st, a day Rwandans later called Liberation Day, was still several weeks away. Unfortunately, unlike a spigot on a faucet, genocide cannot turn off in a second, a day, a week, or even a month.

As we passed through a valley toward the fires that night, I felt my hollow nostrils, having abandoned the seeds from my nose along the trail. Our hands were empty of prop firewood. From that moment on, I never pushed another seed up my nose. I was done pretending to be a Hutu. I was done convincing myself I was an adult when I could hardly keep us fed. I stepped into that village as a child, a Tutsi girl, searching for compassion and protection from God.

The path led us into the center of the village. Beyond the first two houses was a gathering impossible to miss. In an instant, we were among them. The crowd of people were eating, drinking, and resting. Various people were lounging, sitting cross-legged near the campfire, slurping traditional beers. Smoke drifted. A dozen men squatted around a fire roasting meat. Women and children meandered about. Chickens pecked at the dirt. A heap of machetes and wooden clubs lay on the grass near the fire pit. At that moment, I was certain the mayor had deceived me again.

With no trees to shield us, I walked backward, praying that no one had spotted us. I pulled the girls and took a few more steps when we heard, "You girls, come over here."

I stepped away when a man whose sharp eyes were barely visible under his mashed-green military hat loudly called us. On wobbly legs, I slowly came up to the group. Only the man in the green hat addressed me. The others kept busy with their plates of meat and beer. He eyed me up and down, questioning where I've been and why I was there. I told him the mayor had sent us and glanced back at the twins, who were watching. While we talked, the other men lamented how Tutsis could still be above ground in their homeland, taking time to shake their heads in contempt.

Next, I noticed the man's narrow eyes fix on the collection of blades and other killing tools piled up in the grass. The man scratched his head as he judiciously excised a portion of chicken from its bone with his big white teeth. Still chewing, he declared, "I suppose the mayor sent you here to die." I paused, squinting at him semi-spellbound, the trace of a query hanging from my lips. But I lacked the strength to produce another lie to stay alive.

"We are here, and it is in God's hands now," I replied as I lowered my head.

"The case is settled. But you are lucky, cockroaches. You have made it here when we are hungry. Go sit down over there. We will get rid of you in a few minutes." He pointed at some rocks near a house.

"Sit still until we are finished," another man barked out.

I uttered prayers while the twins sat silent, rolling small rocks along the densely packed clay. Teddy appeared preoccupied with the notion of us getting hurt, causing her bottom lip to bend upward. I pulled them closer and swore we would be safe even though I was uncertain about our survival. I realized we had little chance, but telling the twins we were about to die would not have helped.

An hour passed as we sat in silence, waiting to be executed. It was getting darker and the men's voices were getting louder. One of the intoxicated and smallest men in the group was having trouble processing how Tutsi children could still be alive. "Shame! Shame!" he garbled with a high-pitched whine. "What sort of mayor sends cockroaches to us instead of dealing with them himself? Shame on him. Shame on him," he shouted as he shook his head and wiped a dribble of brew from his chin.

As time dragged on, the men drank and ate more. Some played cards and puffed cigarettes as additional empty beer bottles rolled at their feet. A few of them now slumped in the grass, shirts untucked and bellies swollen from their feast. Mostly, their discussion centered on the cards, but periodically the short man would remind the group they had one more task to handle before they turned in for the night.

"You have fifteen minutes. Say your prayers," the short, drunk one stammered, fumbling his cards. But fifteen minutes came and went. As darkness fell, I felt a sense that God was intervening, and somehow we would survive the day. Still, I found it ironic that we were invited to pray while they were planning to kill us. But pray is what I did the minute my eyes met the group. Still puzzled that he could speak of God, knowing he was preparing to kill us, I encouraged Teddy and Teta to pray, too. I watched as they folded their little hands and murmured something quickly.

"Jeanne, are we going to die?" they asked almost at the same time.

I waited to respond and said, "No, we will be fine." When I wasn't praying, I was observing the men. The group, even the drunk one, displayed an obvious and disproportionate measure of respect to one man in particular. The man was called Furaha by the others; they spoke of him with admiration. Furaha stood to relieve himself in the shrubs, his muscular triceps and forearms flexing to display a network of bulging veins that stretched from the back of his knuckles to his neckline. He was at least a half foot taller than the other men and his hairline receded halfway up his skull. When he walked, his shirt stuck to his back and shoulders like an extra layer of skin. He had on baggy green camouflage fatigues held in place by a thin black rope. Aside from one or two vanishing smirks, he wore a serious expression pasted on his narrow brown face. Nearly every physical characteristic showed me he was an important man to the group, and I knew he was our sole chance of surviving the night.

A woman, who I first noticed tending to the grill when we arrived, passed by us numerous times to keep the men's plates full. Each time she passed, her face would soften more. After everybody had eaten and were full, she asked Furaha if she could serve us. The drunken man, now unable to contain his words blurted out, "Waste food on the children of our enemy?" Furaha and the woman disregarded the drunken man's remarks. With his eyes on his lap, Furaha said with a deep, raspy voice, "They will die tomorrow. No reason to make them starve tonight. Feed them."

With that, the woman walked back to the house and came back with a plate of meat, beans, and sweet potatoes. I received the plate and whispered thanks to her. She studied me with sorrow in her eyes and attempted a smile. Such a modest and humane gesture overwhelmed me after being treated badly for so long, and my stomach fluttered, my throat choked, and tears appeared in the corners of my eyes. The twins didn't have a problem eating and enjoying the meal, chewing too swiftly once they realized the consistency was much softer than the raw scraps they had fed on for more than two months.

Like the voice of God had come to me, I was still processing the words spoken by Furaha at that moment, without emotion or the slightest hint of consequence in them, which made the situation instantly clear: we would live through the night and die in the morning. The other men hardly reacted to Furaha's suggestion, only one recommending that we stay the night with Furaha, "their best soldier."

Furaha directed us to his house, situated in the center of the village. He threw open his front door, and entering the main room, I found myself in a low-ceilinged room that when looking to the other side appeared to droop. Furaha yawned and set his beer bottle on one of the two small stools that were the only furniture in the living room.

"Alice! Bring the bedding," ordered Furaha.

Someone else was living with this man. Who could it be? I wondered. *Maybe his wife!*

There were only two rooms aside from the living room where we stood. In a few seconds, a shadowy form appeared in the murkily lit doorway of one of the rooms. It was Alice, a girl I identified as one of the older students in my school. Alice held a folded-up mat under one arm and an oil lamp in her hand. She was wearing a traditional skirt that fell to her shins and was barefoot, like the three of us. Moving toward us, she made eye contact. After placing the mat near Furuha, she came for me, wrapping her arms around my torso.

"Jeanne," she sighed in my ear.

I embraced her tighter, then moved back to get a better view of her. Her cheeks were once full and her shining ebony skin silky and unblemished. Now her cheeks had caved in, her skin was pasty and dry, and her eyes were positioned so far back in the sockets it looked like her skull was hollow. At one time she was one of the prettiest eighth-graders in school, but now her garments hung off her body as if hanging over a stick. I touched her cheekbones, feeling as if I was touching a porcelain doll. The genocide, it appeared, had already seized her life.

Furaha's deep voice blared from across the room.

"You two know each other?" he inquired dryly, making it sound like he had something better to do at that moment.

Neither of us answered him. Furaha kicked the mat in my direction and signaled it was time to sleep.

I unfolded the mat, placing it down on the mud-packed floor, and the twins hastily found a place on it. Meanwhile, Furaha had left us to bring back another thin mat from his bedroom. When I noticed it in his hands, I said, "Oh, one mat is good enough for us, but God bless you."

He shook his head and chugged the remainder of his beer.

"Silly little girl. You think I would allow you to sleep alone? You must think I am a fool," he groaned as he laid his mat down next to ours.

My heart pounded. I had expected he would sleep in his bedroom, giving us an opportunity to slip out his front entrance.

"I don't think you're a fool. But you should be able to rest in your comfortable bed."

"I'm sure you're interested with my sleeping accommodations," he said sarcastically. "Let me warn you in case you think about crawling out while I sleep. Outside my door are the houses of my Twa friends. They don't go to bed. And they may enjoy killing Tutsis more than Hutus, so you are free to meet them if you like."

Furaha removed his shoes, blew out the remaining lantern flame, settled himself between me and Alice, and commanded the twins to sleep on the opposite side of me. Within moments, the twins were fast asleep while I gazed into the blackness toward Furaha's back. Sleeping close to a grown man, who was probably in his late forties or early fifties, and a stranger, felt odd and creepy. It reminded me of the mayor's request to examine our private parts.

But within minutes my mind wandered to the unknowns of tomorrow. *Would Furaha kill us in the morning?* I felt tremendous pressure having taken the twins here; if they died the next day because of me, I would have failed Mom and Dad. While all these thoughts flowed through my mind, I noticed Furuha had moved about, and now his black silhouette was outlined on top of Alice's body. My eyes widened and moved toward the wrestling blobs of darkness. After I heard Furaha's heaving sigh and the thump of skin colliding, I tried to tell him to stop, but struggled to get out the words. "St-t-t...." Then Alice gasped for breath under his weight, and I felt obligated to intervene.

"Stop! Stop it! You're hurting her," I said loud enough to awaken the twins.

"What? Shut up, child. Go to sleep," he said, and then went back to his grunting noises. But I perched up on my backside until he stopped, hoping Alice was not hurt by his crushing weight. When Furaha moved off her, he wrestled with his clothes and resumed his sleeping posture. That's when I finally laid my head down, half wondering why he was harassing Alice while she slept and still obsessed with forming an escape plan.

I tried escaping twice that night. The first time was a good hour after Furaha's sexual attack on Alice. I made it to the doorway and prepared to open it first, then go back for my sleeping sisters. But when I opened the dilapidated door, it sounded like the whole thing might fall apart. The squealing door brought Furaha out of his slumber and to his feet, pursuing me as I crumbled into a ball, shielding my face with my forearms. Angrily, Furaha lifted me with the same ease he picked up his beer bottle and hurled me across the room and onto the startled twins.

My next try came after I heard Furaha's slow breathing transform into heavy snoring. Again, I made it to the doorway, and this time the door mysteriously produced less noise, but when I had the door securely open and peeped over my shoulder for the girls, I heard Furaha's snoring come to a dead halt, as if his creepy intuition had alarmed him. Again, he charged for me, and I folded my body into a trembling sphere. But rather than flinging me across the room, he lifted me up to my feet, pushed me back into the room, and slammed the door as he left the house.

While Furaha did whatever he was doing outside, I paced back and forth and asked Alice what she expected.

"Do you think he is gathering his men to come for us?"

"I don't know, Jeanne, but if he comes back, don't try this again. You're putting us all in danger."

I had tried hard enough and was trembling at the prospect of what Furaha might do or who he would return with. Exhausted, I settled next to the twins and draped my arms around them. Alice dozed off. After a short while, Furaha returned. Without a sound, he returned to his place between me and Alice. Only when I heard his heavy breathing again did I close my eyes and prayed. I was psychologically drained, and concluded that if we were going to die the next day, I might as well sleep.

Chapter Fifteen

I wasn't used to waking to sounds uncommon to the forest, so as I awoke from a half-dreamy state that morning, I tried to interpret the origin of the groans that filled the room. I gradually raised my head and opened my heavy eyes as the source of the grunting came into view. Eight feet from me was a man, well into his nineties, stretched out on his side on the floor near the wood fire pit and wheezing for oxygen. I noted what remained of his hair. It was a scattered cluster of gray wires circling his skull like a crown. The back of his neck was layered with thick folds of skin, and a fleshy pouch of skin dangled from his jaw.

In my experience, elderly people had mostly been caring and sensible, so it comforted me to see him there. I supposed he might comfort us, or at least share his wisdom. I smiled and went to him. But when his glazed eyes settled on me, a guttural sound came from his mouth; he sounded disturbed about something. I assumed he wanted me to help him off the floor, so I crouched beside him. He stared into my eyes but did not smile back. With a friendly, soft voice, I asked him if he needed a hand.

"No, snake!" he gasped. I thought I misheard him, but he repeated himself.

"A snake?" I asked. He emptied his lungs, inhaled, declared I was a treacherous reptile, and demanded that I get away from him.

Puzzled, I leaned onto my haunches; that is when my perception of the old man became even more unusual. He was dressed in nothing more than a maroon shirt—no boots, socks, pants, or underwear. There was only the ancient man's ashy backside dimly lit by the morning sun. I looked at Alice, who squatted on the other side of the old man, meticulously adding wood to the cooking fire. Without words, I gave her a look that asked for an explanation for the nude old man huddled up near the fire.

Noticing my confusion, she cracked a modest smile, stood up, and walked over.

"This is Karl, Furaha's father," she spoke softly, taking a seat next to me. "He sleeps all day in the other bedroom. Other days, he spends his time nestled near the warm fire. He's very old, as you can tell. Probably can't make out a word we are saying right now due to his bad hearing."

"What's wrong with his legs?"

"According to Furaha, until three or four months ago, he could walk around with a stick. Now, his legs are too weak and all he can do is scoot along the floor."

"Why is he naked?"

Alice looked to make sure Karl wasn't trying to listen in on our conversation. Then she leaned toward me and whispered. "He can't control his bladder, and sometimes his bowel movements, too."

"Well, that is sickening," I responded.

"Furaha makes me clean up the excrement from his clothes and I still have to wash them," Alice replied.

When Alice completed her last remark, I sniffed the air expecting to inhale the stench, but the air was stale and musty and only contained a trace of burnt wood.

"It's not that awful, Jeanne. I am used to this now," Alice said, noticing my grimace. "He doesn't relieve himself that often because he barely eats or drinks."

We moved to the corner of the room and exchanged survival stories while the twins and the old man slept. Alice cooked a small pot of beans for Karl, who didn't want to eat because he didn't have an appetite, so we ate them while she filled me in on Furaha's daily activities.

"He normally leaves right as the sun comes up. I think he and his men venture out into the forests and hills hunting for Tutsis. When he returns, he makes me clean his tools and prepare his food. If I'm lucky, I don't see him until the sun goes down." She then described his rules for the house.

"Do you think he goes out to kill Tutsis?" I asked.

Alice looked at me and shook her head. "Don't be a child. He doesn't have a job; every morning he gets up with a machete and comes back late in the evening. So, what do you think he does all day?"

I acknowledged that I did not know, but Alice shared that Furaha gave her regular updates on the Tutsis he saw getting slaughtered, but he never confirmed if he had killed anyone.

I asked why she hadn't left.

"I can't leave, Jeanne, unless it is to fetch water."

"I have to run away before he returns," I said, "today is the day they will kill us, and besides, I can't bear him abusing you or listen to him talk about the people who were put to death." I wandered toward the doorway to catch a peek of who was outside.

"That's a dangerous plan," she responded. "He wasn't exaggerating about the neighbors. Those people are fanatics; they rape, murder, and mutilate women and girls."

I listened to her as I eyeballed a group of Hutu and Twa boys kicking a deflated soccer ball nearby, and recognized one of the Twa boys who used to sell flower pottery to my mom. She regularly gave him food to eat and to share with his family. Despite Alice's objection, I was convinced leaving now was the best option for me and the twins.

"I can outrun those boys. I have to, Alice. They threatened to kill us last night and they know we are here."

Alice stood and came near me.

"There is a reason you didn't die last night," she paused while staring into my eyes. "Furaha caught you trying to escape and forgave you. If he was going to kill you, it would've happened last night. Believe me, those boys, particularly the small ones, aren't your main worry. Not far from them are the teenagers. They are vicious. Worse than some of the adults. They are evil. Besides, how are you going to outrun them with your sisters?"

I reminded her of my time in the bushes, but she shook her head, rejecting my decision.

We remained in silence, staring at the group of boys as they chuckled and pursued each other as free and fun-loving children. Their high-pitched laughter stirred resentment in me. I let out a heavy sigh, sitting down next to the twins and stroked their heads while they slept.

"I know it's scary," Alice said, "but I have been warned a hundred times by Furaha and his men. And look, I'm still here."

As the day ticked by, the dread lessened. Alice knew these people better than I did, so listening to her advice seemed liked the right thing to do. Just as Alice predicted, when Furaha returned, he didn't mention hurting us. In relief, I helped Alice prepare his meal and tend to the old man. That night, when the light went out, I didn't feel entirely safe, yet I didn't feel the persistent fear of dying, either.

THE MAIN CONTRAST in the following night we spent at Furaha's house was that I didn't attempt to get away. Instead, I slept solidly, my arms wrapped over the twins. I only woke once in the night, again to the sound of Alice being sexually abused. This time I held my tongue, which was even more troubling.

In the morning, Karl woke us once again, clearing mucus from his lungs and groaning. This time, I woke with Alice. She had become accustomed to the repulsive image of Karl's private parts jiggling about as he scooted from the living area to his bedroom. Karl proceeded to generate angry grunts at us, occasionally spraying saliva through his discolored teeth. It took me until the end of the day to interpret his offensive language. With Alice's help, I determined that he realized we were Tutsis and he disliked us for that. He demonstrated his contempt at our ethnicity by shouting slurs and insulting us. Some of the profanity he used I had not heard before. After Alice explained their meaning, I grew even more disturbed. In response to his slurs, I secretly mocked him, as he continually went on rants I could not ignore.

102

Teddy and Teta were oblivious to most of the slurs he used except for common insults like "stupid." I had always insisted that they were smart and assured them the old man did not know what he was talking about.

Since the twins were now living indoors, their moods had mellowed. They slept much better, and even the dark circles around their eyes began to fade. Like any other little kids, they darted from room to room, chasing each other and giggling. The girls' jovial moods seemed to irritate Karl, but they saw their interaction with him as another chance to play games. The twins took much delight in pointing out Karl's lack of clothing. "You're naked. Grandpa is naked," they exclaimed as they ran in circles around the elderly man. Hearing them refer to Karl as "Grandpa" irritated both me and him, but I was happy to see the twins behaving as toddlers again. One game they made up on the second day amused all of us except Karl. The girls pulled potatoes out from the tan cloth bag that sat near Karl's fire pit. With the potatoes held in their outstretched palms, they presented them to Karl saying, "Potatoes. Want potato, Grandpa?" When Karl reached for the potato, the girls pulled it away, chuckling, as he struggled to slap at their legs. Being overpowered by Karl was something we didn't have to fret about. Sometimes I purposely passed close by him to watch him waste his strength trying to slap me.

In the late afternoon while Karl and the twins took naps, Alice opened her heart up more after I told her about my parents and little brother. Alice and I had never been close friends due to our age difference. Now, because of our common experiences, I felt closer to her in terms of maturity. She went on about her trials after I fell into a lengthy period of silence, allowing me a chance to wipe my eyes. If anyone could identify with how I was affected, it had to be her. Confiding in her felt easy; like talking to my twin sister Jeannette.

"I have lost many, too," she said, staring at the wall. "My mom was with me when we came here. We were in search of something to eat and heard the news that the government wanted to protect Tutsi women and children. But when we arrived, the men and teenagers gathered around us, shouting and taunting us for trusting the government's lies. They beat and raped her right in front of me." Tears fell from Alice's eyes as I rested my arms on her emaciated shoulders, comforting her.

"They threw her in a toilet hole! Alive!" She sobbed. "Those animals defecate on her every day just a few meters from here."

"My God," I gasped, covering my mouth. After a burst of tears, I bent forward and embraced her. There were no words I could think of to soothe her. After some time had passed, I asked if she had been told any news of her mom recently. She told me the Hutu and Twa boys from the community report to her every three or four days. They do it mockingly, describing the feces stuck to her mom and the moans she makes as they shower her with rocks.

"They say she refuses to die," she said with a helpless gaze.

With all of my imagined power, I assured her I would set those boys straight when they came back again to tell her news about her mother. "They will know they have a place in hell," I added.

"Please, don't. Those boys are not afraid of anything at all. If provoked, they could break in here, or catch me on a water run."

"You must cover your ears next time when they come to update you. They shouldn't torment you and your mom," I said.

"No, I need to hear it. I wish they would tell me that my mom had passed away. I always pray that one day that will be their report, and I will have peace knowing she is in a better place, free from suffering." I wiped away my tears and reached out to wipe hers away, too.

We lay quiet for a while, waiting for the impact of her story to decrease. After some time, I decided to distract her mind with a story from our old school. We chatted about our former schoolmates, wondering where they were and if our schoolhouse was still standing. Then the discussion shifted to Furaha. Aside from his late-night appearances, I had seen little of him. Alice filled me in on how to keep his mood stable, establishing ground rules.

"It's better not to talk until he mentions something to you. Never confuse his intentions. He is not sparing us out of charity. You know that he abuses me every night?" I nodded my head.

Since I only had a little understanding of rape from the cries of victims and the fumbling around Furaha did at night, I wanted to know the specifics. Alice offered an exact description, and when she stopped, I felt sick to my stomach. I had the urge to protect Alice and tried to persuade her again of my plan to get away with the twins, but she promptly disagreed with my proposal.

"Run away to where, Jeanne? There is no one in my family left apart from my mom in a toilet hole. Plus, the men out there have shown how ruthless they can be. Some have HIV and are intentionally infecting Tutsi women and girls who they don't prefer to kill. I'd rather be abused by one man than by a hundred. Trust me. It can get worse."

We allowed the afternoon to pass in silence. When Furaha returned, I looked at him with hostility; I didn't respect him. As I sat silently, I wished he was smaller so I could fight him to save Alice. Even though Furaha never owned up to murdering anyone himself, he intimidated me now that I had a clear understanding of what he was doing to Alice at night. I went to bed praying for safekeeping, especially for Alice who panted for oxygen under Furaha's bulky frame.

My thoughts roamed to my sisters and brothers, and I made an effort to visualize a day we could be together as a family again.

The following few days brought a mysterious vigor to Karl. He woke up bright and early, sat without coughing, and passed up his long afternoon naps. With more spare time on his hands and more strength in his body, he could engage us in more discussion and articulate more precisely. Still, he never greeted us in the morning even though the twins shouted a morning salutation to "Grandpa" as they discovered him scurrying across the floor. After a few days in the house, he may have grown bored of the silence, and inquired how we ended up in his son's home.

"Where did my son find you snakes? Hiding under the rocks?" he asked.

Alice had previously told him, but he wanted to hear it from me or may have forgotten. There was no point in covering anything up, so with minimal detail, I explained getting run out of our house, my parents' deaths,

105

and living in the forests with the twins. For some reason, a part of me believed that when Karl heard my entire story he would have empathy, maybe even exercise the respect accorded him as an elder in the village to encourage others to stop the massacre and rape. I have always believed with old age comes the knowledge to do the moral thing.

Karl listened carefully. When I stopped, he then asked, "You know the issue with the Tutsis?"

I left the question unanswered, as I only saw the Hutu killing squads as the problem.

"The Tutsis only know greed. All of my life I have seen it. Tutsis want, want, and want, until there is nothing left behind to want. Once everything is burned up, they blow up their heads with more arrogance. Always wanting, always believing they are better than us and better than the Twas," he said, looking at me grimly.

I looked at Alice as if to get permission to speak to him. "How can you say that about all Tutsis?" I asked, "How would you know if they are all greedy and arrogant?"

His brows furrowed, and he shook his head in disagreement.

"My parents. Have you ever met them?" I did not wait for his response. "My parents were not selfish. Yes, they worked hard, and we lived a comfortable life, but they gave nearly as much as they received. I can guarantee you that if they were alive, they would share their harvests, offer aid to you and your family." Karl shook his head. "Is that greed?" I asked.

Karl looked toward the ceiling and said, "I can say this because I have lived a long life," raising his voice and spraying saliva onto his chin. "I have seen how the Tutsi king forced Hutus to praise him. You can thank your ancestors for your parents' deaths. Justice is served to your people. If you're Tutsi, you deserve nothing but extinction. We must wipe them out and start over. This land should be Tutsi-free."

The old man's remarks infuriated me. Before I said something insulting, I shut down the debate, but added one last piece of wisdom for him to consider. "My parents," I said, keeping back tears, "told us that hatred toward another person is hatred toward yourself. Mom said that we

106

are all God's children, and to God, Tutsi, Twa, or Hutu really doesn't matter. He loves us all the same."

With those words, he scoffed and swung back to the fire.

Chapter Sixteen

Alice served a purpose for Furaha. His late-night sexual assaults added to her value. Thankfully, Furaha hadn't touched me, but it made me wonder what kind of value he believed I possessed as a young girl. I realized that being pleasant and silent might not impress him enough to keep us around. So I made an effort to pull my own weight as well as that of the twins'. I would begin in the early dawn just before Furaha was up and about, sweeping the fragments of half-burned wood into the inner perimeter of the fire pit. On my knees, I thoroughly dusted the ash and other residues of the firewood until all that was left was the hard-packed mud floor.

My other duty involved organizing the house, making sure everything was dusted and in order. I also helped Alice in the kitchen when there was food to cook. We teamed up to clean Karl's bedroom. With the smell of urine, the room had to be cleaned out as swiftly as possible.

Despite my effort, Furaha griped about the twins, pointing out their failure to cook or clean. I explained to him the twins were only three years old. In his judgment, the girls were grown enough to take part in performing chores at home. So, when Furaha was present I gave the twins small pieces of cloth to help clean, hoping to establish their usefulness to Furaha. Not once did he acknowledge their efforts.

"What use are these girls?" he asked me, suggesting he was doing me a favor keeping them. I reminded him how I appreciated his generosity to let us stay in his house. I pointed out that Alice and I did all the cleaning and cooking, and as a result, the twins didn't have to do any of it.

Hoping to impress Furaha, I involved the twins in all I did; while I was cooking or tidying up, I gave them simple, nearly insignificant tasks to demonstrate their participation. The girls enjoyed helping me around the house. With big smiles on their faces, the twins watched me carefully and imitated everything I did. I called them my "little helpers."

One of the greatest challenges of the housework was keeping enough water. Alice and I used as little water as possible, but now that there were five of us using the water for cooking, face and hand washing, clothes washing, and drinking, it did not last long. The natural spring where Alice filled the water container was on the opposite side of the village. Getting to it meant passing by other members of the village, who detested us for our physical appearance. Alice had it down to an art; she knew how to walk, act, and when to leave the house, specifically during the time most of the dangerous members of the village were occupied. Regardless, most of the villagers had spoken with her and knew of the arrangement between her and Furaha.

One day, Furaha had returned early for lunch and to shower. Instantly annoyed, Furaha tilted the water jug, noticing it was almost empty. He glared at the four of us and complained that we constantly drank and wasted water.

"Now we are out of water, thanks to you," he said, staring at me and the twins. Alice, trying to defuse the situation, suggested that she would refill the water container immediately, but Furaha refused. He declared that we were worthless.

"No," he said, pointing at me, "she will go. It is her time to do some work around here."

Alice knew sending me through the village was dangerous because her first several times refilling the water, Hutu boys pelted her with rocks and tormented her along the way. She made another effort to defend me, pointing out the obvious hazards, particularly being that only a few of the local Hutus knew of my presence, but Furaha was unsympathetic to the risk and brushed it off.

"If it is her turn, then it is her turn," he added. All of this was amusing to Karl, who was observing the exchange with a wide smile on his face.

"I need water now, not tomorrow. Get moving!" he ordered as he doused the rest of the water on his face and scalp.

Without a way out, I wandered over to the water jug and imagined the heavy weight of it when full. Alice gave her final plea for me, pointing out the weight of the container filled with water. She volunteered her services instead one more time. Once again, Furaha dismissed the suggestion. I spent a few minutes talking strategy with Alice, who recommended I fill the container halfway if I couldn't carry it. I thanked and embraced her, and asked her to look after the twins if anything happened to me. I kissed the twins on their temples. With a weakened stomach, I stepped out of the house toward the mud huts on top of the hill.

After a week of being indoors, the sunlight appeared much brighter. I squinted, surveying the trail that led to the water spring. I walked farther down the hill, where the Hutu and Twa boys were quick to discover me. They approached me aggressively, asking questions, and flicking my brow with their fingers. They demanded to know what right I had to show my face in public and shoved me about, knocking the jug out of my hands. At first I remained silent, but then I threatened retaliation from Furaha if I was injured or if the jug was destroyed. The mention of Furaha's name was sufficient to soften their assault, but they pursued me, pointing to the lifeless bodies on the hillside, declaring each dead body as my relative. They followed me to the bottom of the slope and stared as I disappeared into the forest that led to the water spring, shouting, "Tutsi. Tutsi. Kill the Tutsi!"

Shortly after, I stood at the end of a line of a dozen people holding plastic water containers. I carried the jug high, hoping to cover my Tutsi features. The fountain ran slowly, so it took each person a good while to fill up their large water containers. I listened as people spoke of simple things—the sunny weather, planting crops—but nothing about the mass murder. As their conversation dried up, a few of them glanced around and realized that a foreigner was among them. One of the middle-aged women snooping around my jug loudly mentioned my narrow nose and round forehead, pointing out that either the Hutu children are looking like Tutsis nowadays, or I was a cockroach among them. As more Hutus filed in procession behind me, the woman discussed my appearance with them.

"There is an enemy among us taking your water!" she called out.

All the while I held the container high over my face and prayed they would let the subject die down, but the people behind me clucked their tongues and tore the container away from me, forcing a look at my face. Then the men behind me, sensing my discomfort, remarked loudly about the Tutsis they had killed earlier.

By the time I was close to the front of the line, I felt light-headed, as if I had held my breath for far too long. When I stepped into the murky water, all I wanted was for time to speed up, to somehow be transported back to Furaha's house to be with the girls. The water gradually drizzled from the spring into the jug, and voices in the line became boisterous. I wasn't looking at anyone, but I sensed their eyes on me. In my best effort to be hopeful, I began blocking out the insults they threw at me.

As my jug filled, I was hopeful that I had passed the crisis. In an instant, a shirtless, wiry man protested loudly. Everyone froze and fixed their eyes on him. Something awful was about to take place. I had never received a close-fisted punch in the face. The closest I had come to receiving a real punch was the time my twin sister slugged me in the shoulder for telling on her. But this was a hundred times worse. My ears buzzed as a stinging pain radiated around my right eye and up my temple. I was struck once again by the wiry man before I let go of the jug and fell into the mud. Another scrawny man who stood near the front of the line ran up, cheering with the others. Their sweaty faces twisted into scream masks, tight eyes, with stretchy mouths as they announced my demise. A crowd of at least four kicked, punched, and slapped me as I covered my face with my arms and folded into a compact ball. I'm not certain how long the beating lasted or why it stopped, but it did. When I looked up, there were only two men standing over me. They took a moment to spit on me before going away, their saliva bunching and wobbling as it landed on me, running down my face and dripping off my hands as my back sank into the mud. My head spun and I felt disoriented, but all I could think about was Teddy and Teta. *If I die, Furaha will kick the twins out of his home*, I worried.

I then stumbled to my feet; a needle-pointed pain filled my muscles, primarily around my ribs, as I searched for breath. Fumbling for my jug, I sensed another person coming toward me. Flinching, I collapsed onto the ground and back into a fetal position. But the approaching person was not interested in beating me. The woman hovering over me appeared to have pity. Her face contorted in distress at the sight of me. Without saying much, she helped me to my feet and finished filling the jug for me, ignoring the criticism from the other Hutus still present. I wanted to thank her for her good nature, but instead I choked up and my voice became mute. I tried to clear my throat again, but it was as if there was a golf ball stuck there.

I was still delirious from the beating when the kind woman carried my jug to the top of the hill for me. Watching me closely as I attempted to lift it, she quietly apologized for the people's actions. Water splashed out of the jug as I dragged it through the dust and back to Furaha's house. Entering the house, I pulled the jug to the cooking area and ran to Alice, falling down at her side. Releasing a wave of tears into her shirt, I let the emotional pain of the beating flow out of me. Alice wrapped her arms around me and rubbed my back until I stopped crying. Her voice trembled when she asked me what happened.

All the while, the twins stood by, concerned and confused. When I gathered myself, I rolled onto my back. A stinging pain shot from my spine. Alice and the twins tended to me, wetting small cloths and gently swabbing the blood from my forehead and eyes. The flesh above my right eye was raw and enlarged to an egg shape. I pressed my hands against the lumps on my temple. Alice asked me to open my mouth to see if they had knocked my teeth out, pointing out that my bottom lip was split open and I had another gash on my chin.

Karl clapped his hands and snorted lustily, taunting me. "Why didn't they get rid of you?" he asked, chuckling. Karl scooted closer to me, smiling ear to ear. "I want details on how they beat you," he demanded.

As I began to offer the information, Alice brought potatoes to the fire pit and pulled me away from Karl. "Can't you tell Karl is excited about you being hurt?" she asked. I sat next to Alice while she peeled the potatoes. Karl came and joined us by the fire.

I noticed Karl leaned over, dangerously close to the fire, and appeared to be concealing something. When I walked by, I saw he was holding a short stick he had lit on fire. Karl struggled to poke me with the burning stick and I leaped out of the way. He swore as he missed me. Alice looked at him disappointingly and clutched my shoulder. "Jeanne, the devil wants you dead today," Alice remarked. I nodded while glaring at Karl. With his attempt to burn me still fresh in mind, I kept my eyes on him, waiting for him to get sleepy. When I was sure he was sleeping, I took a small stick and jabbed at the smoldering woodpile, knocking bits of lit kindling onto his leg. Karl woke, wailed, and smacked the bits of kindling, most of which landed near him.

"She's trying to kill me! Help! Son, help me!" he shouted.

Furaha was out of the house, and Alice attempted to calm him.

"It was an accident," she said. "She didn't mean to stir the fire that hard."

As Karl continued to disagree, I checked to see if the potatoes were ready. For an instant, the anguish—both physical and emotional—temporarily subsided as my body warmed at the thought of Karl feeling pain as well.

A few hours later, Furaha returned home for dinner, squatting on his seat. He chomped on a potato as Karl retold the conflict.

"These snakes are trying to kill me," he said, begging for my death. Furaha considered the accusations and then shook his head.

"Dad, no one hates Tutsis more than you do. This time, I believe the girls. It must have been an accident. They wouldn't do something that stupid on purpose," he said, eyeing me intensely. I nodded my head.

At nightfall, we gathered on the mats and slept. I tried to disregard the body aches as I reflected on the day. Although Karl was fine after our incident, I thought of what my parents might have said knowing I intentionally burned him. I thought about the beatings I endured at the water spring, and then a loop of pictures filled my head: the death of Mucyo, Joshua, Uncle Edward, and my parents. Then I imagined Alice's mom in a toilet pit with maggots consuming her body, and the desolate expression on Alice's face the morning after the sexual assaults. The bit of guilt I felt about hurting Karl disappeared as I went to sleep that night.

IT WAS A Sunday morning when Furaha told us to prepare a few eggs for the village minister, a barrel-chested man with eager, intelligent eyes, dressed in black slacks and a yellow button-up shirt. He walked quickly through the house and spoke enthusiastically of gathering others for praise and worship later in the day. The man opened his prayer book and delivered prayers over Karl's bedside, something Furaha had called upon him to do regularly since his father became so sick. Karl didn't leave his room and no longer scooted about the house or even had the strength to curse us. Alice and I provided him bedside care, feeding him soft food, mostly boiled eggs, mashed potatoes, and legumes. Every time he raised his finger and touched his lips, it was an indication he was thirsty. I gently poured tiny drops of water into his mouth. Despite how slowly and how little water I poured past Karl's crusty, quivering lips, he coughed and gagged. He looked as if he was in constant pain, and most of his days he spent coiled up on his side. Despite his hatred toward Tutsis, I felt empathy for him. One morning I asked him if he wanted me to pray for him, but he let out a faint "No," which trailed off into silence. But as he slept, I silently asked God to release his pain anyway.

The following days, Karl's condition deteriorated; he stopped eating altogether and made even less noise. Late one night, Karl's final guttural moan filled the house. We followed Furaha into Karl's dimly lit room, watching as he bent over his father's twisted body and listened to a final, hard sigh that seeped from him. Without a tear, Furaha walked back into the living room and proceeded to eat his potatoes and beans.

Little was said that night as we helped Furaha prepare his father's body for the relatives and guests who flooded the house to say their good-byes to Karl. Late in the night, dozens more villagers solemnly walked through the house to pay tribute to the old man. It was difficult to reconcile what I thought of Karl with the images of the visitors crying and praying over his body, as though they genuinely missed his presence.

Some people brought food and drinks. The four of us quietly talked about how we couldn't wait for the visitors to leave the house so we could eat. The whole scene reminded me of something so ordinary, something that could have passed for a memory of my old life.

The last time I saw Karl was when Furaha and his cousin carried him through the living room right before his funeral; Karl's head slid over his shoulder toward me for one last look as they departed. That scowl of hatred seemed to be permanently planted on his face.

The memorial service for Karl took place on a plot of grass only a few yards from his house. Alice and I watched the ceremony through the slightly cracked back window. The pastor conducted Christian prayers and hymns. There were many somber and reflective faces. They gathered in a circle around a heap of dirt where a small, wooden cross had been placed. As they mourned for the old man, I couldn't help but think of the thousands of Tutsi men, women, and children decomposing on the hillsides. They were swaddled in clothing, their belongings and remains strewn about and shattered—macheted skulls, body parts, bones pierced with bullets. All of Rwanda was a graveyard, but no one prayed over those dead bodies or allowed them respectable burials. They were left to be devoured by wild dogs and vultures.

I glanced at Alice, who looked like she shared my sentiment. She stared dubiously at the group in prayer almost in disbelief that they could pray after what they did to her innocent mother. I took one last look at the serious faces in prayer: the children who played soccer by the house; the minister filled with the Holy Spirit; the wiry man who influenced others to beat me at the water spring; Furaha, his relatives; and the sympathetic woman who fed and helped us that first night. If not for this one kind woman among them, I would have dammed them all to hell that very moment.

In these last days of the genocide, a dark silence fell over the country, as if the dead strewn about had asked the living to acknowledge them. From the top of the hill where Furaha's house sat, we could see a few men running up on hillsides searching through bushes for the remaining Tutsi survivors. Many Hutu and Twa families resumed work in their fields or stayed home, attempting to bring a sort of normalcy back to their lives. As for Furaha, his daily routine did not change. He continued to leave the house early in the morning and return in the evening. Without his father to report the village news to, he was quiet.

A couple of days later something pleasant happened: a hot breeze drew me to the window. Feeling the warm wind on my face, I caught the eye of a woman and her child passing by Furaha's house. To my surprise, the woman looked like one of my cousins on my dad's side of the family. To make sure I wasn't delirious, I walked to the door and pulled Alice toward it.

"Tell me, Alice," I said, slightly cracking the door open, "what is that lady wearing?"

Alice looked at me like I had lost my mind. "What lady?"

"The tall woman on the trail. Right there, next door. She is carrying a small child in her arms."

"Um... a blue dress and a black head cover. Why do you ask, Jeanne?"

I hauled her aside to look again. My eyes were not lying to me; it was my cousin!

"Oh my God! Alice, it's my cousin! My cousin Gloria. She is alive!" I rocked back and forth on my toes and heels and clutched my hands together.

"Oh, my," Alice said with a smile. "Call for her. Furaha won't be back for hours. Call her over here," she urged.

I opened the door fully, the sun shining on my swollen face. "Gloria! Gloria! Please come. It's me, your cousin."

Gloria looked at me as if she had been jarred out of deep thought.

"My cousin... Jeanne... Jeanne, is that you?" she said, shuffling toward me, a little day-dreamy and squinting hard.

"Jeanne. My God, Jeanne!" She let go of her water jug, rushed toward me, and crouched down with her baby still in her arms.

"Oh, praise God!" she whispered while looking up at the sky. Tears welled in her eyes as she pressed me and the baby together.

"It is a miracle, Jeanne," she said, unwilling to release her embrace. Alice took her hand and led Gloria into the house, looking around to see if anyone noticed us. The twins recognized Gloria at once and latched onto her legs, causing her tears to start again.

"This is the best day since this nightmare started. My cousins are here, alive, and together," she said with a sparkling smile still on her face. Then Gloria's smile disappeared and her lips twisted as she noticed the fading bruises and lumps on my face. "Come here," she said, pulling me tight against her body. Alice then offered my cousin and the baby some of the beans we had rationed for the day, but she refused them.

"You girls need to eat."

Her thoughtful command took a short while to work on me. After being on my own for so long, it sounded odd to hear comforting words from an adult. It had been so long since I felt lighthearted, and I'm sure Gloria felt the same. We sat in silence, looking at each other and savoring the closeness of family.

Gloria set her baby daughter on my lap as the twins gathered around me. I ran my fingers through the baby's hair, observing as the twins touched her tiny fingers and toes. Gloria was in her early thirties, a newlywed, with her only child in my arms. I had always looked up to her, and she had always shown me and Jeannette so much kindness. She was still as gorgeous as I remembered her but was considerably thinner. Her wrist bones protruded, as did her high cheekbones. She now had dark rings around her bloodshot eyes. And despite the excitement of seeing us, her face looked as if she hadn't slept well in months. Her nice, bright smile was one thing that hadn't been transformed. When she smiled, she displayed rows of dazzling white teeth.

After our celebration, Gloria wanted to learn how we had made it to the village. Unsure of what to omit, I recounted almost everything that had taken place. When I spoke about Uncle Edward, Mom, Dad, Mucyo, and Joshua, plus one of her brothers and a few other relatives who were killed, Gloria sobbed. I didn't know what to say, so I reached out and offered her my hand. She dried her tears away with her shirt, saying, "Oh Jeanne, my heart hurts for our family."

I told her about Aunt Josephine and her husband, and how Mom and Dad made preparations for the others. Her lips grew tight. She wanted to know more about Aunt Josephine and why they turned us away.

"Do you think Jeannette and my brothers are still out there?" I asked, mindful not to use the word "alive" because I had fought with images of their lifeless bodies. She assured me that Dad was a careful man and would have given my siblings the best chances for survival.

"As much as people respected my Uncle, your Dad, I can't believe anyone who knows him would harm his children," Gloria assured me.

She listened closely as I described foraging for seeds, slipping away from the killers by swimming through the river, and pushing seeds up our noses to stay alive.

"Jeanne, you are an extraordinary girl, and I am very proud of you. Your parents would be, too. There are not many young ones strong enough to survive like you have." I did not think I was particularly special, but I was grateful to be reassured that I was doing the right things. Since bringing us to Furaha's village, I had felt a lot of guilt about our situation.

We sat in silence for a few more minutes, and then I asked Gloria how she survived. She was unwilling to tell me her own survival story or how she ended up with the Hutu family who lived next door. Instead, she gently caressed my cheek. She inquired about the bruises and bumps on my body. I filled her in on the attack at the spring and explained that I was angrier at those who had killed our family than those who had beaten me.

"Jeanne, I know it is painful. This has been challenging for all of us. But do not allow your heart to harden. The last thing your parents would want is for you to keep hatred for others," she said, her face now tensed. All of this discussion about forgiveness was disturbing me. As she continued to preach, I noticed my attention wandering. I felt my hands clench into round balls and my face flushed. Finally, I interrupted her.

"How can I forgive these devils? Have they been responsible? Any of them?" Bellowing, I repeated the last question. Immediately, I held my head down toward the infant, and the silence around the room told me I had done something far from my normal character.

When I raised my eyes to Gloria's face, it was grim. Alice turned away, and the twins stared at me nervously.

"Jeanne, there is a future after all this pain. Soon, the RPF military will overtake the country. Peace will be brought back, and we will restore our family. If it is only the six of us left, then we will be a family of six. We will be together, and we will have many reasons to be thankful." Alice's face brightened up when Gloria included her in our family.

We spent the afternoon discussing our new world after the genocide, which brought optimism to us all.

Gloria took Alice aside and they discussed something privately. When she returned, Gloria reiterated what she had said about peace being renewed and told us what she had heard on the radio about a refugee camp set up for Tutsis. "The French had returned to Rwanda and were attempting to help some of us." She went on to say that between the French's presence and the RPF fighting to conquer the Hutu extremists, some people in the village were becoming fearful that their offenses would be found out. Some Hutus and Twas in the community were preparing to flee the country.

"Please, Jeanne, you've managed so well, and this is nearly over. Justice will prevail." She embraced all of us warmly as a parent would, kissing my swollen eye and forehead. She swore to stop by whenever she could and waved farewell with a tender smile.

That night, my pleasant mood was suppressed when Furaha rolled near me. Disgusted with his foul breath blowing in my face, I scooted away, and turned my backside toward him. Minutes later, I felt his breathing on my neck. He planted his hand on my leg. Instantly, I swiped his hand away. He clucked his tongue and seized my bicep, pinning it against my body.

"You believe you are stronger than me, girl?" he breathed into my ear. Thankfully, he rolled over and went to sleep. I didn't sleep for the rest of that night. My heart pounded, and I was uncertain of what to do.

The following day, Furaha didn't go out on his usual excursions. Instead, he remained in the house all day, making us nervous. It felt like change was in the air, and Furaha made sure we knew it. He spent the daylight hours on his stool, drinking banana beer and complaining. Surprisingly, the majority of his grievances were aimed at Alice. Despite how thoroughly Alice tidied up and served him, he found something trivial to gripe about. For some reason, he excluded me and the twins in his criticism, which was unusual.

After lunch, Furaha's brothers and nephews stopped by the house. As we served them, they joked that we were Furaha's "young brides." Hearing this made me nauseated. Alice, too, looked disturbed. He chuckled in response and said, "Two wives are too many for any man." When the trio weren't engaging in such awkward and disgusting talk, they chatted about politics, mostly the approaching occupation of the Rwanda Patriotic Front (RPF). Furaha was certain the RPF would be defeated, but his brother was obviously worried about the stories floating around the village.

There was a different mood in the village. People seemed anxious about the lack of governance and leadership in the country, but many were even more concerned about the RPF taking over.

Chapter Seventeen

All this talk about the RPF put Furaha in a volatile mood. He shouted in agitation, mostly at Alice. As night fell, he drank excessively as he and his companions played cards. When his friends staggered out late in the night, Furaha's anger intensified. He kicked an orderly pile of firewood, startling the four of us. He was shirtless, flexing his muscles as he cursed about all the food we consumed. Suddenly, he became obsessed with an egg he swore he had placed near a bag of grains. I had not seen eggs in the house since the minister visited to pray for Karl. Still, he was convinced his egg had been eaten by one of us, and we could no longer evade his line of questioning.

"Who ate the egg?" he yelled out, kicking the sack of grains and spilling them on the floor. "Who ate it?" He said, staggering toward the four of us. We were all frozen and confused.

"Alice, you're responsible for the food in this house. You ate it! Didn't you?" he shouted, pushing his face into hers.

The four of us huddled closer together. Finally, I spoke for all of us, reassuring him we only ate the small portion of beans he allowed us and nothing more. Ignoring me, he continued his rant. I expected him to vent a little more, and then give it a rest, but he continued to curse louder. I realized that this time he wasn't cooling down. After a while, I thought he might have been upset about something else other than the egg. Thinking one egg wasn't worth all the screaming, I decided to take responsibility for it, assuming the punishment wouldn't be severe. But Alice beat me to the confession.

"I ate the egg," she declared remorsefully. I then quickly went to her defense.

"We've been eating the same food for days. Shouldn't she be allowed one egg at least?"

Furaha took a step closer. "Am I hearing you correctly? Allowed? You aren't ALLOWED anything! You should all be dead by now, and thanks to me you are not. I am not your father! You are not my children to care for! Get out! Get out! I want you out of here, right now!"

Terrified, we watched Furaha take a seat on his stool, glugging his beer while he continued to bark at us to leave. We remained still because Furaha was basically sending us to our death. Earlier in the night, a group of Interahamwe had camped near his house.

Alice and I tried to plead with him. She apologized repeatedly, but Furaha wouldn't accept her apology. I promised to borrow money from my cousin to buy more eggs, but again Furaha refused. He said he had made up his mind and we had to leave in the middle of the night, which we were grateful for. We assumed we had a better chance of surviving if we left when the Interahamwe were asleep. Alice and I mapped out a plan; we would stay in the banana plantation near the river. This way, we would have access to river water and possibly sweet potato fields. We sat in silence as the hours ticked by, waiting to depart. But when it was time to leave, the twins cried that it was too dark. Alice and I picked up the girls. When we were at the door, we heard a group of people walking towards Furaha's home. We begged Furaha to allow us to stay for few more minutes.

To this, Furaha agreed, but shockingly, he decided that Alice would be the only one leaving. "Why does she have to go by herself?" I asked, but he ignored me. Again I pleaded to let us go with her, but he had made up his mind that my sisters and I would remain. The hours leading up to Alice's departure were heart-wrenching. She had not survived as long as we had in the bushes. I offered her every bit of information I thought might be helpful, including directions to our favorite bush near our Aunt's house, hoping to meet up with her after we survived this horror.

Finally, Furaha decided her time was up, and led her by the arm to the door. Trying one last time, I dropped to my knees and begged him to change his mind, but he shook his head and pushed past me. I shuffled to the door and Alice slid past Furaha, squeezing me tightly as our tears fell to the floor. She extended her hands to me, and as she touched my hand for our last good-bye, I felt a vibration of nervousness in her body. I watched her small frame disappear into the morning light, a brave and loving soul.

The following days leading up to the village's evacuation left many people feeling uncertain and suspicious—uncertain that the Hutu government could be overthrown by the RPF's military, and uncertain if the killers, including the civilians who took part in the genocide against the Tutsis, would have to explain their crimes to a new government. Various-sized groups of Hutus and Twas had passed through the village with more reports about the RPF, and many more were preparing to leave the country. The dread of RPF retribution wasn't the only motive to leave; many of the Interahamwe and Hutu soldiers had stated their distrust of the Hutus and Twas staying behind, accusing them of betraying the Hutu power government. But most of their reluctance to travel came from the difficulties they were sure to encounter being on the road for days, if not months.

Then there were more discussions about whose side the French soldiers were on. Some people in the area believed the French stood with the Hutu government as they provided them food, water, weapons, and shelter in the refugee camps; very few thought the French had arrived in the country to protect the remaining Tutsis. The majority of the Hutus seemed to view the French refugee camps in the Southwest as unsafe for Tutsis.

There was another question that seemed to linger in every Hutu and Twa's mind: everyone wanted to know where to flee to and how far to go from Rwanda. The majority of Hutus were headed to a country known as Zaire at the time, now the Democratic Republic of Congo. Others intended to go to Burundi, Tanzania, Kenya, or Uganda. Still others wanted to go as far away as Canada and the United States.

Furaha and his immediate family were united about their need to flee and had mapped out a plan of where they wanted to go. More and more neighbors knocked on Furaha's door with worried faces and discussed strategies on how and when to flee the country.

One early morning, I peeked out the door to find some young teenage boys who always came to update Alice about her mother's status in the toilet hole. "Is Furaha home?" they anxiously asked. Afraid they might kill us or call other killers to kill us, I told them Furaha was out of the house but was likely on his way back. Without any sensitivity, they began to tell me how Alice had been raped and later murdered. They provided comprehensive details on how she was tortured to death. I held tears back and listened.

When I was overwhelmed, I held my hands over my ears and screamed, "That is enough." I closed the door and sat behind it. The twins came over and wiped away my tears, all the while assuring me that everything was going to be okay. I forced a smile and hugged them tightly. Alice wasn't my blood sister, but our circumstances had made us a family. I felt like I had lost another family member.

About the time of Alice's death, things were happening very quickly. There was no time to grieve. People were afraid of the unknown; I watched the neighbors anxiously gather in front of Furaha's house in large groups. All the tension probably caused Furaha more angst. As a consequence, he became more controlling of me and the twins. He reminded me how incompetent the twins were, likely as an implicit way to make me work harder now that Alice was dead. I was entirely responsible for preparing the food and keeping things orderly. Unfortunately, the changes didn't stop there. Now that Alice was dead, Furaha chose a new recipient for his sexual abuse.

For me, that meant discovering a new degree of humiliation. The day he forced Alice to leave, once it came time to go to bed, I felt his hand slithering onto my leg. As I did before, I tried to push it off. What commenced was an intense exchange in the dark of night. I, searching for one last hope, tried to reason with him, reminding him that I was a child, and told him to look to his conscience as a mature man. He laughed off my insight and when he came back at me, he was more forceful. Feeling helpless, I threatened to tell my parents. He snickered at that slip-up and said that he "wasn't frightened of ghosts." The struggle proceeded for a good while. I fought him off, staggering to my feet and attempting to escape after he touched my private part. After being caught again, I wiggled relentlessly, at times digging my nails into his forearms. When I tried to bite his forearm, he became more hostile and pinned my arms above my head. All I could do was gnash my teeth together as the pain rushed up through my insides. When it was all over, my face wore an unbroken flood of tears and a hopeless trance.

The morning after the first time I was raped was a blur. There was unrelenting physical pain, embarrassment, but mostly an excessive sense of disbelief. I remember paying more attention to my shadow, feeling like I needed to somehow crawl into it. There was something so enticing about the darkness that it even provoked me to think about committing suicide. But when confronted with this, the twins gave me a purpose to stay alive. Over and over again that day, I reminded myself that the twins needed me. Each time he abused me, it felt like a battle he was winning. Still, I pressed on. I pledged to myself that he would not control me permanently.

Once Furaha had left the house, I made preparations for the twins to run away and go back to the bushes, but I needed to say good-bye to Gloria first. I peeped through the door; the entire village was now on edge. There were more people walking through the area and gossiping with neighbors. My other alternative was to leave without saying good-bye. However, the longer I thought about it, the more I did not want to lose communication with her. She was the only adult member of my family I knew was alive. I needed her, and I needed her guidance. More than anything, I needed to tell her about the rape and the cloudy feeling I had over my head. I also needed her advice on where the twins and I should go once the RPF took over the country. But since the rumors about the RPF had become more widespread, Gloria had been locked up in the house.

After days without speaking to anyone other than the twins, I missed having conversations with a mature person. I thought of Alice and wished she was around to share what I felt. I knew she would understand since she had endured the same pain. Then the images of her dead body began to torment my mind and reminded me that the twins and I could easily face a similar fate if we left. I decided to crawl back into my shadow and stay in Furaha's house.

A COUPLE OF nights later , once Furaha's relatives had left his home, the twins and I were ordered to gather in the living room. We took a seat on the floor to listen to Furaha speak. Appearing calm and certain, Furaha made clear his preparations for our departure to Congo. He pointed out that almost everyone in his village planned on fleeing the country except for a handful of elderly people. After he finished, he ordered us to get our belongings ready and prepare to leave the house. I wanted to laugh because all we had were the clothes on our backs. The whole plan about fleeing to Congo left me confused, and I began to ask myself, *why would I go to Congo with the same people who killed my family? Why run away from the RPF who fought long and hard to save the remainder of the Tutsis, like me?* Many more questions rushed through my mind, but my thinking was interrupted by Furaha when he swung the door open. He looked upset about something. The twins and I watched him storm to his father's old room and back to the living room. Without any explanation, he told me and the twins to be ready to evacuate his house promptly. He claimed that the Hutus and Twas passing through the area suspected our presence in his home, and we were all in jeopardy, including him. He also added that this was the same reason he sent Alice out.

On one hand, I was relieved at the thought of being free from Furaha's abuse and hopeful the RPF would soon be in the country to protect us. But on the other hand, according to Furaha, the Interahamwe had made it clear that they would kill anyone left behind. The risk of death by an Interahamwe group terrified me.

Obeying Furaha's request, the plan was for us to leave later in the night. Furaha slept next to us as usual, and I was grateful not to endure his rape that particular night. As the twins slept soundly and Furaha snored, I stayed up, planning where the twins and I needed to hide until the RPF could rescue us. A few times I stood up to check if it was quiet enough for us to leave.

Finally, I woke the twins and then Furaha to let him know we were leaving. "We will stay in the bushes until the RPF captures the country," I said. I thanked Furaha for allowing us to stay in his home and for the food he provided, and then I led the twins toward the door. Furaha stood silently.

I proceeded toward the door, but when I reached the door handle, Furaha grabbed my sleeve and pulled me aside, smiling, and shaking his head.

"I don't want all of you to leave," he whispered in my ear.

I felt goosebumps rise on my arms and the hair on the back of my neck stood up.

"What?" I asked, trying not to sound angry.

"I want you to take them elsewhere and come back," he said, pointing at the twins. The twins cried and said they wanted to stay with me.

I looked up at him and said, "I have nowhere to take them and I will not leave them behind. I will never abandon my sisters. You can abuse me if you like, but without my sisters, I have nothing to live for," I cried.

"Jeanne, if you die, then who will take care of us?" Teddy asked. I took her hand and told her to stay silent.

"I have been clear," Furaha said. "Take them elsewhere and return here. If you don't come back, you will deal with the consequences," he threatened.

"What consequences?" I asked. He grinned and walked to his stool. Again, he pointed out that the three of us would draw attention from the killers, and it would be safer if we split up.

127

At this point, my mind was racing. I was overwhelmed with anger but without time to figure out a new plan to keep the twins alive. Hoping that getting away from Furaha would give me an opportunity to process what I needed to do, I walked outside to see if it was clear to leave. It was a quiet night, and the only noise came from a few howling dogs and crickets.

The twins appeared confused and uneasy. Teddy, who was sucking her finger, looked at Furaha and begged, "If you let us stay, we will be good girls and won't eat your beans again."

Furaha opened the door wide and paused for us to step out. His last words were directed at me, to be sure to return without the twins. In that moment, I nodded yes as we walked out.

We started right for the forest while the twins cried about the darkness. It was as if they had forgotten about living in harsh conditions outside. Trying to be confident and hopeful, I explained to them how we were heading to a safer area, meanwhile assuring them that the chaos was nearly over.

I stopped when we arrived near a banana farm. Many scenarios played through my head like a bad dream: *I can take the girls into hiding and not go back to Furaha, but on the other hand, I might be captured and put to death by Furaha or his people.* His threat to return had left an impression on me. *Perhaps somewhere out there is a generous Hutu family that might be willing to take the twins in.* We carried on, walking farther into the forest while I thought of alternative plans.

Once we left the forest, we arrived at a river near an evacuated village. Since it had been pouring for the past few days, the river was full and fast. We stopped next to the edge, the twins standing at my side. They were oblivious to the dark idea I was now considering. With limited choices, I thought the fastest way to kill the three of us was to drown. *At least we will die together and I won't have to leave the twins behind.* I closed my eyes and muttered a quick prayer. I assured myself that God would forgive me for the sin I was about to commit while I lifted the twins and prepared to jump in, but my body felt numb. Standing at the edge, I looked at the twins' faces one last time. My hands were shaky and my heart raced. I felt the need to say good-bye to them, but I did not know how. *Perhaps they should die without knowing what was coming,* I thought. *I will count to five and then jump in.* On the count of three, I looked at the girls once again, but this time my stomach turned and I vomited. Placing the twins down, I knelt beside them and gagged as they patted my back with their little hands and asked if I was going to be okay.

The thought of the twins dying was making me ill. And when I thought of my parents, brothers, and sister, I knew they would not forgive me for giving up.

I wiped my mouth. For the first time in almost three months, I asked the twins for their advice. "What should I do, girls?" I whispered.

The moonlight was reflecting on Teta's eyes. With her uncertain voice she said, "Wwwe can... go... go back to Furaha and tell him... that we're going to be...nice kids. We won't eat his... his beans anymore."

Teddy smiled while agreeing with her twin. "We will clean his house, and then we can stay!"

Their words warmed my heart.

"Okay, I have an idea. Before we try Furaha again, let's go back to Aunt Josephine," I suggested.

They both nodded.

Late in the night, we arrived near Aunt Josephine's house. We crouched in the same flowery bush we had hidden in for weeks. I instructed the twins what they needed to do when they arrived at Aunt Josephine's door.

"Knock on the door, and when Aunt Josephine comes out, tell her you don't know where I am, okay?"

"But that is lying. We know where you are," Teta said. I sat down and placed their palms in my hands.

"Girls, let me explain something; it is like a game. You have to pretend that you do not know where I am, and then Aunt Josephine will allow you to stay with her. She will take good care of you. You will be able to stay in the house, sleep in her comfortable bed, and eat delicious meals." They smiled and nodded. "Just promise you will tell her that you don't know where I am, alright?" They nodded again.

I hugged them, told them I loved them, and then directed them to Aunt Josephine's fence. Over and over again I thought, *the worst Aunt Josephine and her husband can do is to tell the twins to go away. But how could they be callous towards these precious little girls?*

I waited as they beat on the door to the house. Within moments, they came back to the bush, explaining that no one came to open the door. I insisted they go back, and this time I suggested they knock harder and wait until someone opens the door. They had distressed expressions on their faces.

"Girls, you can do this. You are strong and smart. Please, go back out there. I am right here, and I promise I won't go anywhere until someone opens the door and lets you inside," I said, giving them each one last squeeze.

I vowed to pick them up when this chaos was over. "I will take you back to our beautiful house." They nodded and went back to knock. Luckily, a few minutes later, someone unlocked the door and let them in.

I stayed behind the house making sure Aunt Josephine and her husband didn't kick them out. A few hours later, I returned to the bush and laid my head down for a while. When I woke up to birds chirping, I looked at the fence in front of the house a while longer. Still, Aunt Josephine had kept the girls inside. As the next day rolled around, I thought of what to do next.

Assuming that the twins were now safe with their aunt, I thought through what I needed to do. Returning to the bushes sounded like a better option for me, but Furaha's words came flooding back in my head, "If you don't come back, you'll face consequences." I was well aware that Furaha was a powerful man in his community. With that authority, he could send a group of men to search for me. *What would he do to me if they caught me? What consequences would I face?*

After a few hours thinking of how to avoid his sexual abuse or being taken into a refugee camp, I considered approaching the Interahamwe and asking them to give me a swift death.

The voice in my head kept telling me, *"The twins are safe now. You can end your life."* For the next few hours I battled the voice, but it was winning. Finally, with the voice in my head getting louder and assuring me that dying seemed like the best option, I began to welcome and accept death. The sunrise filled the sky. The birds sang. It was a beautiful day for those who were free.

I headed toward the closest killing group, but the closer I got, the more I felt like I was about to make the biggest mistake of my life. There was now another inner voice that kept saying, *"Don't do it! Do not go forward!"* Unsure of which voice to listen to, I stopped walking. I then shook my head vigorously, hoping to think straight or to at least silence one of the voices in my head. More questions rushed in my mind: *Who would take care of the family if they survive the genocide? What happens if Aunt Josephine kicks the twins out of her house?*

I avoided going to the killing squad; instead I found a tall bush and sat in it. I spent the rest of the afternoon rethinking my decision. Finally, after hours of contemplating, I decided that despite Furaha's abuse, he might keep me alive. Then I could at least check on the twins from time to time, and I would have a chance to reunite with my siblings if they made it. I would also have an opportunity to stay close to my cousin Gloria.

My decision made, I headed back to Furaha's house.

Chapter Eighteen

My first two days back at Furaha's house were excruciating. Apart from the sexual abuse, I missed my little sisters. Although I had no other option to keep them safe, I felt a heavy responsibility and criticized myself for delivering them to Aunt Josephine's house. A mixture of guilt and anger began to drive me into a deep sadness. While preparing to leave Furaha's village, a crowd of Interahamwe and their families stopped by to share stories about the RPF's attack in Kigali. Although this news offered me a glimmer of hope, it was provoking the already maniacal killers. Furious that they might be forced out of the country by the RPF, they hunted any remaining Tutsis in moderate Hutu homes, fields, and bushes. "Interahamwe have been encouraged not to leave any stone unturned," Furaha said, adding that I should avoid stepping outside for the next few days.

Early that night, Furaha told me to hide under his late father's bed. Once it was quiet outside, he told me to come back in the living room. However, at about two in the morning, we heard the Interahamwe chanting their killing songs as they pushed their way through the homes in the village. In an instant, they were between Furaha and the family next-door's compound. I scrambled to hide behind the living room door.

"We were told that one of these homes has cockroaches in it," one remarked.

They pounded on Furaha's next-door neighbor's door, demanding to be let in. Their voices grew louder as they shouted. Next, the whistles sounded, which always indicated a Tutsi had been discovered.

"Please, God, protect my cousin and her baby," I prayed.

Sweat gathered on my forehead and dribbled down my face. Then I watched Furaha go outside. They were arguing, and then I heard a man shout out, "She's running away. Get her. She's running!"

Next, silence. Then, a wailing baby. The mixture of men's and women's voices grew louder again, but I couldn't make out what was said. It was as if the entire neighborhood had come out to watch. I could only imagine what was about to take place. I leaned my sweaty forehead against the wall and whimpered.

A few hours later the neighborhood became silent again, as if everyone had gone back to bed. Furaha returned and it didn't take long for him to begin snoring. I did not sleep that night. Part of me wanted to know the details of what happened to Gloria and her baby, but the other part of me was afraid to learn about the cruel acts done to my precious family.

As I expected, bright and early the next day, people in the neighborhood were talking about what happened to my cousin and her baby. They said she would have lived if her baby hadn't cried.

"Furaha and his brother had persuaded the killers to continue on until the baby cried out for her mother," one of them said. I wiped away my tears. "Gloria ran back for her baby girl and that was when they caught her."

I folded my shaky hands under my armpits.

"They raped the mother and stabbed her and her little girl."

Another family member I had to mourn, another wound in my heart, another question for God.

Late in the afternoon, still shaken by the previous night's event, I remained still for hours. I sat on the floor absorbed in my thoughts until a gentle knock on the door brought me to my feet. Silently peeking through the holes in the wooden door, I saw what looked like little children standing on the other side. I slightly opened the door and to my surprise, it was Teddy and Teta.

"I can't believe you made it here!" I jumped. With a fluttering heart, I swung the door wide open, and they scrambled into my arms with enormous smiles. "My God, how did you two get here?" I asked, scooping them up. "Did anyone come with you?"

"No…we came alone," Teddy responded with a smile on her face.

They told me how Aunt Josephine and her husband kicked them out and ordered them to find me.

"I missed you two so much," I said as they smiled and hugged me tightly.

I took them to the pot to eat. While gazing at the fire, I pondered how to keep my girls safe. I had already looked the girls over and there were no bruises or scratches on their skin. To this day, I don't know how they returned to Furaha's house. Nevertheless, I was thankful that they were okay and they were with me again. The only question was how to keep them with me, and keep us all safe. As I grappled with what to do next, a simple idea popped into my head. I tested the girls to make sure they understood the plan.

"So, when we hear Furaha coming home, where are you going to go?" I asked.

"Under the bed," they replied in agreement.

"And when can you come out from under the bed?"

"When you say it's safe," they responded.

"Very good, girls. Remember, no talking."

At first, the twins did well staying under the bed, but soon they had concerns.

"Jeanne, there is a monster under the bed," said Teta. Teddy nodded her head, agreeing with her twin. I took a lantern under the bed to show them it was safe. Teddy said the monster did not come out during the day or early in the night, but only late at night.

"Monsters don't come inside the house. They only live in big caves outside," I emphasized. "Here, under this bed, you are safe."

They nodded in agreement. Thank goodness they trusted me and went back. Throughout the day, they did a good job remaining silent. The one exception was Teta's cough, which traveled freely throughout the small house. I did my best to help her hide it by giving her a cloth to cough into. I begged her to be quiet, though I knew how unreasonable that was.

When Furaha returned, things went smoothly for several hours, but Teta's muffled cough grew stronger. I attempted to cough along with her to drown out the sound. I mistimed a few, however, and her coughing was easily noticeable.

"What was that?" Furaha demanded.

I coughed even louder. "Just a cold," I answered, coughing a few more times.

He jumped up and went right towards the bedroom. Before he reached the room, I fell to my knees and began to beg. "It's my mistake. It's my fault. Please don't hurt them."

He jerked them out from under the bed. "Get out. I want you out of my house!" he roared at them. Then he turned to me. "Wasn't I clear? I want them out of here."

"Yes, you were clear."

He walked back and forth. "Do you understand the entire country will evacuate soon?"

"I see people evacuating every day, but you should know that I will not leave without my sisters. If they are not safe, I am not safe. If they die, I will die. They have kept me alive more than you or anyone else has."

Furaha shook his head. "Well, you better figure out a place to keep them, but not here." He let the twins sleep in the house, but reminded me that the three of us had raised suspicions in the entire neighborhood. We were putting him and his family in danger. "I am sure you don't want anything like what happened to Gloria happening to you and the twins," he remarked. Before going to bed, he stressed that I had this one night to make a plan for my sisters.

Before daybreak, I had settled on two options. One was a woman right near the edge of the village. I did not know her well, but she used to say hi to me and Jeannette when we were coming home from our old school. The second option was a Hutu family that my parents had given a cow and its new calf to support with milk for their young children. But this particular family lived miles away.

In the morning, I tried the friendly woman first. When we arrived, I started off by asking if she needed help, especially with her youngest baby. When she said yes, I told her the job wasn't for me, but for my sister, pushing Teddy a little closer to her. She chuckled at my suggestion.

"I was going to say that you are too inexperienced to take care of my child, and now you want your baby sister to watch my child? She is a baby herself," she snorted.

"Look at her, she is tall. She is not a baby," I replied.

"How old is she?" The woman asked.

Before I could make up a story, "We are three years old," Teta responded promptly.

"Almost four," I added.

"Don't you think three years old is too young to take care of themselves, let alone another child?" she asked.

"I know; but I need your help for now, and I don't have anyone else who can take her."

I promised I would come back for Teddy and that she would be helpful in the meantime. After I told her more about Teddy's strengths, the woman finally consented.

I returned to Furaha's house without Teddy and told him of this development. Unsatisfied, he asked, "What are you planning to do with the other girl? I want her out." I promised I would think of a place to take her.

"Please give me time. I will have it figured out soon."

I could tell that he was upset. He marched straight to where Teta was squatting and picked her up, something he had never done before. Teta looked at me, yelled, and stretched out her arms for me to rescue her. When I reached for her, Furaha pulled her away. I begged him to let me take her, but he refused.

"I told you to have both the girls gone by the time I returned, and you did not listen. Now, let me take care of her for you," he announced as he stepped out of the door. Teta cried over his shoulder, begging me to help her. The farther he walked, the quieter her cry sounded. I wanted to run after him, but I realized that I may put her in worse trouble. I went back inside the house, sat on the floor and sobbed.

A few hours later Furaha returned, and said she was "safe," which I didn't totally trust. Despite the anger I felt towards Furaha, I gathered the strength to pray and begged God to watch over my little sisters.

The next day, the village evacuated.

WE WERE NOW refugees. That dawn, the residents of Furaha's village gathered into one enormous group by the road. Mothers impatiently ordered their children around. Children complained in response, and babies screamed in their mothers' arms. The men were detached and looked agitated. Those in disgruntled spirits filled the day by arguing about which direction was safest to take, presumably to evade the gun battle between the RPF and the Hutu military. Almost every face looked nervous and already worn out.

In the group, I felt more lonely and intimidated than I did at Furaha's house. Though Furaha had loaded me down to cover most of my body—a stout stick balanced over my left shoulder that had sizable black cooking pots attached to either side, and over my right shoulder was slung a bedsheet stuffed with Furaha's clothes—I was still frightened that I'd be identified.

I stood in formation with the others, waiting for the elders to tell us which direction to travel. Soon I was being forced along in the crowd of refugees. The pots on my head clanged together as the voices of people blended with the bleating of goats. The conglomeration moved slowly at first and then picked up speed, creating an opening so that I could examine the landscape in the distance. I took in the changed scenery before me. The Rwanda I had once experienced as a lush paradise was now what I imagined hell to be like. We looped around paths and hills. Bodies lay along almost every road and trail. Corpses were everywhere, their bodies split wide apart. Some of these victims were still alive, twisting and groaning while little groups of Interahamwe and a few refugees rejoiced.

Along the path, a few miles from Furaha's area, were fragments of sheet metal pillaged from houses. Clothes, trash, and possessions of the dead littered the ground. One area, which seemed to have been densely populated, had a few burned vehicles around brick buildings. The smoke drifted up the surface of the wall, winding up and exposing the side of the burnt buildings. Dirty pots, cracked plates, and cups were scattered around along with suitcases that had been left behind. Around a corner, more houses burned. I watched from a secure distance as the flames fluttered in the breeze, seemingly swaying as if in misery.

The parade of refugees wound around the quiet countryside, neglected farms, and dense forests. As we neared a mountain, the woods on the other side seemed to have a life of its own, as if the poor souls of the Tutsis that were slaughtered there now lived in those forests. The branches were twisted, barren, and interlaced with other trees as if they were embracing in memory of the departed. Because so many were unwilling to mourn for them, it seemed like nature was warning us all that you cannot silence the dead.

As we rested, the refugees around our camp discussed everything surrounding them except the dead Tutsi bodies that were everywhere. They talked about how they would allocate the rations, the sunny climate, the last time they drank banana beers, the RPF — "the enemy" — but not the endless heaps of Tutsi bodies in these mountains and hills. From their exchanges, I gathered most had somehow justified the deaths and assigned responsibility of those murdered to the RPF. One old man, who seemed to dominate the conversation, rolled up his sleeves and told the group that "the Tutsis in Rwanda would have been safe if the RPF had stayed in exile. They tried to come and take over our country, and this is what their people get."

The following morning, I woke up to a feverish discussion between groups of men. They spoke over one another. One man who seemed to be the head of the Interahamwe group put his rifle on his shoulders and explained how he killed four hundred men, women, and children. "I understood if I didn't get rid of these snakes, they could have taken over our country and stolen our belongings." Other soldiers saluted him for a job well done.

Another young man in the crowd yelled out, "I killed at least fifty children because a son of a snake is a snake, too." The men patted him on the back and cheered him.

These conversations taught me who to avoid in the camp area. I covered up my head to mask my features and sat close to Furaha's family. The sun blazed down on us. Sitting around our parcel of the camp, Furaha's family turned to a discussion I didn't want to have: what my fate might be. They walked out of earshot of the others and Furaha sent me to fetch water from a nearby stream. When I returned, they were still deep in the subject of "traveling with a Tutsi." It was obvious that some members of the family opposed bringing me along for the most obvious reason, which they recited to the others. "If we are caught protecting a Tutsi, they will shoot us. We cannot risk our lives for her," said one of Furaha's cousins.

A few of them nodded in unison and recounted stories they had heard of moderate Hutus being executed for hiding Tutsis. Furaha's aunt, the same lady who had given us food the first night we arrived at Furaha's village, advocated passionately for me. She pointed out that I had made it past many groups of Interahamwe and came through. "Also," she paused and reflected, "we cannot dismiss the child's willingness to help us. She carries clothes and pots; fetches water and firewood. She is more valuable to us here." After she finished, she went and sat in the corner.

"I do all the jobs the other children don't want to do," I added, hoping to add to my value or the reason why I should stay alive.

Some concerns were brought up in opposition, mainly from a younger relative I had not communicated a lot with. He talked about the fear of being perceived as a traitor and offered to kill me. In the end, the group respected the wishes of the elders and decided to continue on with me.

With my temporary membership in Furaha's family accepted, we gradually advanced through Rwanda to a destination that came to be known as "Munkambi." In Kinyarwanda, it means refugee camp, although the camps were just larger crowds of people living and wandering through the wilderness.

The sun's rays outlined our shadows along the dusty path as we marched. The boys who regularly played soccer by Furaha's house occupied themselves by poking fun at my struggle with the pots, pans, and rolled mat that I had added to my cargo. What I noted most was how others crumbled under the harsh conditions. We had been on the move for a short time and I felt my resilience had yet to be tested. Having spent months in the bushes, I had built up a tolerance to brutal conditions. Others twice my age complained and became ill. Still, exerting energy on traveling, scavenging, and transporting cargo was leaving its mark on my body. Weeks before, I had rolled the top of my brown skirt so it remained fastened to my narrowing waistline, but the rolls were not as effective now that I was down to my bare bones. Luckily, I came upon a discarded piece of yarn along the way and tied it around my waist to prevent my skirt from slipping off.

When we finally arrived at a large refugee camp, there were thousands of people. Later in life, I realized just how enormous the Hutu refugee migration had been. The government estimated upward of two million Hutu refugees exited Rwanda. In our area, hundreds grew to thousands day by day.

Meanwhile, the recurrent fear passed around in the camps was that the RPF would enact a killing campaign in response to the genocide against the Tutsis. We never saw any RPF soldiers, let alone witness any retribution killings. Most of the travelers in the camps appeared to be inciters, participants, or families of the Interahamwe caught up in a state of fear. As for the millions of Hutus who stayed in Rwanda, they may have had little to fear as it was evident that they were only witnesses to the killing. Some moderate Hutus even died while protecting Tutsis or denouncing Tutsi killing campaigns.

The Hutu hardliners continued their discussion on how to attack and defeat the RPF. Others pledged to kill every Tutsi that ended up in the refugee camp. While these discussions were taking place, I was busy praying for the day when the RPF would reach our refugee camp. However, most of the refugees appeared certain that the French military would not allow the RPF to come anywhere near the camps to rescue me.

In the following weeks, the refugees' plans for a killing campaign became clear, so I planned my escape back to Rwanda's capital city, a place everyone believed the RPF had conquered. I staked my chances for survival on finding some of those elusive RPF soldiers and praying that their cause would involve protecting a Tutsi child like me. But the question was how to distinguish between Hutu and RPF soldiers. Without disclosing my plan to escape, I asked Furaha's numerous relatives and friends the uniform difference between a RPF and Hutu soldiers. Most dismissed my curiosity and described the RPF soldiers as insects or some kind of animals.

"How will you identify an RPF soldier?" one man repeated after me, confounded I would even ask. "They will have skins like lizards and some will have tails like monkeys. Or, if they are the clever type, they will look like a cockroach," he responded with a big smile that exposed all his front teeth. Of course, this all sounded ridiculous. Not ready to give up, I wandered around the camp hoping to find an elder who might answer my question about the uniform. I asked about twenty people, and everyone seemed to agree in their description of RPF soldiers as some sort of animal. I had exhausted my energy for the day and found a secluded area to sit down. I did not give up, though. In the coming months, I continued to inquire about how to distinguish the two groups.

SHORTLY AFTER, WE gathered among a massive group of refugees. They were squatting, sitting, and standing shoulder to shoulder in the valley before us. A few groups possessed tattered tarps and shaped them into basic shelters, dangling them over tree limbs or stringing them by rope, but most of the refugees were exposed to the elements. Sauntering into the arms of the camp, we collected branches and bushes for a fire while Furaha attempted to exchange our food for a tarp. There was no barrier, no sanitation, and no United Nations forces. At least, there were no foreign forces that we could detect. At this point, the gathering appeared to be people who had evacuated without thinking hard enough about living in the wild. I watched Hutu government soldiers and regular citizen loot houses nearby, carrying expensive supplies instead of things that were practical in the camps such as mats, tents, cooking pots, clothes, and blankets.

Glancing around, it was apparent from the expressions on people's faces that this place was another hell. Bitterness was engraved on each refugee's face like a permanent marker. When discussing their previous work before the genocide, as it turned out, many had been farmers, traders, doctors, and educators. But now status didn't matter, especially for those who had run out of money. We were all refugees.

Out of boredom, I followed the never-ending lines of people moving to and from the water. They hauled water in containers, pails, plastic bags— anything that would carry liquid. People fought over basic items, even tree limbs. Hundreds left the camp and others were quick to take their places and possessions. The environment was harsh and unpredictable.

To remain valued, I kept up my duties. However, trips to the stream always brought on a feeling of dread, particularly because more often than not, Furaha insisted I go alone. He often made the request so that he could catch me alone in the forest, pin me to the ground, and rape me.

Passing through the camp, more people talked of a "better refugee camp" as a place of salvation where United Nations workers were handling security and handing out tents, food, and medicine. Yet many refugees feared getting entangled in the remnants of fighting between the RPF and Hutu militia soldiers. As a result, some refugees prolonged their decision to leave.

In contrast, I feared the Interahamwe in our camps who routinely worked their way through crowds in a procession, eyeballing as many people as they could, hoping to find those with distinguishing Tutsi characteristics: long arms, tall, narrow noses, and well-rounded foreheads, all reasons to be investigated. To my luck, Furaha's family members had a system in place to protect me. They warned me when they saw the killers prowling in the distance or near our tent.

Most days when Furaha was around, I could stay inside. I always assumed the killers were somehow afraid of or respected Furaha, because they never searched our tent when he was around. When Furaha was away, the family directed me to hide in a nearby bush.

Surprisingly, Furaha's relatives weren't the only ones watching out for me. Unsure whether it was because of Furaha's influence in the community, or other unknown reasons, I gained additional Hutu allies. The few moderate Hutus who learned that I was a Tutsi kept the secret to themselves and joined Furaha's family in helping to keep me alive. While struggling to reconcile with Furaha because of his ongoing abuse, I silently rejoiced knowing I was accepted by some refugees despite my ethnic background.

But the most peculiar action from Furaha had yet to take place. It all began when Furaha's cousin, David, and his refugee group settled in our camp.

DAVID, A CAPTAIN of his own Interahamwe group, was a thick-shouldered man with fleshy bags under his suspicious eyes. He strung up a tent a few meters from ours and settled in uncomfortably. It didn't take much observation to tell that David had a deep hatred for Tutsis and had likely been traumatized by all the people he murdered. A simple discussion with him could quickly escalate into shouting, as David had limited control over his rage.

The second morning after his arrival, I heard him arguing with his mother. Then he charged out of her tent and vigorously swung his machete at the nearby trees until sweat streamed off his face and his voice went hoarse. When he was worked up, he not only pushed us children to the ground or spat on our faces, he also kicked and knocked over anything that was in his way. The look of terror on everyone's faces told me that they were afraid of David. All except Furaha.

The first day David showed up in our camp, he pressed the group to let him murder me. Openly disgusted at my presence, he became more agitated upon discovering that some of his family members had basically accepted me as one of their own as long as I completed my daily chores.

One night, David wouldn't let the problem of a Tutsi in his presence rest. He started off with a variation of two questions. With his two hands placed on Furaha's shoulders, he asked, "Tell me, Cousin, why do you keep snakes around your people? Do you know how dangerous snakes are to humankind?"

David's questions were left unanswered, so he began again. This time, he was talking to everyone around. "For these last few days, I've raped and killed little girls who looked just like her," he added, his eyes locked on me. Coldness seemed to flow effortlessly from his voice, causing my legs to shake as I raised my downcast eyes to see the flesh under his eyes twitch.

David cut the silence with his throaty voice again. "Could it be this girl is a ghost? Or have I neglected to do my duty?" He hesitated, looking at everyone. "I know I couldn't have pardoned a Tutsi like her...forgiving a Tutsi is not within me, so it must be that I missed her. I must've failed to kill this little Tutsi." He pronounced the word Tutsi with heavy emphasis and in a loud voice, like it was some dreadful affliction.

David awkwardly chuckled, and then Furaha addressed him. "She searched all morning for the corn you are eating. There is value in that, isn't there?"

"Oh, yes," David answered, sucking the kernels from the cob while staring hard at me. "Great value," he said sarcastically.

There were other men in the camp like David—men with twitchy eyes and aggressive, paranoid personalities. These men were traumatized by the killing they had done, who gazed blankly into the trees. Like David, they launched into discussions with no one in particular, sputtering fragments of propaganda, then stopping sometimes to grin and then stare blankly again.

These indoctrinated men sometimes saw images and people that others couldn't see, images of people they had killed who now hunted their minds. "Look," they would say, "can you see her? That lady, I killed her. Why is she here?"

Little children were the most prolific ghosts to disturbed these men. One man who staggered by us explained that the children he had murdered followed him every day. At night they woke him up, asking why he had killed them. Somehow my presence appeared to trigger even more trauma in David and his men. However, unlike some of the others who remained trapped in fear, David's trauma manifested as pure violence.

David and his Interahamwe groups spent a good part of their day combing through nearby forests and patrolling the camp, scouting for Tutsis. Everyone seemed to be at ease when David was gone. The minute he returned, a sense of fear and negativity spread through the atmosphere like wildfire. David's unpredictability kept everyone on edge. He challenged the others to do something about the "snake in the camp." But again, a few came to my defense, especially the women who outlined my services to the others. Then Furaha would get involved after it spun out of control. Even David's own mother, a humble and even-tempered old woman, found herself between the two of us. But David was persistent, blaming the "snakes" for all his troubles. He went on about the annoyance of the smoke, the waves of stench from the refugees' sweat, the odor of excrement, and the nearby decomposing corpses. As far as David was concerned, he and the others who had taken part in the genocide were innocent victims of their circumstances.

No matter how much time Furaha spent attempting to reason with David, justifying my value by predicting I would be "the last Tutsi in the country" so I would be worth a lot of money and many cows someday soon, David still wanted me dead. "Jeanne is going to be a symbol of what Tutsi people once looked like," Furaha told David. But these rebuttals only inflamed David's hatred. The screaming escalated, sometimes resulting in pushing and shoving between the two.

Often David and Furaha's arguments and threats caused a ringing in my ears and a numbing, tingling sensation in my fingers and neck. Soon, others in the camp began to take these arguments more seriously, causing our entire group to be in a perpetual state of angst. I spent a large part of the days hiding from David. Even when I wasn't there, others told me that I occupied his mind.

Finally one day, the group called for a meeting in the forest nearby. All were in attendance except David. It was the first time I heard the group proposing to kill David. Relatives and nonrelatives, men and women, all were in agreement. They had likely been either thinking about it or discussing it for some time before the meeting. Even though death surrounded them, killing a family member wasn't something to take lightly. Following this initial meeting, there were other meetings about how to handle David. Surprisingly, other children were asked their input, but no one sought my opinion. Even if they had, I didn't have a solution. Some of the family members wanted to give David more time to accept me and adjust to the refugee lifestyle, but most were frightened that he might kill them for sheltering me or for other, unrelated, reasons.

Even David's own mother feared for her life. "David, my poor son, has become mad. The killing of Tutsis has changed him," she said, wiping her tears.

The tipping point came a day or so after some boils formed on my upper calves, causing me to skip my water and foraging runs. For the past few days, I had wakeful nights as David's threats carried over into my dreams. Everywhere I went or sat, I looked over my shoulder, worried that at any given moment he would plunge his blade into my body.

One afternoon, my nightmare became a reality. I found myself lying flat on the thin grass mat in the tent. Standing at my feet was David. Like in my dream, I found him staring at me, and my heart leaped. *God, please don't let him kill me.* He stared as his mother tended to my wounds, wrapping a scrap of cloth around the open sores. Seeing the care his mother was giving me may have caused him to snap, and he lunged at me. "Mom, if you let me finish off this snake, you will never have to take care of it." As David reached over to seize me, I rose up and ducked behind his mother. His mother attempted to guard me as she extended her arms to keep him away. David pushed her into me and we both shouted for help. Quickly, Furaha ran in and was able to separate David from us.

The others gathered around while Furaha attempted to calm David. In a fit of rage, David swung his machete at a nearby tree, splintering it.

"You feed her, take care of her wounds!" David screamed.

"Calm yourself," his mother pleaded again.

"Why? Why do you care for an enemy?" his words tore past her. The others attempted to restrain him, most asking him to walk away.

"I will go, but when I return, she better be gone or else I will kill her!" he screamed. I breathed deeply to loosen the pressure in my chest as David left, kicking anything that stood in his way and warning that he would murder whoever stood in his path.

There was a moment of solidarity as everyone watched David's departure. After some silence, everyone looked at each other in disbelief, and a last meeting was called. Everyone gathered behind our shelter. Listening to the unthinkable, David's own mother advocated for the execution of her son. With David's mother leading the cause, it did not take long to reach an agreement. The other relatives gave their consent. They believed David was controlled by a demon and would likely kill me and the others in our camp.

The plan was drawn up by Furaha and others who were to carry out the murder. We children were told to carry on as if everything were normal. When David came for me, Furaha and the others would cut him down. As I listened to everyone, I felt a knot in my throat and stomach. My head spun in confusion and I was petrified. Everyone else returned to their usual activities. The more I thought about what was about to take place, the sicker to my stomach I felt. I rolled to my side and choked up yellow bile that stung my throat. Knowing David's death was soon to come, and that I was the primary cause, gave me a crushing guilt that worsened when I looked at David's mother. I wondered how she would live the rest of her life after witnessing the death of her son.

A few hours went by, and finally David returned. Time stood still. Everything stopped moving. He casually sauntered toward me and the other children, calling out for the "snake" and declaring that he was going to finish me. My heart pounded and my face warmed up. I felt like I had been crippled.

"Jeanne," one of the little girls in the group called. I couldn't answer. My mind simply stopped. Even the flames twisting around the wood in the fire pit appeared to pause.

David kept walking toward us, looking into my eyes. "I will kill you. I will get rid of you!" he screamed. Then I heard the thump of a machete plunging into his neck. Two or three more blows followed, and then David released a sound somewhere between a sigh and a moan. I fluttered my eyes as I realized David's blood had splattered onto my forehead and was quickly pooling around my knees. David was on the ground, crawling a bit, and stretching his hand out toward me. There was absolute quiet, and then a chorus of screams broke out among the children. I joined the other children shrieking. I remember wishing that it was just a dream, but it was real. My child's mind failed to comprehend how such an event could happen. Later that day, I wailed loudly in the tent as the others napped. I felt sad for the pain David experienced.

That evening, guilt drove me to pick some pink and lavender flowers I found on a foraging run. I brought them to David's mother. She knew what they meant. She looked at the flowers carefully and then pitched them into the fire.

"I gave birth to Satan," she said, shuffling away from the smoldering flowers. David's body was carried away and buried in a hollow pit by Furaha and the other men. There were no prayers said for him, no tears that I saw besides my own. It was as if no one had died.

For the next couple of days, I noticed an eerie silence over the normally boisterous camp. A heavy fog came in the morning and hung like a black tarp over everything.

Looking back, I didn't realize that my tenth birthday had come and gone as I had endured this bleak and dreary time living with my fear of

David. A year earlier, I couldn't have conceived of a world like this. Despite being a year older but still a young girl, I had the sense that my age would no longer matter much. My childhood had completely faded, and any age that my physical body might attain would be of no consequence. My soul felt already old and weary, although not yet wise. It was as if the world had nothing left to show me.

Chapter Nineteen

A few days after David was buried, we went back to our daily routines. The trees and water around our camp had been depleted by the unrelenting flow of refugees. If lack of water and firewood weren't reason enough to leave this particular site, refugees passing through continued to tempt us with the promise of a better camp toward the northern part of the country. For many among us, including Furaha and his family, it was time to pack up our scattered belongings and travel north toward Congo.

We walked for days through Rwanda's blood-soaked landscape, along unpaved roads pitted with holes the size of trenches and through forests ringing with the clap of bullets. The roads wound around terrain I had never seen and images of the dead I'll never be able to remove from my memory. Children cried at the sight of the piles of dead bodies along our route. Some victims were freshly killed; others were bloated and ready to burst from their clothes. Insects fed in delight on human remains while we grimaced in anguish. Legions of dead Tutsis formed heaps as tall as me. The victims were neighbors, brothers, sisters, friends, mothers, fathers, and toddlers. They were twisted and bent, some naked and others still clothed. Blood flowing, faded, and stale. The crimes were months old and hours or minutes old. It was a hellish scene.

Some of the Hutu and Twa refugees died along the way as well. Mostly they died from disease, but also killed each other over possessions, simple arguments, or food. To them, death was becoming meaningless. Their burials, which used to be just a step better than what was given to the

Tutsis, were now just as irreverent. Human value was so inconsequential that bodies were unceremoniously pitched along roads and into forests, with pallbearers only pausing to clear sweat from their faces before continuing on. Family members and friends would stand over the dead, sad for a few minutes, then return to the business of survival.

Most of the refugees had never traveled beyond their villages, and a compass or maps were not readily available. Lacking experience and leadership, navigating properly in the chaos was almost impossible. Sometimes we broke away from a larger group because Furaha and the others disagreed with the direction they were leading us. Our group would shrink from hundreds to a couple dozen, then swell again into the hundreds a few days later.

One day, we ventured through the center of a forest to a clearing where there were numerous farms. The locals, a couple of large Hutu families, were inviting and generously offered us their crops. We enjoyed a few peaceful nights until the numbers of refugees grew again. The families' generosity dried up as their crops were consumed. We spent weeks in this "squat-and-go" lifestyle, all the while searching for the "better northern camp."

Some days, the fighting between the RPF and the remnants of the Hutu Power Army found its way to us. Depending on the size of the refugee group, disorder could spread throughout the crowd in an instant. But, regardless of the size of the crowd, any sound of fighting prompted the masses into a fear-filled gallop. Shortly after we left the farm, we crossed paths with Hutu militarized forces with machetes, rifles, ammunition, and grenades. I carefully paid attention to the group's officers giving out orders to their soldiers: "Shoot toward the trees where the RPF are coming from and make sure to watch out for refugees."

Now that some Hutu soldiers had abandoned their uniforms, I asked a woman near me how the Hutu leaders were able to distinguish between who was a soldier and who was not, and she answered, "As long as people had weapons, they were soldiers." We stopped to watch the men open fire and throw their grenades. The gun and grenade sounds continued for a brief while and everyone in the camp covered their ears. When the soldiers began firing in all directions, bullets and grenades spraying in the distance sent refugees dispersing into the woods.

In our large group, we used a method to remain together that included abandoning the possessions in our arms and locking elbows with the person nearest to us or staying in a single-file line like children in school. We did this regularly as the trees began to shake, bullets flew, and the mass of people spread and fled like a flock of ducks.

When the dust cleared, we rested a moment, though my heart never really slowed down. I noticed the veins on my arms bulge as I rubbed my neck, which had become hardened and achy. I was unsure how long this lifestyle would last.

After the sound of fighting stopped, a handful of our group went back to recover our refugee belongings, occasionally adding to our reserve. Other times, we lost items to others who picked them over and took what they wanted. Then the dull rumble of voices from the crowd would surge again in response to the sound of more bullets, which meant it was time to run again. One of my hands clasped Furaha's aunt's hand, and the other was in the hand of one of the other children as we charged past the others. The line split. Families were in disarray. Children cried out for their parents. Mothers roamed the forests for hours in search of their children.

One day, the walk ended. We had walked and run and hauled our tired bodies for days, and many of us were dehydrated. Luckily in the distance there was a shallow lake. I recall walking toward the water in a trance, and instead of slurping the water with my cupped hands, I walked straight into the lake water like a cow, collapsing and resting my wet face on the bank of the lake and cooling the blisters on my feet. I must have fallen asleep because when I woke up, it was night, and fires were flickering around the camp. Furaha and the other men had made some useful trades, and we ate well for a few days.

We rested before we were to pass over a large nearby river. In the days leading up to passing the river, hundreds more refugees camped around us. Once again, as the camp's population grew, so did the presence of

Interahamwe and former Hutu government soldiers. It was clear that they had been defeated, and their only solace appeared to be locating and killing any rare Tutsis. As their presence increased, so did rumors about RPF spies. I heard outlandish stories of the RPF planting Tutsi women and children in the camps to observe and report back to the RPF. To my knowledge, this could not have been the case, as our group of refugees were far from the RPF stronghold at the capital. Nevertheless, this rumor was used as justification to kill women and children who looked Tutsi.

On the march again, we approached another large body of water. But I wasn't certain of the name of this new river. Many refugees assumed it was the Nyabarongo River, a place occupied by Hutu hardliners. Around the fire, Furaha's aunts and children cautioned me to stay close to the camp during the day, retelling stories of Tutsi spies getting killed near the river. Regardless of the threats, I was still expected to fetch water and scour the area for food and firewood.

On the second day of rest, my search for firewood led me to a narrow section of the river where a sparsely populated group of refugees camped. I was wearing a checkered shawl around my neck and let the sleeves of my oversized shirt dangle below my hands. I pulled the string tightly around the top of my skirt, plucked up a few branches, and ventured farther down the river's edge. The area had been nearly picked clean by those who came before us. The smoke from their fires now filling my nostrils, I drifted even farther, noticing the crowds grow in size. Still unsuccessful in my firewood pursuit, I continued to a low-lying area of land that had been flooded. Moving around this area, I expected less people and likely more firewood. However, when I passed the marsh and went through numerous foliage and trees, I came upon an enormous group of refugees. I couldn't say exactly how many people were there, only that I felt eyes locked on me regardless of the direction I walked. For the most part, I tried to keep my eyes on the soaked ground before me. I drifted back toward the river where a squabble had broken out. Insults flew from one man to the others surrounding him, then he spat on them. He was quickly killed. I felt tightness in my esophagus and picked up my speed, passing women who were hauling water buckets. Beyond the women was another hostile gathering.

Heads were weaving for better views as they watched a group forming along the river's edge. I felt the rhythm of their hearts like a drumbeat in between my ears. I hoped my frightened eyes would not signal them.

I am a human. No need to stop and examine me. I'm just collecting firewood for my Hutu people, I repeated in my head, wishing any onlookers could hear my thoughts. Furaha and his family were nowhere near to defend me.

Then a man's voice cut the air, and all the background noise seemed to shut down except for his booming voice. "Little girl! Little girl! Come here! Come here, you foolish little snake!" His last word sent my body into an instant tremble. Pretending his call was meant for another little girl, I sauntered forward, my eyes down at my feet. But the man's shouts became louder, and a large ensemble joined him.

"Snake! Cockroach!" screamed the crowd as one of the men came up to me.

"Why are you pulling at me?" I questioned as the man's hand folded around my arm. He answered that I looked like a snake. Afraid to confirm or deny, I murmured to myself, *I am not a snake. I am not a cockroach. Can't you tell that I am human?*

The men led me to the back of a line of two dozen people. I don't know if they were all Tutsis, but they looked like shells of humans consumed with worry and shock. Circled around them were the bystanders—mostly men and older women—encouraging and cheering in chorus at the top of their lungs, chanting the ethnic cleansing song: "Eh yay tubagandagure, Eh yay tubatsembatsembe!"

Yards before them, the dead floated in the river, a look of melancholy surrender on their watery faces.

Yet outrage was carved onto my ten-year-old face. I felt like a complete stranger to this madness, but I wasn't. *Had I suffered so much just to die here?* I wondered.

One by one, the men ordered us forward to meet their weapons: a steel blade, a long, wood-handled hatchet, a stick fixed with long nails. The main killer was a stiff and uncoordinated man. He fumbled with his blade, as if his mind was a thousand miles away, yet he continued on. The others assisted him, using various weapons to hasten their "work."

I watched as they fell, one by one—boys, wives, and children younger than me. These were Tutsis marked for death by their identification cards or their noses, arms, and height. They were martyrs, lost in space, suspended in time.

"You! You! Long arms," barked the same man who fetched me. He was now directing another unfortunate soul in line behind me. I watched as the killers cleansed us of our ethnic labels, bathed in blood and sweat, taking turns with the duties. Their voices were hostile and intense.

"Be still," commanded the captor of the boy in front of me.

"Don't make this difficult," warned another captor, who was busy adjusting the collarbone of an elderly lady as she stared helplessly into her palms. Her eyes looked as if they ached into eternity. The clumsy man swung his machete down on the base of her neck, spurting blood like a faucet onto his jaw. Anxiously smearing the blood across his cheek with his shoulder, he stood aside. The others picked up the woman's corpse and tossed it into the river, which splashed and parted the other dead with her wake.

The man called for more, and more people fell.

God, give me a miracle. Reveal yourself here, I prayed again in my head, noticing the boy in front of me tightening his muscles out of fear.

Protect us, God, save us, I muttered through my trembling lips. A rush of urine drizzled down my legs. Then, the flexing boy's body in front of me was heaved into the river. I stood still. It was my turn. In that moment, everything before me seemed to stand still and quiet. Time seemed to have stopped.

"Let's go! Come forward," a voice called to me. I tried shuffling my feet to break my trance, but my entire body stiffened. I couldn't even blink. With machete in hand, the awkward man approached me. I imagined my body lying dead at the feet of the murderers like the boy before me: my neck opened, my checkered shawl cut off, blood saturating my shirt. My bare feet shuffled toward him and then quit working. At that moment, an awareness that I was truly going to die entered every part of my body. The dread that paralyzed me flushed away. I accepted death like an eager child, beckoning to be lifted to heaven by my parents. A warming sensation pulsated from the crown of my head to the soles of my feet. My last thoughts were of my siblings. I asked God to keep them safe and give them a decent life.

The man raised his blade high in the air when a voice called out in the crowd.

"Stop! Stop!" shrieked a woman. "My girl. Don't hurt my daughter!" Everyone looked around, puzzled. *My mother is dead, she can't be talking about me*, I said to myself.

The people cleared a space for the woman to pass through while the awkward executioner lowered his blade. The murderer's companions stared. Some demanded that this unknown woman explain herself. The only explanation that made sense to me at that moment was that she had misidentified me. Perhaps I looked like her daughter, possibly the girl had disappeared. Like everybody else, I watched the woman, waiting for her expression to change once she realized that I wasn't who she thought I was.

The killers stared at the woman while she approached me. She wrapped her arms around me, filling me with an almost incomprehensible sense of relief. In a short time, we were separated without exchanging a word to each other. The killers explained they were going to investigate and ask us the same questions, and if our answers didn't match up, they would kill us both.

I was asked a series of questions by a man who was staring fiercely into my eyes. "How old are you? Where were you born? When is your birthdate? What's your name?"

I answered all his questions, but paused for an instant at the last one. Then I said, "My name is Jeanne Umutoniwase."

I'm not sure why I chose my nickname instead of my official last name, only that I felt it was the response I needed to give at that time.

Afraid that I was about to be killed with this strange woman, my heart pounded faster. After the investigation, the killer walked me back to the edge of the river where his partner was examining the woman's identification card.

Amazingly, our answers matched. The disappointed men confirmed this, mumbled something, and thrust me into this woman's arms.

Still puzzled but thankful of my hero, I strode away from the killers and looked at her vibrant face. I ached to know who she was, but it was crucial to wait until we were alone. She gripped my hand and we walked casually away from the crowd.

When we were far enough away, she leaned down, looked in my eyes and whispered, "Jeanne, my daughter, go on, continue traveling with these people and don't be afraid. I will be by your side, protecting you." I nodded and turned my head to face the crowd. When I turned back, the woman was gone. I ran around searching for some of the afternoon, but could not find her.

After exhausting all my energy, I made my way back to Furaha's camp. I spent the next few days watching for this woman, but I never saw her again.

SOON AFTER I was saved by the woman, a number of people in our group packed their possessions and lined up to pass over the Nyabarongo River, the place where I was nearly killed. There was no bridge, only two large logs as high as telephone poles that had been chopped down, hastily trimmed, and laid across the river linking it to the opposite bank. When it came time for me to cross, I froze, gazing down at the broad river, horrified by the clear sight of lifeless bodies manipulated into movement by the flowing water. My eyes fastened on a dead woman and an infant child. This delay caused the people waiting to cross behind me to squeeze into a jumbled heap. They promptly became annoyed, and many complained and suggested I be tossed into the river. As their patience dissipated, I pushed myself into motion across the tree logs and onto the next refugee camp, which became my home for the next several months.

It must've been a few days later when I laid eyes on the largest group of people I had ever seen. With pans clanking together over my shoulder, we topped a ridge where we could watch the immense masses of uprooted people. They were like ants in a colony. For as far as my eyes could see, refugees standing shoulder to shoulder, united together in harmonious confusion. No barricades, no toilets, only thousands of blue plastic squares propped up into huts serving as their residences. Near the middle point of the camp, I located a parcel of white canopies, which I later learned were United Nations food stations. The concept of humans willing to help became the only remnant of hope that hovered over the group of people.

We mixed with a never-ending procession of women and children who wandered along the pathway, bearing stacks of firewood piled high on their heads. Peppered throughout the procession were children dragging branches and twigs that scraped along the dirt path, creating trails of dust behind them. When we reached our destination, we unloaded our possessions and settled.

In the coming days, my eyes became acclimated to the burning of dense smoke from the countless fires warming the refugees. It hung in the air and caused us all to cough. The camp was a remarkable and somber sight. On my first trip to the white tents, I marveled at the sounds of the camp, tens of thousands of people conversing at once, producing an incessant buzzing in my ears. Occasionally a truck horn sliced through the noise, sending my body into a more heightened sense of awareness. From where our blue tent was set up, I could look into the center of camp, or what came to be known as the "Capitol," and a sort of trance would fall upon me. The trance resulted from watching thousands of bodies moving about, zigging and zagging quickly, like bees in a hive.

Most of my first trips to the "Capitol" were in small groups, usually led by Furaha and a handful of his relatives. But in the coming weeks, the others trusted me with solo excursions. On these initial expeditions, I made mental records of the most important places and pathways, counting rows and tents like a detective. One of the most important routes to remember was the path to the streams, as collecting water was still one of my main duties. Another vital area I had to learn about was the market, where the refugees and locals from adjacent villages flocked to barter and purchase goods. Everything from rifles to bananas were swapped there, but mostly people sold food like corn and rice and beans, all laid out on dusty plastic covers on the edge of the tracks. I recognized a lot of the food items from the humanitarian relief supplies. Now that I was entrusted to make trips to buy sacks of grains and porridge, I felt a little bit of freedom.

It didn't take long for me to single out the most relevant area in camp, the only place that could deliver me from a life of abuse and possibly return me to my hometown to find out if any of my relatives were alive. It was basically a system of large white tents surrounded by a ten-foot barbed wire fence near the middle point of camp. The allure of this area was the crowd of children who surrounded it. Many of the youth gathered there looked like me, uncertain and in need of parents. Excited to learn that this place was built to help displaced children and orphans, I was more hopeful. Many people referred to this organization as "Umuryango Ufasha Abana," which was equivalent to UNICEF. I came close to the barbed wire fences, watched the children in line, and wished I could be there. But the question was, how? I returned to our tent and didn't mention a word to anyone about the organization.

A few days passed; I returned to the Capitol to buy salt. On the way there were soldiers in green- and-baby-blue helmets handing out samples of crackers to waiting children. I pounced on the opportunity and forced my way past the younger children to claim a broken piece. I made eye contact with the soldier, but when I spoke, he looked perplexed. He replied in a language that sounded like gibberish, and I went on my way, slowly enjoying the pleasant taste. The following day, I observed a long green truck packed with children rumbling down the path away from the camp. Although I had no idea where those children were taken, in my young mind any place was better than the refugee camp lifestyle.

From that day, I used most of my camp time attempting to become a passenger in one of those trucks. Besides, I was still a Tutsi who could be subjected to death, an inferior class even in these times of hopelessness and intense poverty. I lived on a smaller share of rations or nothing for days, was still expected to work despite the boils that persistently infected my legs, and when away from the others on a water or food run, was subjected to rapes by Furaha. To make matters worse, there was a cow herder in his late twenties or early thirties who disgustingly leered at me on my way to the market. All those reasons justified my desire to escape back to my hometown, or any other place but the refugee camp.

One sunny evening, the same leering cow herder arrived at our campsite. He introduced himself as Gahigi. Furaha, likely looking to form a relationship with more prosperous locals, uncharacteristically welcomed Gahigi like a familiar friend. From that day on, the two sat down by the fire nearly every night, drinking beer and trading stories. Whenever I strolled by them, their discussions often stopped or became hushed.

When I saw Gahigi snoring a few spaces over from me the following morning, it did not take long for me to figure out the purpose of his and Furaha's relationship and his objectives. Even though Gahigi was an adult, it was obvious he wanted a child wife. More precisely, he wished me to be his bride. To communicate this desire, Gahigi smiled at me regularly, presenting his spaced teeth and chafed lips, whispering that I was "beautiful." Needless to say, the idea of marrying a grown man at the age of ten evoked the level of disgust I felt when suffering through Furaha's perverted violations.

This behavior, which developed over the course of a few weeks, inspired me to stop by the UNICEF tents more often. Despite my numerous visits, the sheer number of children waiting to be helped and the amount of Hutu screeners made it difficult to find my way inside the white tents. All the lines were sprinkled with Hutu extremist screeners positioned unwittingly by the humanitarian relief personnel. I recalled their faces from the killings at the river. I also recognized some of them among the group who had sung the extremist songs throughout the camps, but the relief personnel had put them in a position to interpret and translate for refugees from the Kinyarwanda to French or English. I stood in line behind dozens of children, pretending to be mute, not even answering the children who tried to get me to speak, some even poking and pushing me to get me to break my silence. When the skeptical Hutu screeners approached me, I stood silent, only staring blankly in reply to their inquiries about ethnicity. During these instances, I was sometimes led away by the screener as they warned me, "This isn't an area for Tutsi children."

Even with a foreign presence, the camp was still highly politicized and militarized. Though the killings of Tutsis were less bold, they still occurred periodically in pockets of the camp. However, natural death did not discriminate; many of the Hutu refugees began facing their end as well. Their deaths were not carried out by a blade or bullets, but by nature itself: the executioners came in the form of malaria, dysentery, and cholera. Their presence was unmistakable. I saw it on my way to the heart of the camp, in the faces of the women with deadpan expressions and the restless infants wailing in their arms but unable to generate tears.

Their slumped shoulders slanted the same way my friend Alice's had when she was a captive in Furaha's home. Discouragement seemed to be everywhere I turned: a woman talking to herself, her head swinging to some rhythmic arrangement of words aimed at soothing her misery; a man bent over, his fingers locked behind his neck, dusty white film around his lips, grieving for his kin and himself. Their eyes were sunken and void of life. Some of them looked the same way that many of the Tutsis did right before they were killed—people suspended in time in a state of perpetual disbelief.

A portion of me had hardened toward the extremists the same way my heart had hardened toward Furaha's father. But now, in the face of torment, I felt for them. There was no part of me that rejoiced when I saw another human in misery. Somehow, my young mind recognized that we were all human, and that pain and suffering were the same for us all despite our identity.

Apart from the boils on my legs, I also experienced another indiscriminate contagion in my body. I couldn't say what it was except it

161

acted like malaria or perhaps dysentery. My body was scorched with fever, and within a couple days, I was vomiting bile. I found myself lying flat on the grass of our tent wondering if this sickness would bring me to the end. Without the strength or desire to eat, Furaha's niece, who was my little companion, brought me water. Everything I consumed found an immediate exit. The fever, body aches, and headache continued, and I was hallucinating. I do not recall going to a doctor or seeing a physician for evaluation and without a formal diagnosis, I was not provided medicine except some herbs. Unable to leave the tent, Furaha and others lifted my shivering body and lay me outside to soak up the sunlight. The warmth of the sun lifted my spirit and brought a sense of peace, but hours later I was interrupted by Furaha's aunt, who said I had been lying on my right side for hours. She helped me lay on my back and told me she was going to find me a cure. "Thank you for taking care of me," I whispered.

For hours, I laid in the sun, closed my eyes, and prayed that I somehow would beat this illness. I then heard Furaha and Gahigi coming toward me. Furaha looked shocked. "Oh, you don't look like you are going to make it, and if you do, it will be by the grace of God," he announced with his hands placed on his head.

"She looks like a ghost," added Gahigi. Trying not to cry, I closed my eyes, but Gahigi went on telling Furaha that if he gave me to him, he would take me to the hospital or find a cure. The men continued to discuss how my illness needed to be handled, but I prayed that Furaha would not hand me over to Gahigi.

I was relieved when I heard a woman's voice coming toward me. And even better, it was Furaha's aunt. She brought another lady with her to my side, and they sent both Furaha and Gahigi away. Without telling me the name of the lady, Furaha's aunt explained to me that she was a village doctor, basically a witch doctor. She was middle-aged, with fat cheeks and deep cracks in her forehead. The witch doctor knelt down at my side and picked up my hands. She chanted in a foreign language after placing some money in my hands and rolling it about. After more chanting, she dropped a pinch of ash in the center of my palms and blew it at me. All the while, my jaw hung wide and I fought to keep my eyes open. Terrified at my first encounter with a witch doctor, I prayed I wouldn't end up with a worse illness than what I already had.

After looking carefully at the boils and sores, which now covered my thighs and oozed puss and blood, she talked in my native language, Kinyarwanda, asking about my past. Furaha's aunt, who watched me struggle to speak, volunteered information about my parents and relatives who were killed in the genocide. That's when the witch doctor decided my illness was due to deceased family members haunting my body. She prepared a grass-type mixture in a bowl and forced me to drink it. They thanked her, and she departed.

After vomiting up the mixture, I floated into sleep to the sound of little girls laughing. For a moment, I was convinced it was Teddy and Teta. The laughter brought me to a euphoric state, a place I assumed was heaven. My twin sisters and parents were waiting for me. Then, all of a sudden, the laughter ceased, and all I saw was darkness. Furaha's aunt told me that I was still hallucinating.

Chapter Twenty

D ays passed and my condition improved to the point I could now walk on my own. It was during this time I decided not to throw away my next opportunity to place myself at the front of the UNICEF line to claim a seat on the large green truck with the other parentless children.

When Gahigi noticed that I was back on my feet, he resumed following me around the camp. One particularly sunny day while I was on my way to buy beans, Gahigi followed me to the market. While Gahigi pursued me relentlessly, describing what our life together would be like, I zigzagged through the shelters and people, desperate to lose him. But he clung to my heels, each scene he detailed causing me to wince in revulsion. When I reached a hill nearby, I looked back and was delighted to discover that I had lost him. I merged back to the main road and was about midway to the market when someone tickled my ribs from behind. I turned around, stunned to see Gahigi's toothless smile. I screamed and scratched him when he tried to cover my mouth.

He yanked me off the main road and into the bushes. "Stop fighting," he said as he attempted to pull my skirt off. "You know you will be my bride one day." I scratched him again and slapped his hands. Unlike Furaha, Gahigi was a lanky, almost frail man, which made it possible for me to break his grip. I ran away as fast as my legs could carry me. He pursued me to the market, but I lost him in an open mass of people.

I headed straight for the UNICEF line, determined to make it into the white tents. After arriving, I noticed the lines looked shorter. Only a few dozen children, just as determined as I was, waited ahead of me. We stayed all afternoon and were given a small pack of crackers. Ripping the pack open, I placed an entire cracker in my mouth. Going without food for days made it taste delicious. I remember not wanting to swallow because I wanted the taste to remain in my mouth. As it was getting dark outside, a UN soldier sauntered before us and declared that no further applicants would be seen for the day.

Hoping to buy a bus ticket to escape back to Nyanza, I went to a place where people gambled anything from clothes to money. There were a few people around, and one man who looked like he was in charge explained the simple gambling rules. I stood there watching others play, but when it was my turn, I told the man that I would try next time. Everyone around persuaded me that I could win a lot of money.

The man in charge allowed me to practice a few times. My first three trials I won. With a little bit of confidence, I put Furaha's money down. I won my first two rounds, but not enough to buy me a bus ticket. My next round, I lost what I had won. Taking a risk, I continued, but lost half of the money to buy beans. Hoping to at least gain the other half back, I played again. This time I lost everything. Although it wasn't a lot of money, I was petrified of what the consequence would be. Without the beans from the market and no UNICEF prospect in place, I returned to camp to find Furaha and his relatives in a state of angst. I failed to produce a sufficient reason for coming back empty-handed. Angry, they sent me out to collect firewood.

Upon returning, I listened in on a hushed conversation. As I drew near, the voices of the shadowy figures became easily detectable. It was Gahigi, Furaha, and a few of Furaha's relatives. I crouched behind the tent for a few minutes until it became evident they were talking about me.

"She could be the last Tutsi in Rwanda," declared one of Furha's cousins.

"Yes, valuable, rare, and beautiful. Definitely worth more than two cows," added Furaha.

They haggled over the cows. Three. Four. Back to two. Gahigi brought up my strong will and unwillingness to accept his advances. Then Furaha pointed out that at my age, practically all wives are unreasonable.

A wife? Six months ago, I was playing with dolls and now these donkeys were arranging my wedding with a man almost my father's age! I stayed until the discussion stopped, then walked to the campfire.

That night I slept next to Furaha's aunt, lying on my side and watching the flames burn out in the fire pit while contemplating a life with Gahigi. I imagined a life where I could never go back to Nyanza to learn what remained of my family. I foresaw my days living in a poor home, spending every waking moment of my life with a grown, perverted man. Something inside me stirred. The image of becoming a child on that UNICEF truck disappeared.

The fire flamed out except for a smolder. The people in the tent, including Gahigi, who slept at my feet, fell into a relaxed state. It was the middle of the night. I heard a voice in my head, *Get up! Go! Go! Now is your chance.* I listened as the voice repeated. The more I recoiled from it, the louder the voice grew. *Go! Go! Go!*

I exhaled a deep, heavy breath. As I inhaled, I held my breath as if I was preparing to jump into a dark lake. My heart thumped against my chest as I slowly turned on my belly. *You can make it,* declared the voice. *Move quietly.* Once on my feet, I cautiously stepped in between the slumbering bodies. The first was Furaha. With my legs split over his body, one hand clinging to my bunched skirt, he snorted, prompting me to hesitate like a cat in the darkness. I caught my breath again. When his breathing became normal, I stepped by the others, slowly, carefully, ever so quietly. My toes touched the cool soil outside the tent. I took a dozen more quiet steps. Then, as if driven by a lightning blast, I sprinted.

The blue plastic blurs and glows from smoldering fires seemed to merge in my peripheral vision as I tore through the camp. I leaped over things I could see and slammed into those I couldn't. I came to the main path in a matter of minutes, my thin legs pumping like a machine.

When I reached the lower range, the tents and fires grew farther apart. I rushed past them, stumbling in a hole and falling to my knees. Without pausing to examine my wounds, I continued my dash, reaching the forests I collected water from every day. I must have run miles by the time I eventually stopped. Panting and heaving, sweat drenching my body, I looked up at the sky. A thousand stars sparked bright above and a silvery moon dimly lit the trail before me. I turned back toward the direction of the camp, back to where my abusers slept soundly, back to the place where so many killers lived, where death and a life of suffering were inevitable. I gathered my breath, turned, and continued running up the path.

Throughout the darkness I continued my journey, running then walking then running again. By the time the sun's golden rays rose over the horizon, I had come to a dense jungle. Finding a covered area, I sat down at the foot of a tree. I looked down at my bloody legs; running all night and falling had cracked open the scabbed boils. None of this troubled me. I let the rays from the morning sunlight warm my face. I took a whiff of fresh air and closed my eyes.

That morning, I took my freedom. I never saw Furaha, his relatives, Gahigi, or a refugee camp ever again.

THE DAY AFTER my liberation from my abusers, I was drained and indulged in a day of rest. The area was unfamiliar. I calculated where the camp might have been located, but at best, it was just a hunch.

I didn't have a clear direction other than the knowledge that I was running away from the refugee camp. I listened to my conscience and guessed the direction I needed to take. For weeks, my guesses led me through a vast wilderness. Sometimes the earth was soft and claylike, and an immense valley unfolded before me; other days, the landscape I passed was rocky and muddy. This cycle repeated itself, so I gathered I was walking in an enormous circle. To make progress, I placed mental marks on the landscapes and found myself in a dense forest. After walking endless miles, I was worn out, and I did what I had not done for days—napped in a low-hanging tree. At night, I stared at the moon and stars. During those nights, it seemed like the moon was my only friend. It accompanied me through rugged terrain and under misty clouds. I stared at it and even spoke to the moon every night. This was the first time in my life I was utterly alone, and I realized even more the intense misery of separation.

Like it had been during the genocide, my diet was simple—flowers, wild seeds, and if I was lucky, wild fruits. Looking for more food, I ventured into a bamboo jungle. As I struggled through the bamboo, I sensed eyes on me. I looked up to see a group of short black monkeys with straggly white whiskers. Being so lonesome, I wasn't frightened. I stopped to smile at them, but my affection wasn't appreciated. The larger one screeched in a high-pitched tone, which I took for a warning, and scurried along.

Without further alarming the monkeys, I took a different path that led me to human voices. I followed the voices to a site where two women and a handful of kids sat around a fire speaking a foreign language. I determined they weren't refugees from Rwanda, and approached them, greeting the startled faces that looked at me like I was an alien.

"Rwanda," I said again, "Which way to Rwanda?" I pointed my finger in a way to help them realize that I needed to know whether Rwanda was in the East, West, South, or North. Confused, they answered me in their native language, so I waved and departed.

After traveling for days, I saw hills and mountains, and then came across a large body of water. I found a group of villagers and was delighted to learn they spoke French and Swahili. They confirmed I was still in Congo. I asked an elderly man among the group the name of the river ahead. He laughed and said, "That's not a river, but a lake." Smiling, he added, "Lake Kivu."

After rounding Lake Kivu, I felt a sense of victory. I was on the right track home. "Yah! I made it," I screamed. Joyfully, I jumped up and down but stopped when I realized a group of people were staring at me. Still feeling a sense of freedom, I encountered yet another family of travelers in the forest. Hiding behind a shrub, I listened as they talked to each other in my native language. More eavesdropping made clear what I assumed—they were a Hutu family returning to their homes from Congo's refugee camp. I intended to follow them through the terrain since I had no clue which path to take back to Nyanza. As they journeyed on, I followed from a safe distance to avoid attracting attention. But soon their daughter, who was close to my age, and her older brother found me on their way to gather firewood. They didn't look startled by my presence and neither was I by theirs. They came closer, wanting to know my name, age, and where I was from. I told them more than I should have because I thought they were sympathetic and friendly. The girl looked me over. I could tell she was troubled by my frail frame. Without asking, she went away and returned with an uncooked sweet potato and a partial yucca root, placing them in my hands.

I continued to travel behind the family while the children continued to sneak out and sometimes share their tiny meals. They told me they never mentioned me to their parents, which surprised me. One evening, we finally said our good-byes. My little friend explained that her parents planned on traveling to a provincial town on the eastern side of Rwanda. She handed me one last meal and we shared a silent hug. I watched as the family disappeared down a desolate dirt road.

Now that I was moving at my own speed, I ran rapidly through the trails and valleys. Advancing farther into the country, I caught sight of those all-too-familiar roadblocks: this time around, the barricades weren't manned by Interahamwe, but RPF soldiers. They appeared to be over seven feet tall and skinny to the bones.

My initial communication with a couple of lean, tall, stone-faced Tutsi soldiers standing guard was anything but dramatic. As I drew near them, one asked, "Where are you going?"

"Nyanza," I responded.

Without further inquiries, the officer nodded and stood out of my way so I could go on. Down the trail I met several more, and I experienced similar interactions. They wore serious faces, but were nothing like what the people in the camp described them to be. "I was told you would have tails," I joked with one group.

They smiled, and one of the tallest in the group said, "We have been called many things."

Farther down the road, I came to an area I was familiar with—the forest near one of my aunts' homes and a destroyed school. As I pushed myself through the thick forest, the breeze picked up and the sky became gray. The wind brought the whispers of my parents, the giggles of the twins, and Jeannette's voice, as if they were calling me home.

I traveled past my aunt's home, which had been reduced to ashes, and there was not a person to be seen. As I journeyed past the secondary school, I noticed piles of dried human bones picked over by crows. I kept moving as a flashback of hiding in the forest with the twins ran through my mind. Everything seemed to have just happened. I stood still to reflect on how long I had been away. It was now the midpoint of December, nearly nine months since we had been forced out of our house. There was barely six miles of road between me and my home.

It hit me that I was just minutes away from all the answers to my questions about what had happened to my family—and about my future.

Chapter Twenty-One

The pathway to my house bent south, setting the sun straight in my direction. The sky was open with nothing but a few wispy clouds. Questions flew through my mind as I stepped onto familiar dusty trails that led to my home.

"What if I am completely alone?"

"What if my sisters are dead?"

"What if I stumble upon their corpses?"

I passed by the first set of houses a few miles away. The familiar faces of my Hutu neighbors, former friends, and past employees of my parents gathered along the road with astonished expressions. The first, a young family of four, were all tongue-tied; the mother, a woman my mother often prepared care packages for, gasped when she caught sight of me. They spoke quietly, and I went on without a single spoken word exchanged.

Not much farther down the road were a bunch of young boys carrying water. Dropping their responsibilities, they trotted alongside me, watching with contorted expressions of curiosity fixed on their faces. Some of them looked at me as if they were seeing a ghost.

"What are you doing here?" they demanded, reminding me I had no business here. Six months ago, I would've run for my life, but now that the RPF controlled the country, Tutsis like me were free to return to whatever was left of their homes. I continued walking, straight-faced and measured. I said little, ignoring most of their unwelcome remarks.

"Have you seen Jeannette or my brothers?" I asked.

One of the boys answered, "I haven't seen one Tutsi in this town for months, except you." His words were the nightmare I had shunned for months. "If you're smart, you should go away and never come back here," he said as they left.

Now within a mile of my home, I felt a strange mixture of emotions. The strongest yet were feelings I now noticed all too well—resentment toward every human being in my neighborhood, and anger that was rapidly advancing to hatred.

Topping the hill, I saw where my home and the homes of my relatives had been.

I passed more neighbors, rubbernecking and eagle-eyeing me. Neighbors I had wandered by countless times without a second thought now viewed me as if I was a foreigner, or even worse, a fugitive staking out "their" property—the property they had taken from Tutsi families like mine.

I walked past two homes that my uncles had owned: one Joshua had lived in and the other had belonged to my Uncle Edward. I wanted to enter what remained of the houses, but the fear of finding remains kept me away. The houses were deserted, obliterated and silent as a graveyard.

A few minutes away, I noticed a middle-aged woman effortlessly balancing a sack on her head. It was Kalisa's mother, a woman who had always been kind to my family. From the look she offered me, it was clear she was as unprepared as the others to see me.

"Oh, my, you're alive! Are you Jeanne or Jeannette?"

"Jeanne," I answered.

"I cannot believe it...I can't believe you survived." she said, setting the bag at her feet.

Tilting her head, she went on, "No one thought any Tutsis survived...especially in this town." I listened to her, but I had no words in me except an outrage that prompted me to gasp. "I'm sorry... so sorry... they ruined your house... your parents... and all your relatives...well...My God! You're alive, I can't believe it."

I looked through her, praying she would soon tell me she saw my sisters alive and together. But she was obsessed with my condition.

"How did you survive? You must've holed up in the bushes from your looks." I nodded my head and stared at her curiously. She hesitated, and then began again. "Pardon me; I am startled to see a Tutsi made it. That's great news for you!"

Again, I didn't know what to say, so my silence lingered.

"You know, your parents were good people, I never had an issue with them...they were respected by all in this town," she said gloomily.

I nodded in approval and mumbled, "They were."

"This skirt...it may have belonged to your mother or one of your relatives. I can't recall who gave it to me," she remarked, placing one hand on her hipbone and peeping down at her torso, brushing dust from her blouse.

"Yes, I remember it," I said. The anger boiled inside me, but I forced an evasive smile to match hers.

She then rambled on about our furniture, clothes, and livestock seized by other neighbors, running down a list of items and matching them with people in the village as if she had studied them for weeks.

"But," she said, abruptly interrupting herself, "... it may lead to trouble if you go around asking for your family's things. A long time has passed, Jeanne. People are starting over," she said, nodding rather wildly.

After thinking about what she had said, I cleared my throat and replied, "I'm not here for our belongings. I'm here to see my brothers and sisters. Possessions are not as valuable to me as my family," I assured her, making evident her skirt was safe and sound.

"Are you sure? You may need some of those things to keep your family's memory alive," she said, softening her eyes a bit.

"If my siblings are alive, that will be enough for me. Things are replaceable, but people are not."

She nodded in approval. "Very wise... Jeanne... very wise... you remind me of your father... you're like him. He was a clever man. I see him in you. No doubt you will grow up to be like him."

That was possibly the highest compliment she could've offered me. With those words, I moved on, but she offered a final piece of counsel. "Be sure to check the orphanage in Nyanza for your sisters. There are hundreds of kids there," she said loudly as I wandered away.

I walked onto our field with a queasy stomach, over tall weeds, and past the area where our wood fence once stood. It was now dismantled, leaving an eerie silence to linger before me. I remembered the landscape, but it looked strange. Where there were once fields of vegetables and fruits was now replaced with weeds and lonely trees. Even the bamboo trees Jeannette and I played around appeared to mourn something, and the chirping birds in the trees sounded detached and estranged. I remembered a lush paradise, but our farms were incinerated. Nothing more than blackened wooden frames remained. Before the genocide, cattle bellowed on our fields behind our house, but now all I heard was the melancholy wind sweeping the overgrown shrubs. Not one goat, cow, or chicken remained.

Standing before me wasn't the home I cherished but only a part of its foundation, charred back walls and a few side walls.

At my feet was debris—a cracked vase, pieces of burned pictures and papers. Noticing a shiny object reflecting the sunlight in the weeds at my feet, I went down to my knees. Parting the weeds and sweeping aside the dirt, I picked up a wallet-sized chunk of shattered mirror and held it up to my face. A few cards stuck to its surface, so I removed them, revealing my reflection. The girl in the mirror was recognizable, but much like the landscape in front of me, she looked different from what I remembered. Her thin face was dirty and pale. Her hair was thickly dreadlocked and entangled with small twigs and leaves. Her sun-chapped lips were dry and trembling. And her eyes were sunken, dull, and isolated. They revealed nothing but sadness. Lowering the cards and mirror to my side, I looked closer at the remnants of our house, spotting a blackened table leg that was all that was left behind of our dining furniture—the place we had gathered for family time, to play card games and laugh, to poke fun and communicate our concerns, to eat, pray, and be a family.

Suddenly, I saw my Dad's face in my mind, then my mom, then my brothers and sisters. We were playing games at the dinner table, laughing, and listening to Dad's folktales. We were eating meals and celebrating birthdays. Every image seemed more animated than the next. Then, their voices came to life, as clearly in my head as if I was talking to them in the flesh. First, my father, clear as day, "Help your brother with his homework, Jeanne." "Don't be late for class." Then my mother's voice, "clear the dishes before you head out." The longer I reminisced, the more real it became.

"Time to go, Jeanne," Mom said, in her soft, soothing voice. "Time to go, sweetie."

"Mom," I replied back to her voice, "Mom, can you see me?"

Tears were gushing from my closed eyes.

"Mom?"

"It's time to go, honey." Everything seemed real.

"Oh, God," I said aloud, "This can't be happening." I opened my eyes widely and slapped my face. *Am I going mad? Is this what trauma looks like? Please, God, help me.* I swung my head wildly and my chest heaved. The images then flew faster. School. Church. Family gatherings. Walks through the banana fields with my Dad.

Looking around, my face twisted in confusion and anguish.

God, is this why you rescued me? To take me this far so I can live alone with nothing but an image of my family? Why, God, why did you save me? I thought you understood my prayers. I begged you to keep my siblings alive. Now, here I am alone.

I stumbled forward onto the dirt; saliva hung from my lip and drizzled onto the soil. My jaw was wide, suspended in pain, as a high-pitched siren wailed in my ears. Then, in an instant, the noises stopped. I'm not sure how long I stayed on the ground, but when I looked up, the sun was still high in the sky.

There were tiny fragments of shattered vase embedded in my leg, and I still had the cards clenched in my fist when I finally pulled myself up. Looking around to collect my bearings, I dropped the cards on the lawn and removed the pieces of vase from my skin.

Walking back toward Nyanza, I saw a couple of well-muscled longhorn cattle with spotted white-and-black coats meandering about Fatuma's house. Fatuma, the old woman who offered her grim prediction before the genocide, stormed from her house, her eyes suddenly flashing. "I told you. I told you how this was going to go, but you didn't pay attention," she said, smiling a long, cunning smile.

I stopped in the middle of the road to look at her. It was then her words before the genocide came streaking in my mind, *we will take everything you have.* She babbled something, but it wasn't clear. I asked her to repeat it again, and she did, "You shouldn't have come back to this area. There is nothing here for you."

I turned around, looking at the ghost of my home, and then my relatives' and all the destroyed Tutsi houses, and nodded my head.

"I know. There is nothing here for me but memories of my family," I said, wiping the lingering tears from my eyes.

ON MY WAY to the Nyanza orphanage, I struggled with the possibility I was the last of my family alive. The remnants of houses and shops I once remembered were visible on the path. A few miles from my home, I passed the first handful of Nyanza's residents—a man on a bicycle, a woman carrying a baby, some shopkeepers tending to their shops. I remembered the leaves and the blades of grass and little rocks on the trail outside of town, but now the outskirts looked like another place entirely. The massacre had left its signature: houses and shops pockmarked with bullet holes, doors torn from their hinges, stores ransacked, and trash in the streets.

Most of what I remembered about Nyanza's beauty had disappeared, but I recognized a store Jeannette and I used to call "the Buttermilk Shop," and more memories rushed back. The shop owner sold more than milk products, but buttermilk was the one treat we always asked our parents for when we went to town. The structure had sustained limited damage. As I walked by, I thought of the early summer mornings when Jeannette and I knocked back a generous bottle of buttermilk with beignets, watching people pass by the window. I recalled the shop as always being full of light and moving air.

Rousing myself from my reverie, I approached the orphanage, which was on an upward-sloping hillside. I heard children's voices giggling, calling, teasing, and arguing. Shortly after, the children came into view. The boys were running, kicking at each other's feet, hooting and creating clouds of dust. The girls were calmer, yet some were hurrying about in their identical blue uniforms. As I came closer, a few took notice of my condition, pointing, gesturing, and whispering. I couldn't really condemn them for staring; I looked dreadful. If I were in their place, I would've been entertained by the looks of me as well. I looked like a stray street girl with holes in my soiled clothes, bare feet, and mud on my face.

I examined each orphan student's face, hoping to find one of my siblings. Working my way through the crowd, more of the group stared at me and some made faces. Unapologetic about my ragged appearance, I proceeded up the middle of the group when I heard a girl say a name that caused my heart to leap. "Jeannette!" the girl repeated. But I didn't notice who she was talking to. Moments later, I located the source of the girl's call—a lanky girl standing straight before me, frozen in a state like the others.

"Jeannette," I muttered to myself as an unexpected flood of air filled my lungs.

I slowly walked up to my sister, my twin, my best friend, Jeannette. Our eyes locked. But the closer I drew to her, the quicker she backpedaled.

"God, what is this? No, God Almighty! No!" she cried, still backing up. "My sister's ghost. Oh, no!" she cried once more until her friends forced her still.

"No, she's not a ghost," one of her companions yelled, attempting to reassure her. "It's your twin! It's Jeanne, your twin. Can't you see she looks just like you?"

"It's her," added one of the other girls, "the one you talk about every day who you thought was dead!"

Jeannette clasped her hands and then covered her face while the girls nudged her forward towards me. We could only stare at each other for a few moments before more tears streamed down our faces. Soon after, we ran into each other's arms.

"Oh, Jeanne, is it you? Is this real?" she asked, hugging me as tightly as she could. She barely got her words out, so she touched my face and I in return touched hers. We both wept in each other's arms. It was a surreal moment.

"It's me," I assured her, "I am alive, Jeannette. You are alive!" To make certain I was indeed there in the flesh, Jeannette took a step back and punched me in the stomach with her fist. "Ouch! That hurts," I said while holding my belly. We both giggled.

"God, if this is not real," she added, "I will never trust you again." Once more we laughed.

A few passing people and Jeannette's playmates circled around us. Some watched our reunion with smiles. Others even cried, enjoying our relief and happiness.

Immediately, Jeannette wanted to show me to her dorm room. With her arm around my shoulder and mine around her waist, we strolled to the administrator's building to obtain permission for me to visit the orphanage. My spirit was flying, and I couldn't even feel my feet on the ground. I couldn't think of another occasion when my body felt so light, when anything and everything seemed possible. Still, all the months away from Jeannette caused me to ask, "Were you hurt?"

She grinned through my question and told me we had a lot to discuss. Her smile made me smile, which grew as her friends accompanied us to the building, singing, "Jeannette's twin is here! Jeannette's twin is here." This occasion was extraordinary beyond any reality I could ever imagine.

As Jeannette sought permission, I waited with her friends outside the large concrete brick house. She returned quickly, full of enthusiasm. "Let's run," she said excitedly, pulling me toward the attached white house.

"This is our dorm area," she said as we strolled into an immense room crowded with metal bunk beds and steep wooden dressers. Leading me to her bunk, she sat me down and asked her companions to wait with me. "I have something to show you," she declared as she hurried across the concrete floor toward the doorway.

Within a few minutes, Jeannette returned with the pitter-patter of bare feet on the cement following her. When Jeannette stepped aside, I gasped. Teddy and Teta were marching toward me. I sprang off the bed and lifted my hands in the air, "Oh, my God! Oh, my God! Thank you! Thank you!" I shouted as the little ones rushed to me.

Teddy put her head in her hands for a few moments, getting excited at the sight of me. Her jaw fell open and her eyeballs popped wide, while Teta flapped her arms like a bird. Falling on my knees, I folded my arms around them and squeezed my head against theirs.

"Thank you, thank you, God!" I repeated while I spun their tiny bodies around. Jeannette's friends proceeded to celebrate our reunion by clapping as I squeezed the twins. Even with all the excitement, I thought of my commitment to Mom to protect them, and the tears flowed and wouldn't stop.

"Stay here, I have another miracle," Jeannette said as she left for a second time. I had barely caught my breath when Jeannette returned holding our youngest brothers, Kayishema and Byiringiro.

"My boys made it, too," Jeannette said as she neared us. I couldn't restrain my joy; I was jumping up and down.

"Jeannette, this feels like a dream," I said, squinting through my tears of joy. I gripped the boys' hands, placing a kiss on each of their foreheads. Jeannette nodded, still sobbing and laughing as she watched us. I took a heavy breath and looked at them all. Just the expressions on their faces made my spirit overjoyed.

"Let's go to the playground," interrupted Jeannette.

Speechless, the six of us and Jeannette's entourage poured from the white house and onto the playground, where a crowd of boys were kicking a soccer ball. I hummed while I waited for the next revelation, knowing it would astound me. *Glory be to God. You are worthy of worship, my God. Praise forever. Praise God forever!*

We watched the group of boys for a short time, but Jeannette couldn't control herself any longer.

"Michael! Michael!" she screamed. "Come see your sister Jeanne!"

The crowd of boys stopped playing and stared at us, then our brother Michael shoved his way past his playmates and galloped right for me. He nearly knocked me to the ground when he flung his arms around my bony body.

With the biggest smile on his face, he took hold of my hands while bouncing up and down. He roared with joy, "You made it. You made it, Jeanne." I attempted to catch my breath. "I'm so happy you made it, Jeanne!" Michael yelled and hugged me repeatedly.

"This is a miracle, Michael, a miracle," I said, still gripped in his embrace.

"There's more," Jeannette said. She paused and took my hands. "Aimable and Cyiza survived as well. They were removed from the orphanage, but they live outside the city and sometimes they visit us," Jeannette cried. Again, I dropped to my knees and lifted my hands to the sky.

Thank you, God. Thank you for protecting them. My siblings now formed a circle around me, watching, crying and laughing along with me. In fact, we were all crying except Teddy and Teta and the little boys. Confused, Teddy asked me why I was weeping while rubbing my back.

"We are happy," Jeannette said, answering for me.

"I cry when I am hurt," said Teta, accompanying her twin by my side.

"These are different tears, girls. These are happy tears," said Michael.

"Happy tears? That is odd," said Teta, prompting the three of us to giggle.

But I didn't only feel happy, or exhilarated, or grateful at that moment. I felt like a person risen from the dead. What had died in me suddenly came to life. The others watching us were also overwhelmed by the happiness that enveloped us. Bright-eyed with tears and joy, my family and I celebrated life in that field as if every possibility in the world was now open to us.

Before the dinner bell rang, Jeannette went to the matron in charge and asked if I could join them for dinner and stay overnight. After dinner, Jeannette's second order of business was to meet with the Italian priest, Father Leonard, the chief administrator, and ask that I be admitted into her dorm. She was convinced that he would approve.

Once the young ones returned to their dorms, Jeannette and I walked away to catch up with each other. For the most part, we avoided talking about the genocide. Neither of us mentioned Mom or Dad. I kept what I had witnessed to myself. Instead, I talked about the old days.

Jeannette made me laugh by poking fun at my hair, suggesting I was related to a sheep. I was thankful she hadn't forgotten her sense of humor, although I detected in her an underlying sadness.

After our long conversation, she plucked a bag from her pocket, unfurling the top of a brown paper bag and extending it to me. We took a seat in the field, shelling roasted groundnuts and rubbing off the red skin tissue with a rolling movement of our thumbs and index fingers. We slowly savored the oily flesh, discarding the husks on the ground as we gazed at the orphanage before us.

When I asked her how she came across the groundnuts, she replied, "From one of the elderly woman I helped in the dining room."

She reflected as she snapped another one in her mouth, and then added, "I was saving them for a special day."

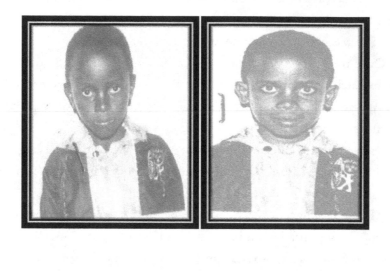

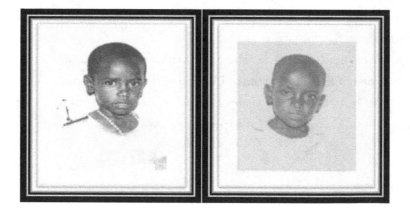

Top left: Teta, Top right: Teddy.
Bottom left: Byiringiro, Bottom right: Kayishema.
Photos taken at their orphanage a year after the genocide.

Top: Ruins of our home and guest house, destroyed
during the genocide.
Bottom: Remnants of my Cousin Joshua's house.

Top: The view from behind our house.
Bottom: Myself and a relative serving as flower girls at a
wedding, two years before the genocide.

Chapter Twenty-Two

That evening, Jeannette made good on her promise. While her companions set out to a prayer service, she tiptoed across the concrete floor and outside, then across a swath of field to the administrator's building where she waited for Father Leonard to arrive. Father Leonard, a sincere but strict priest, listened as Jeannette pleaded my case to become a resident in the orphanage. Unfortunately, the priest told her that the orphanage was already at capacity and could not accommodate any additional children.

In Jeannette's eyes, he might as well have said the opposite by the way she outlined our morning routines. She couldn't wait to introduce me to her classmates. She was convinced the priest would change his mind once he learned what had happened to our parents and relatives.

To make sure I looked presentable for our meeting with the priest, Jeannette brought along one of her tan skirts and a pink T-shirt that had been donated to her by the orphanage. She also brought with her a metal bucket, a bar of soap, and a set of blue flip-flops, all of which she "borrowed" from the orphanage. Accompanying me to bathe, Jeannette painted our future days at the orphanage together. She highlighted meal breaks, recess, and study times while reminding me how much I liked school. She also provided inside information on the orphanage politics, details about who was friendly, who to avoid, and how to handle the matrons.

We carried our supplies, and I washed months' worth of dirt off my body. Once clean, I disposed of my genocide clothing and put on the new clothes. It was refreshing.

Jeannette pulled a comb from her pocket and attempted to separate the knots in my hair, giggling as I struggled with her. "Has anyone mistaken you for a crazy child?" Jeannette laughed.

"Oh, I don't look that bad," I replied as we both chuckled. "Or I guess I do look a little like Bob Marley," I joked. Though it was a dark period for us, I was pleased again to see she had kept some of her lighthearted demeanor intact even though she now sighed more than she laughed.

Now that I was cleaned up, it was time to meet with the priest. As we walked to his office, Jeannette and I spoke about our casualties. As far as we knew, except for our Aunt Josephine, her husband, and their children, our other relatives in Nyanza were dead. Jeannette then told me what she learned of our brother, Adam, who had set out before the genocide to fight alongside the RPF.

"Adam is alive. He made it, too!" She explained that he was distraught to hear about Mom and our other relatives' deaths.

On the walk to Father Leonard's office, the clouds billowed over the blue sky and it grew dark. Heavy rain accompanied by thunder and lightning sent the animals around the orphanage scurrying for cover and into silence. We beat on the door and soon noticed it was locked. We then moved to the dining area. Entering the mess hall, I glanced around and saw several ladies handing out plastic dishes of rice and beans. I wasn't in any kind of rush, but I was anxious to get my hands on a warm meal. Still, I waited patiently alongside my twin to get our plates without getting in front of anybody.

"The look on your face tells me you haven't had rice and beans in months," Jeannette observed. I nodded and told her that I was starving. Finally, I picked up my plate and stuck my nose into the heat rising off the food. I allowed my soul to rejoice, delighting in the warmth of fresh clothes and the pleasure of eating a cooked meal, topped off with the company of my siblings. I don't recall if I had a smile on my face, but I was beaming on the inside.

I finished my plate before everyone else and Jeannette pushed her plate in front of me. I declined, although I could have used a little more food. After eating our meal, Jeannette pulled me toward the administration building once more and was excited for me to meet Father Leonard. With Jeannette clutching my hand, we made our way through the office and stopped in front of Father Leonard's door. "He's always here this time of day. Watch," Jeannette said, looking delighted.

After a couple of knocks on the heavy wooden door, it squeaked open and in the doorway stood Father Leonard. He was a short, slender man, his face withered and strewn with tiny creases around his eyes. Thin silver hairs remained above his temple. His bright eyes fixed on Jeannette and me. Smiling, he opened the door wide for us to enter.

"What can I do for you, girls?" asked the priest in perfect Kinyarwanda. Impressed with his grasp of our native tongue, I watched as he sat down in an old-fashioned armchair. He steered us to stand against a wall even though there were two unused chairs at his desk. There were a few pictures of orphaned children hanging on the wall. I noticed Teddy and Teta among them. A long crucifix hung from his neck, and another large crucifix hung in the entrance of his office. Next to the cross was a picture of Mother Mary and Jesus. Everything in his office resembled my old Catholic church.

"Father, this is my twin sister I told you about. Her name is Jeanne."

"Nice to see you," said Father Leonard, nodding his head and again talking in our native language. Jeannette then provided a rather frantic explanation of what had taken place since the genocide started, describing what she had seen and the little I had shared with her. The priest's face revealed empathy. First, he offered his sympathies for our parents, and then he talked about the minimal resources he had been allocated to assist orphans. "Girls," he said, pausing to savor a drink from his cup, "I want nothing more than for the two of you to remain here together, but it's not possible. Until we find homes for the current orphans, we are not taking any new ones. As it is, we have two or more children sleeping together."

Jeannette nodded in agreement but offered a solution. "But she can sleep in my bed with me. She won't use up any extra space, and we will divide my meals."

"I am sorry, girls. I can't approve that."

Jeannette wasn't satisfied. "Please, Father! Please let her stay." Jeannette's voice cracked like she was on the verge of crying.

I tapped her back and told her it was okay. "Father, do you think sending her to the streets is worse than letting her sleep on our floor in the dormitory?" she begged.

"I don't want her in the streets. There must be a relative who can take her in," he replied.

Outside the rain pounded against the window.

"Tell me, how old are you, young lady?" He took another slow, deliberate sip from his mug.

"Ten, Father."

"Ten…Unfortunately, there have been quite a few younger children I've had to send to their extended relatives. It is our reality at present." He reflected again and continued, "Surely you must have one adult family member who survived; an aunt, cousin, or an uncle. I am confident you will find someone who can take you in."

I shook my head, thinking of Aunt Josephine and her husband.

"Thank you for coming, girls, I have to get back to work."

After leaving the administration building, Jeannette and I found a dry place to plan our next decision. While my mind was working on options outside of the orphanage, Jeannette fixated on overturning Father Leonard's decision. The following week, she tried again and again, returning to his office door almost every day for the same debate. Finally, after much pleading, crying, and shouting, Jeannette conceded to his decision and searched for other options, one of which was the widowed genocide survivors who dropped by the orphanage home to find young house servants.

Naturally, the notion of being a maid was unappealing. As the weeks ticked by, Jeannette continued to reach out to visiting widows, and I returned to my life of homelessness on the streets of Nyanza. Ironically, our favorite shop, the "Buttermilk Shop," was also my favorite place as a homeless orphan. It was one of the few buildings in the town that had an overhang that sheltered me from the falling rain.

Chapter Twenty-Three

I am an early riser, the sort who springs wide awake out of sleep as if an alarm clock is connected to my brain. Normally, I can estimate the time within five or ten minutes. However, when one is homeless, you have little choice but to rise with the sun and the chirping morning birds. In some ways being homeless in Nyanza was a step forward, as some aspects of surviving became easier. For one, I was not in immediate danger as I had been in the months of carnage and at the refugee encampment. I had a daily routine; I wandered around the city, watching people pass in the markets. At first, I kept to myself, as I had become apprehensive and mistrustful of people. At night, I found my way back to the milk shop.

The first several weeks, I was tired. However, I didn't exactly lie awake, yet I did not fall into a deep sleep either. Maybe it was the enthusiasm of reuniting with my family and knowing they were alive, healthy, and just a few minutes away.

During these nights of wakefulness, I begged God to find me a home, one with love and support, and most importantly, one that supported my education, my only chance at independence and security.

On the streets, I became observant not merely of my surrounding environment but of people as well. To say relationships between Hutus and Tutsis in Nyanza after the genocide was awkward would be a grave understatement. Mostly the two ethnic groups stayed clear of each other. Many times, I saw Tutsis move to the opposite side of the path to avoid a conversation with a passing Hutu, and the Hutus did the same. The politics of the country was still a sore spot. Many genocide participants perceived the RPF as their enemies, whereas most of us Tutsis considered the RPF as our heroes. Personally, I believed without the RPF's intercession, the Génocidaires would have exterminated our entire population. Not only were Tutsis destitute, many of the survivors were traumatized by the grief and horrors locked in their minds. I watched as mothers wrapped their trembling arms around their offspring. They tried to console their children while grimacing in a persistent state of hunger and emotional pain. Some nights at dusk, a group of homeless Tutsi families gathered behind the milk shop to spark a fire just to be together. The firewood lit our stone-hardened facial expressions as the wisps of smoke rose toward the sky.

However, the Tutsis weren't alone in their suffering; many of the Hutus who witnessed mass atrocities and who took part in the killings also suffered from anguish. I recall passing by a young Hutu girl who lived in a clay hut. She had on a ripped sweatshirt on top and nothing on the bottom. She spoke to her mother about dead people while pointing to a pile of dirt. She hallucinated and yelled out names of the people she saw being murdered.

The contempt that had led to the genocide did not disappear with the elimination of roughly 90 percent of the Tutsi population. The Hutu citizens watched in spite as survivors crept out of the forests and bushes. But now the spirit of hatred seemed mutual.

Beyond the traumatized girl's mud hut was another, where an old Hutu man dwelt. I caught his eyes following me from his home. They burned like little flames. Awkwardness was in the air, in the basic gestures and glances of the people.

The man's look reminded me of others who chuckled at me for living in the streets. It also reminded me of other Hutu men I passed in the street who expressed regret at my survival abilities. These looks and comments raised in me the harsh, dirty taste of prejudice. I reflected on people like Fatuma, the faceless extremists who killed my family, the band of demons who murdered my father, the attitude of old Karl and his rapist son, Furaha. The consolation of surviving with my siblings, but powerless and abandoned in a broken world, was very little comfort at all. Thinking about my house in ruins and my parents' bodies discarded like garbage enraged me to no end.

Still, there existed other complex feelings to reconcile. The acts of moderate Hutus who had risked their lives to help me tempered my feelings of ill will. Kalisa, our security guard, for instance, will forever remain a hero. Uncle Gustave's father, who permitted us to stay in his house for a day while putting his life in danger, will remain a great man in my heart, as will Furaha's aunt, who showed me compassion through my stay at their village and in the refugee camp. I am sure there were thousands other unnamed, moderate Hutus who died saving others, and many who died just for speaking out about the genocide against Tutsis. But the violations perpetrated by the majority of Hutus largely overshadowed those noble actions, allowing bitterness to remain lit in my soul. My only glimmer of hope was something my mother taught me about forgiveness. She said that a hateful heart cannot connect with a loving God. Although I respected my mother's wisdom and believed it, practicing it at that time was another story.

But among all these bitter feelings, I still had my siblings. I was grateful to God for such a miracle. One Saturday, Jeannette came to surprise me. We jumped on a motorbike for about an hour-long trip up a rugged road to where Aimable and Cyiza stayed. Our first visit looked much like my homecoming with my other siblings. There were lots of tears and plenty of smiles, yet little conversation about Mom, Dad, or the genocide. Aimable joked that I looked "thin as a twig" as he folded his arms around me. I noted he had lost a good deal of weight as well. He wore a worried look on his face. Like Jeannette, he tried to make jokes. When I updated him on my living situation, his face showed sadness, but then his face changed as he counted how many of us had made it. "We are blessed to be alive," he reminded me. Cyiza reached out and hugged me, brushing his bony elbows against my waist. They invited me to live with them.

I would have moved in with Aimable and Cyiza, but their situation rivaled mine. They had settled into a narrow wooden shed marred with holes and cracks. The shack lacked a toilet, electricity, or furniture, and was packed with four other orphan boys close to their age. Hutu neighbors had assured the boys that they could stay there until the owner returned home from the refugee camp. The boys fed themselves by selling bottles of Coca-Cola and candies to the locals and merchants around town. Their enterprise barely produced a day's meal for them. Not wanting to consume their hard-earned food, I decided my free meal at Jeannette's orphanage was better for all of us.

Before we left, Aimable reached into his pouch of goodies and picked out two bottles of Coca-Cola for me and Jeannette. A frown crossed his face as we rejected them at first, but Aimable persisted, "This is the only thing I have to give you. Please take them." The four of us stood outside his shack, drinking Coca-Cola and gawking at the people passing. I told him that was the first Coke I had since the genocide started. He looked delighted.

Jeannette and I said our good-byes and returned to Nyanza. Over the next few days, Jeannette stepped up her efforts to find me a home. She established connections with women around the orphanage, but mostly talked with her matrons about a widow from Kigali who was interested in helping children. This particular woman was called Ms. Nadine; she was a genocide survivor and widow who made numerous trips to Nyanza, returning to Kigali with orphans. Depending on the orphans' age, they were either set up as live-in servants or adopted by families she found for them. Without a legal or formal structure, these arrangements exposed many children to exploitative conditions, but Ms. Nadine was a genuine orphan advocator. She showed compassion and was a sensitive, soft-spoken lady who wished to find loving homes for every child she met.

Jeannette talked about the possibility of finding me work through Ms. Nadine. But the notion of full-time employment was not all that appealing or comprehendible. Every time she brought up working as a maid, I brushed off her intentions and refocused her on finding a family to raise me and put me back in school. After weeks of indecision and discouragement, I recognized that remaining on the streets was dangerous. I began a process of self-talk as a way to reduce my fear and suspicion of people. In the coming weeks, I found the courage to ask local shopkeepers and random families if they would adopt me. I kept my pitch simple and stuck to the details about my orphan status. With persistence, I drew interest, but there was no one willing to commit to taking me in.

My lunchtime discussions with Jeannette continued to revolve around the possibility of finding me work as a housemaid in Kigali. As usual, I rolled my eyes at her suggestions, to which she responded, "You have to get off the streets. You don't belong out there, Jeanne." This was true, and Jeannette remained motivated by my lack of shelter and the embarrassment she felt explaining to her friends why her twin was a "street girl."

I quipped, "Let your friends know I am not homeless by choice." I could tell the more I rejected her advice, the more frustrated she became.

"Jeanne, have you counted how many people passed and said, 'There goes that beautiful homeless girl?'" she asked.

I nodded.

Jeannette kept on, "If you are someone's maid, at least you will have a place to sleep, food, and if you are lucky, they will put you in school."

A couple weeks later, I met Jeannette outside the orphanage, although this time she invited me to her dorm area. First, she finger-combed my hair, then passed me a bowl of water to clean my face. She dried my face with her T-shirt and then applied Vaseline to my cheeks and forehead. She said I looked pretty and we both grinned. We entered the hallway to join Ms. Nadine, who was relaxing on one of the matron's chairs. Ms. Nadine was a youthful-looking woman with immense brown eyes. She received me with an affectionate hug and a smile. She then told me about a mother in Kigali who was in need of a maid for her and her two teenage sons. The woman agreed to provide housing, food, and pay 3,000 francs, the equivalent of $3.00 per month for wages. As a child, that seemed like a good amount of money.

After Ms. Nadine left, Jeannette and I stood in the field talking about the distance and how hard it would be to save for a semester's worth of school fees. In the end, we agreed this opportunity beat the alternative.

After missing me for so many months, my siblings had grieved for me as much as I ached for them, and the last thing we wanted was to live in separate places. Jeannette felt awful for me and suggested that Father Leonard might allow us to change places. Touched at her suggestion, I rubbed her back and assured her, "Don't worry, God will make a way for us."

I spent my last evening in Nyanza saying good-bye to the displaced families I shared the streets with. After living with them in the aftermath of the darkness of the genocide, they had become like relatives. Without money to go back and say good-bye to Aimable and Cyiza, the following morning I met Ms. Nadine at the entrance of the orphanage and began the next phase of my life.

I HAD LIMITED possessions to take along with me to Kigali—just a bar of soap and a comb that Jeannette gave me. I wrapped them in a paper sack and packed them into my pocket, drawing my fingers across their outline against the fabric of my clothes as the bus hummed along the road to the capital city. When the bus stopped at the city center, the effect of the genocide was still detectable. The majority of structures showed some sort of damage from bullet holes, looting, or grenade blasts. Garbage blew across the paths like tumbleweeds, but city officials had removed the human remains. That evening, I visited with Ms. Nadine in her home. She introduced me to other orphaned children whom she had adopted. For the first time since the genocide, I felt secure in a stranger's house.

In bed that night, I thought about the tearful farewell I had shared with my siblings. I pledged to myself that I would work hard, set aside money, and put myself through school. Perhaps, after graduation, I could take care of the young ones, who weren't shy about letting me know they were counting on me as we had said our good-byes.

The next day, I followed Ms. Nadine through the streets of Kigali to my new home and place of employment, a neglected house on the edge of the city. It took three months for me to determine that this place suited me no better than the streets. The causes were twofold: first, probably disturbed by the genocide, my new employer, Ms. Anne, took her alcohol-fueled fits of hysteria out on me. Second, she made excuses to withhold payment. So, not only was I unlikely to step foot in a classroom again, I was also unlikely to visit my siblings because I didn't have money for the bus fare.

Ms. Anne introduced me to her mental disorder on my second day at her house. I had settled into the narrowest room in the house, which contained a twin-sized bed and a hook pounded into the wall to hang my belongings. Having little experience as a professional cook, I struggled to prepare the family of three's breakfast on my first morning. I rose well before the sun came up to become acquainted with the layout and contents of the kitchen. Succeeding at boiling and preparing tea, I felt confident until I realized I didn't know how to prepare the porridge Ms. Anne had asked for the night before.

Ms. Anne stood barefooted in the kitchen early that morning, her gray-streaked hair exposed below her head wrap. She was straight bodied and pale, and had a twisted look to her mouth as if she was moving it or chewing on food. This nervous tick was the most visible sign of her discomfort level and angst. Her twisted mouth made her appear disconnected from her surroundings, and her evasive eyes compounded that impression. But soon the shouting came. That morning, she woke her children with her shrieking voice, complaining about my incompetence and abruptly announced my salary would be cut in half.

Life only grew more complicated at Ms. Anne's home, as she soon discovered that I lacked other domestic skills that Jeannette and Ms. Nadine had promised her I possessed. But an inexperienced maid was the least of Ms. Anne's difficulties. Ms. Anne appeared to have experienced a good deal of the same horrors I had witnessed during the days of the genocide, and likely suffered from post-traumatic stress disorder. This was made clear by her lack of a regular sleep schedule, continuous use of alcohol, and uncontrollable outbursts.

A widow who still wore her wedding ring, Ms. Anne was thin with a worn face and darkened skin around the base of her eyes. Her daily routine was erratic but always included an early meal and a cigarette. Then she would withdraw and reappear throughout the day. Sometimes she returned in the early afternoon, smelling of whiskey and tobacco, and dragged herself into her armchair in the living room. During this time, while she sank into a state of alcohol-induced sleep, her experience during the genocide would reveal itself. After a few minutes of sleep, Ms. Anne's skinny arms would swing at the space before her. Phrases I had heard in the months of killing then tumbled off her sedated lips, "Stop. No… no… no… no… stop," she cried in a state of disturbed sleep. She would invariably awake at some point, glance around the room, and then go back into her nightmare, repeating those two words at various volumes.

Suffering from this brutality and persecution, she found a kind of satisfying release by shouting at me about my imperfect work performance. When the screaming alone didn't satisfy her, she escalated her relief by striking me. At first, the burn of her slap caused me to wince. After a month or so, I became accustomed to the sting on my cheek.

My list of tasks was intimidating for a ten-year-old. I was responsible for maintaining fires, preparing the lamps, cooking breakfast, lunch, and dinner, washing dishes, sweeping and mopping every room in the house, weeding the garden, fetching water, washing everyone's clothes, and many other tasks that were not defined. Another important duty was lighting up the charcoal stove to heat and serve food I had prepared regardless of the time Ms. Anne returned home. This procedure proved to be challenging, particularly when Ms. Anne arrived home in the late hours of darkness, sometimes after 2:00 a.m.

Some days, I was fortunate to avoid her beatings, and on happy occasions I could go an entire day without ever speaking to her. I always speculated she had a boyfriend, friend, or possibly a group of drinking companions that she stayed with when she didn't come back for the night.

A turning point came soon after my fourth month of living with Ms. Anne. Earlier that morning, I had asked for my previous four months' wages, the equivalent of $6.00, to take a trip to Nyanza to visit my family. After shooting down that request, Ms. Anne returned in the afternoon. She shuffled past me to her bedroom then returned quickly, trudging toward me. Seizing the back of my neck, she pulled me to her bedroom. Barefoot and smelling of whiskey and cigarettes, she held me against her wiry frame.

"What is that?" she asked, clasping my neck tighter and shoving me deeper into the room. "Maid, are you deaf? What is that on my bed?" She walked to the bed and pointed to a stack of folded sheets lying on the end of her bed. I had folded them but had forgotten to place them in her cabinet. Returning, she pushed the sheets into my stomach, secured her grip around my bicep, and slapped my face with her free hand.

"Sorry," I replied over and over as the slapping continued.

"You are sorry?" she declared, swinging harder. "I will tell you when you are sorry," she garbled. She continued the beating, using her fists, and then lit a cigarette. When she lacked the strength to continue, I slipped away and ran out of the house.

My only choices were to go to Ms. Nadine or return to the streets. At this point, I was more than prepared to exchange the living conditions at Ms. Anne's with the uncertainty of life on the streets.

The next day, standing in front of Ms. Nadine, I touched my nose and swollen forehead and described the confrontation. Ms. Nadine ran her forearm against her brow as I detailed the conflict. In tears, I explained Ms. Anne's rigid rules; how she beat me for waking her after she fell asleep in her armchair, and yet another time she beat me because I didn't wake her after she dozed off under identical circumstances. Ms. Nadine grimaced as I shared how Ms. Anne became enraged and slapped me for reading newspapers and still had yet to pay me a coin for four months of labor.

A troubled kindness was moving into Ms. Nadine as I recounted these episodes, and I saw the discomfort on her face. When I stopped, she embraced me and went on about the prospects for children like me, how fortunate I was to be alive, and that she would do her best to find me foster parents and not an employer. She was eager to find a family to care for me.

But her stipulation was a bitter one to accept: Ms. Nadine asked that I return to Ms. Anne's house until she could make arrangements for me.

That night, I wandered the streets of Kigali, staring at the star-packed sky over the treetops and dreaming of a better tomorrow, one that involved school and a little peace. After two more months, just a few days after I received another beating from Ms. Anne, I went back to Ms. Nadine's home one last time. As I tapped on her door, I imagined another conversation in which she asked for my patience again. But when Ms. Nadine opened the door, I found a smile on her face.

We walked together to the living room, conversing. I was impatient to understand why she looked so pleased. "You seem to be happy today," I said.

"My girl," she replied, "when Ms. Anne leaves tomorrow, prepare your bag. I found a family for you!" I looked her in the eyes as if I didn't understand what she was saying. "That is right; a foster family."

I didn't jump up and down, but I smiled, pressed close for a hug, and thanked her.

That evening, I felt weightless as I went back to Ms. Anne's house, leaping and bouncing up the road. I kept this new arrangement quiet. As usual, I cleaned and then cooked my last meal for Ms. Anne's household.

Chapter Twenty-Four

The next day, I walked the streets of Kigali with Ms. Nadine to meet my new foster family. I admired the various automobiles, restaurants, and minimarkets along the way. Ms. Nadine must've sensed my excitement. She stopped to buy me a grape-flavored soda and a sweet cookie, then we continued on our way.

After we turned down a shadowy street, she reached for my hand the way my parents would have. I pulled away for a second, but then returned my hand to her. It was clear that she cared about me. As we walked, the soda foamed in my mouth. Ms. Nadine explained that my foster family was a business-minded family and financially secure, adding that they had also lost many relatives in the genocide and would understand my situation.

As we got closer to their house, Ms. Nadine reminded me to work hard and participate in chores in my new home. I assured her that I was ready to work diligently and would not disappoint her. A bit closer to the house, she looked at my face, brushing cookie crumbs from around my mouth and running her fingers through my hair. "You look nice," she said as we approached the Bernards' gated house, which was surrounded by a brick fence.

Ms. Nadine rang the bell, and a security guard verified us and opened the gateway. He escorted us into the living room, where Mrs. Bernard sat on an enormous red sofa next to her two young children. After introductions, the five of us lingered in the living room waiting for Mr. Bernard, who was cleaning up, to join us. I peeked into the kitchen where the laminated floor gleamed and everything was bright and polished. The dining table was topped with a spotless white tablecloth, sparkling dishes, and fresh breads. When Mr. Bernard joined us, their maid escorted us to the dining area and served sautéed beef, mashed potatoes, and vegetables. I inhaled in delight, almost powerless to keep from peering into the kitchen and wondering what was to come next.

My foster parents looked to be in their late thirties. The husband, Mr. Bernard was a bulky man just about under six feet tall, with a narrow face that made his eyes bulge. His eye-catching wife was in much better shape— lean, quick stepping, and had taken time to apply crimson lipstick to highlight her full lips. Their oldest child, Martha, was a few years younger than me, and her younger brother, Xavier, looked to be about six years old. Martha and Xavier, my new "siblings," grinned at me sheepishly throughout the entire dinner while Mrs. Bernard conducted herself in a self-conscious manner. She was formal and careful in her speech. Mr. Bernard did the same, only he was more blunt.

When dinner was over and Ms. Nadine had disappeared into the darkened streets of Kigali, Martha and Xavier walked me through the house. With my plastic sack in hand, I followed them down a long hallway. Opening the door for me, we entered a spacious, simple room. The bed looked comfortable, covered with a fuzzy blue bedspread. Outside our window was the garden and an enormous mango tree.

Martha placed her arm around me and said, "We'll play here, in our room, but we have to be careful because Mom and Dad's room is on the opposite side." I grinned at her and set my plastic sack in the closet.

Martha and Xavier glued themselves to me after that initial night. Xavier came into our bedroom to play nearly every night. And even though the kids and I formed a unique connection, the first several weeks were uncomfortable while I relearned how to rely on adults again, struggling to adjust to this unfamiliar situation where everyone seemed compassionate towards me. There was so much uncertainty, especially the fear of how long this family would care for me. Even worse, I worried they could become abusive like Ms. Anne. Despite the acceptance they showed, I couldn't help feeling like an awkward visitor settling into a strange family's home.

My morning routine during this time was simple; I woke up with the children and helped prepare them for school, which included making their snacks and organizing their backpacks. I also made an effort to be helpful in all areas at home. I felt delight knowing I had a purpose in working with the children and helping around the house.

I picked my words carefully, generally opting for silence in the presence of the parents. I basically adhered to Rwandan culture's norms, which stress a child should remain quiet before an adult. Even if I had the opportunity to express myself more, I felt mixed-up in the world and in disbelief that I had a roof over my head and what seemed like a normal foster family to care for me. When I communicated, I often spoke about what the children learned in school, hoping they would register me in school at some point, too. During school and business hours, I organized the children's closets and cleaned the parents' bedroom. The rest of the time I spent around the maids with a newspaper in hand, asking for definitions of Kinyarwanda words I didn't recognize or testing my spelling and mental math skills.

I longed to get back in school. It was all I thought about. However, I didn't want to be a burden to my new family, as I understood they were doing me an enormous favor by housing me.

For the next few weeks, I kept up with my routine, but grew bored of reading the newspapers and chatting with the maids. One sunny afternoon, Mrs. Bernard returned early from work and called for me to meet her at the dinner table. She asked me various questions about how I was settling in and if I wanted to attend school. Immediately, I opened up about my enthusiasm for school and how I used to be an excellent student. The news made my heart warm and I wanted to hug her and tell her how I appreciated her offer. Instead I grinned and said, "I am delighted to go back to school!" She spent the next few days accompanying me to different stores to buy a school uniform, shoes, clothes, and other school supplies.

In a country where free public schools did not exist, this was a rare opportunity. I was restless to get back into school and even daydreamed about what the classroom setting might look like, promising myself to be the best student.

The morning finally arrived when Mrs. Bernard escorted me to a nearby schoolhouse. The Bernards' children went to a different school, a more prestigious kind. Their school was better equipped than mine, but that didn't change my attitude toward my humble schoolhouse. I kept in mind that if I worked hard, I would have a greater chance at life and could eventually support myself and my siblings. Repeatedly I focused on the opportunity before me and resolved to make a difference.

I hadn't forgotten what it was like to be a student. My parents had valued education so much that it was well entrenched in me. But sitting in class, paying attention, completing homework, and making friends were altogether more challenging. I struggled to focus on assignments as my mind strayed when spontaneous, painful memories from the genocide surfaced, interrupting my concentration. I tried to suppress these disturbances at first, focusing on the task at hand, yet inevitably the feelings of distress, sorrow, and isolation appeared with such force that my ears rang and my head buzzed. Images of lifeless people plagued my mind and random shocks jolted their way up my spine. I could never be sure if the other kids noticed my indiscriminate twitching, but I was always highly self-conscious of my trembling. At recess, I wanted to be alone to avoid the other children's screaming or loud noises, which triggered the voices of victims from the genocide.

While trying to adjust, it dawned on me that I hadn't sat in a classroom in nearly two years by that time. It made me realize that I needed to work harder.

After a few months, I felt a sense of safety and began to relax around the Bernards, who showed that they cared for me. After all, safety and love were all I longed for as an orphan.

One night at the dinner table, an unusual feeling stunned me. As we ate, a memory came in my mind. It wasn't a specific day or time, just an image of eating with my biological family. Then I thought of our sharing ritual, how we offered thanks and then shared our daily challenges with the other family members. These feelings mixed in me throughout our meal. As I sat at the table, I thought it was time to tell my foster family about my past. Every time I started, I stopped myself, afraid to release the gloomy images in my mind.

Finally, neglecting the food on my plate, I placed my utensils down and cleared my throat. A soft, subdued, voice that sounded like mine then forced itself out to the dinner table.

"Thank you... for sending me to school," I said, "... thank you," I repeated louder to make sure they heard me. Mr. Bernard stopped chewing and stared at me wide-eyed, nodded slowly, and then glanced at his wife.

"I love school," I went on, in the same soft tone. Mrs. Bernard and the kids now joined the father in staring at me. More silence and time passed as I shared a little about my survival story. I paused when Martha interrupted to tell me how they, too survived the roadblocks and various checkpoints on their way to Congo. Martha and her brother recounted all the narrow escapes they experienced throughout their journey.

When the children finished telling their experience, I began again, this time focusing on the fact that I had siblings in Nyanza whom I missed and wanted to keep in touch with. After a few minutes, I realized my foster parents sat silent, not chewing, not blinking, just maintaining their empty stares. I stared down at my food when I realized the silence was not going to be broken, and although my throat had almost swollen closed and my stomach twisted, I put a slice of meat in my mouth and slowly chewed.

That night was the first and final time I attempted my family's "sharing time" at the Bernards' dinner table.

NOW THAT I was eating regular meals and feeling safe at home, my weight came back. By my twelfth birthday, I looked like my former self. My clumps of hair were trimmed down to a buzz cut, and my tattered orphan clothes had been replaced. I was more enthusiastic about life and had built up more hope about my destiny. The Bernards even gave me money for a bus ticket to visit my siblings and a little bit of cash to buy them simple gifts. Things seemed to be going normally, better than I ever expected.

However, in my twelfth year, a damaging incident took place. It was a sunny day when I arrived home for lunch to discover the house empty, even the security guard positioned at the entrance had taken the afternoon off. Walking through the main corridor and past Mr. and Mrs. Bernard's bedroom, my thoughts were on my studies. That year I was in the top 10 percent of my class, but my aim was to be in the top five percent by the end of the semester. As I passed the opened door to the Bernards' room, I heard some weak coughing. Out of the corner of my eye, I caught Mr. Bernard near the end of his bed, staring at me. I hesitated and took a few more steps past the door.

"Jeanne, is that you?"

"Yes, Dad. It's me."

"Come here for a moment."

"Yes, let me put my books away and I will be there."

"No. Don't bother with the books," he replied. "I need you to do something for me, right now."

I took a few steps closer to the half-open door.

"What is it, Dad?"

"The maids…" he said, "they did not make my bed this morning. Will you fix it for me?"

"Okay, I am coming."

I slipped my backpack off my shoulders and rested it against the hallway wall. Instantly noticing the bed was perfectly made, I looked at him with confusion.

"Your bed is in order."

Mr. Bernard then passed by me and shut the door, turning the knob, locking us in.

My heart pounded against my chest as I backed away from him. But he pursued me until my back met with his bed. With room to move, I asked, "May I be excused? I need to study; I have an exam this afternoon."

205

He pressed his body against me, but I slipped away and stumbled backward toward the door. "Dad, what are you doing?" I screamed.

He lunged for me, but I jumped out of his way. I then spent a few minutes spinning and twisting from his hold, all the while he ordered, "Come here!" Breathing heavily, he pinned me on the mattress.

"Let me go!" I shouted while he maneuvered to remove the rest of his garments and mine. His bulky body crushing my ribs, I recall making one final plea before he raped me.

I pressed my head against the mattress, wiped the tears off my face and said, "Dad, please don't do this to me."

His response accompanied with his stale breath pierced me in my fragile heart. "Don't pretend like this is the first time this has happened to you," he said.

After the assault, as he dressed, my eyes locked on the white ceiling and tears flowing down my face, he added something else that stayed with me. He buttoned his pants, took a step, then another, pulled out his handkerchief and mopped the sweat from his face. Now standing above me, he lingered over my crushed body. "Don't tell anyone about this."

My head twitched to the sound of his voice, but I remained quiet in my tears.

Letting his command linger for a few minutes in the soundless room, he stared deeper into me and said it again, "You will tell no one about this."

I never answered him, because from the beginning of the assault, I vowed to myself to one day tell as many people as I could.

The abuse continued, but I never gave up fighting with him to defend myself. Recognizing my protest another time, he soon delivered another message many survivors of sexual abuse hear, "If you tell, it can lead to problems." This remark was a heavy one, one I was aware had a ring of truth in it. The life of orphanhood was showing me the harsh lesson of what it meant to be without a voice.

For years, in front of others, I still called him "Dad," although from the day he assaulted me I never again allowed him the honor of that title in my heart. He was nothing compared to the man who raised me before the genocide, the father who loved me and defended my mind and body from the unpleasantness and horrors in the world.

Over the following six years, Mr. Bernard proceeded to assault me. He was even brazen enough to leave his wife in bed in the middle of the night and slither into my room after he asked Martha and her brother to sleep in their own room together. I considered running away, but every time I was ready to leave, the danger of being in the streets that my twin highlighted flashed in my mind. Not knowing anyone else other than Ms. Nadine and Ms. Anne in the city, I felt trapped.

Luckily, Mr. Bernard was a businessman who took multiple trips a year. When he was out of the country, the atmosphere at the house always brightened. His absence meant a therapeutic release for me, as well as for his children, who were always frightened by the sound of their father's voice.

When Mr. Bernard was in Dubai, we played longer hours, ate and slept past our usual wake-up times. Even at the dinner table, we told jokes with Mrs. Bernard. The absence of Mr. Bernard brought glimpses of ordinariness that allowed the three of us to be kids and sometimes make mistakes.

Almost two years later, at breakfast, Mrs. Bernard delivered exciting news about the possibility of all of us going to the United States. I don't remember how Martha and Xavier reacted to the news, but I remember smiling ear to ear. It was a thrilling moment. Even though I was only fourteen years old, I was exhilarated about my chances in America. Yet at the same time, I was uneasy, having never been on an airplane nor ever traveled outside Africa.

Mr. Bernard returned and claimed that everyone had been issued a Visa except me, and that I would remain with him until my Visa arrived. After his wife and children left, I assumed Mr. Bernard had purposely withheld or delayed my Visa, postponing my departure to abuse me. Months later, Mr. Bernard finally announced I would join the rest of the family in St. Louis, Missouri.

Excited about the trip, I continued to learn English words and practiced common phrases like "What is your name?" and "How old are you?" The following week, I used my English skills after we boarded a connecting flight in Europe. As the flight attendant moved through the aisle and made her way to my seat, I was certain she offered me three entrée options, but all I heard was gibberish. When she repeated them, I said the one that was easiest to pronounce.

"Tom-a-to," I repeated back to her, smiling. She smiled in return, nodded, scrawled on her pad, and continued to advance her cart down the aisle. Minutes later, she came back with a can of cold tomato juice and a piece of bread.

Looking across the aisle, I noticed others eating chicken breast and vegetables and I laughed at myself. Right there, I had my initial lesson in the power of understanding English.

Soaring high in the clouds, my thoughts wandered to all that I knew about the United States, which came mostly from the handful of American films I had watched. Because of those movies, I assumed that America was a country of wonder and opportunity, a place with boundless wealth, where everyone enjoyed luxurious cars and lived in magnificent houses. Those fictional images disappeared once we arrived in Detroit, Michigan.

Leaving the airport, I shivered as the cold worked its way into my clothes. Lights gleamed on the surface of everything, and the freezing temperatures made me wonder how people survived in such a climate. In the morning, we ventured to some supermarkets. Impressed with the elevators and sliding doors, I knew I had much to learn about this unfamiliar country.

The first time I noticed tiny white specks dropping from the sky, I excitedly shot my tongue out to catch them, thinking the sky was melting. Hours later, the drive through St. Louis was also fascinating. I spotted a remarkable arch bending over a body of water and marveled at the towering buildings and fascinating web of light poles and wires.

That night, I laid in bed with Xavier and Martha, wondering what this chilly place had in store for me and what it would mean for my siblings back in Rwanda.

Chapter Twenty-Five

My first year in an American school was challenging. On day one, an English as a Second Language (ESL) teacher greeted me at the office to accompany me to my first class. At that point, my English vocabulary was under one hundred words, and I used only a few phrases. The instructor led me to a chair at a table in the center of the room. With a stiff back and alert mind, I listened for any words or phrases I knew. The students were friendly, and I smiled at them but didn't try to use my new language.

As we moved to the next class, I was curious why the teachers spoke so fast and moved through topics with high speed. With a language barrier, I failed to grasp what was being taught, and was even more frustrated when the teachers erased the board before I could copy down the notes. Everything seemed to be moving at high speed and was fascinating. What was even more surprising was watching girls apply lipstick and makeup in the middle of a class or students disrespecting a teacher. I imagined students getting scolded for such behaviors back in Rwanda.

By the end of the first day, I had met all my teachers, learned my schedule, and how to get to each class. In each subject, many questions loomed, but with insufficient English I refrained from asking for clarification to avoid embarrassing myself.

To better my English, when I wasn't busy cooking, cleaning, or babysitting my young brother, I watched American TV, read books, and listened and sang along to American pop music. I recall the Backstreet

Boys, Britney Spears, Destiny's Child, and Christina Aguilera being some of my favorites. I also developed a habit of watching peoples' mouths when they spoke, hoping to learn how to pronounce English words correctly. At the library, I checked out children's books. Once I mastered them, I moved on to the young adult section. There was a treasure of fictional stories, like *The Adventures of Huckleberry Finn*. Later on, I read true stories about Holocaust victims like Anne Frank and survivors like Elie Wiesel.

Still, even with a French and English dictionary, my assignments took hours to read, interpret, and understand. Frustrated by my low grades, I worked longer hours and tried harder. I was moving along, guided by the respect I had for learning fixed in me from my childhood. Thinking back to Rwanda and recognizing that so many children like me had been stripped of their chances, I pushed myself onward, feeling I ought to achieve something on my own.

As I advanced through school, I took fewer ESL classes and more general classes. Mathematics was my strongest subject because it was the least affected by the obstacle of language, but my French class, taught by a middle-aged lady with chestnut-colored eyes named Madame Silvia, left the greatest impression on me. The moment I entered Madame Silvia's classroom, I felt a connection to her. After only a few weeks, I enjoyed full discussions in French. Her eyes and body movements burned with enthusiasm, and she was clearly passionate about education and her students.

Even though I had developed an inward life of intense privacy stemming from the genocide and abuse, I cracked the door open for her. The reason was straightforward: I trusted Madame Silvia. She had learned a little about Rwanda's history and my ethnic group. She also noticed my sullen and introverted behavior. One day, she waited for me after school. She told me that she had heard about Rwanda's turbulence and wanted to know if I was there in 1994. I nodded and let her go on talking about what she knew. She used her knowledge as an ice-breaker to bring it up a few more times, persuading me to talk about the genocide in broad terms.

Usually I could only utter a remark or two before angst gripped my chest and visions of lifeless bodies shot through my mind.

It was that year—somewhat because of the interest Madame Silvia showed and also my desire to remember and recreate "sharing time" as my parents had taught me—that I got inspired to journal about my experience. In the dark of night, I picked up my journal, clicked on my lamp, and wrote about whatever I felt. Most of it was to process the grief and horror of my family's deaths. Soon the notebooks piled up below my bed as I detailed specific days of the slaughter, writing in my native language because I could readily access the appropriate word. Remembering once more Mom's wise words about carrying hatred, I prayed for God to remove the anger I felt toward my abusers and my family's killers.

A point in the year came when Madame Silvia had extracted from me the basics of my genocide experience: being segregated by ethnic groups in the classroom and hiding in the bushes. Once in high school, after telling another approachable teacher about my experience in Rwanda, I was invited to tell my account to a world history class. I was reluctant, but as I was not accustomed to refusing an adult's wishes, I hesitantly agreed. She arranged my presentation the following week. Walking into the room that day, I noticed dozens of eyes following me as I stood in front of the class.

In addition to the students, some assistant teachers and a few teachers who were invited crowded around to hear my experience. From the minute I started speaking, a fiery pain gripped my throat. Feeling as though my chest was being squeezed, my head sweated and my eyes watered. Without being prepared to excuse myself, I cut my presentation short by giving general facts about the genocide and leaving out more of my ordeal. Afterward, the students had questions. To avoid bursting into tears, I gave vague answers and withheld details about my family.

However, the discomfort of speaking about my personal experience and the genocide against the Tutsis later got better. Little by little, I felt stronger emotionally and was growing into a young woman in the United States. At school, I became more sociable, made a few friends, and even signed up for volleyball. I kept a busy schedule, which helped me not to focus on myself or my past. The Bernards were active in the Mormon Church, which also took up a good chunk of my spare time, attending morning seminars, hosting Sunday dinners with missionaries, and praying.

To outsiders, the Bernards looked like the near-perfect couple and family. One day, at a meeting with the Bishop, I conjured up the strength to share the abuse I suffered under Mr. Bernard, but the Bishop caught me off guard by asking if I had improper relations with boys. When he asked me if I was "romantic" with them, I froze up. He went on about chastity and how it was a sin to have sexual relations before marriage. As I listened, my heart pounded in my chest. I wanted to speak up, but I could not get the words out.

As I matured, I thought of other ways to shake off Mr. Bernard. At night, when he was feeling brazen and knocked on my door, I would go out my back door and take a seat behind it, sitting quietly, gazing at the night sky while Mr. Bernard jiggled the doorknob and tapped on the door. Other days, I stayed in the shower until my skin turned white. Inevitably, he would go back to his bedroom. Some days I wasn't as fortunate. Fighting off or hiding from Mr. Bernard always left me shuddering with fear. I never forgot that he could overpower me in an instant, that he could decide that I was no longer fit as a foster child in his house, and that I was more trouble than I was worth. But in the darkness, alone, I was doing what I thought I needed to in order to defend myself through even the slightest attempt. I wanted to tell the world, even if no one but me and Mr. Bernard could hear, that I believed what he was doing was wrong and that I deserved freedom.

After one of his invasions on a chilly fall night, I went down to my room and punched my pillow until I collapsed onto it, weeping heavily. As I cried, I envisioned myself roaming through the house, room by room, staring at everything: the kitchen table with six plates arranged for dinner, the skillet and the pots and the kettle on the stove. Everything was falsely perfect. I wanted to rip the tablecloth off and slam the plates against the wall.

A few hours later, I went to the kitchen for a drink of water. After I finished drinking, I stared intently at the glass. Right then, the culmination of all the suffering in my life flashed through my mind like a movie reel: running away from our house; squatting in the rain with the twins, wedged between bushes; Mom, Dad and my baby brother's lifeless bodies. The insults. The rapes. The beatings. Something inside me snapped. I raised the glass above my head and slammed it into the sink. Shards of glass splintered and flew in all directions. I remained motionless over the pieces, sobbing once more, wondering when it would all end.

After I swept up the broken glass, I stepped over to the dining room table, discovering a letter that had my name written on the front. The writing looked to be that of a young child. I opened it and began to read. It was written in Kinyarwanda but translated into English:

To my big sister,

The main reason I am writing you is to ask you how you are doing. How are you doing? Me, I am fine. I am doing well in school. I was in the top seven in my class. I tried and hope you are proud of me.

Our younger brothers wanted to greet you but they do not know how to write yet. Please come and visit us. Everyone in our family misses you and they are doing okay.

Please continue to pray and work hard in school. Everyone is counting on you to help us have a better future.

Well, I don't have much to give you except my picture so that you can always remember me. People tell me I look like you, but I don't know.

If you have a picture, maybe you can send it to us.

Please don't forget us.

Love, Teta

From left: Teta, Teddy, Byiringiro, and Kayishema.

The last line stung my heart as I read it. I pictured Teta, who was now older than I was when the genocide happened, writing this letter at a flimsy desk.

I imagined her sitting at the desk thinking about what she would write, and then slowly writing out each word perfectly. I pictured her folding the letter and then using whatever money she had begged for or scraped together to print the photograph she included. I envisioned Teta and her twin waking up to the harsh voices of strangers and marching to the schoolhouse on an empty stomach. I saw their dirty clothes and tattered schoolbooks.

I then cried one more time, not for myself but for them, for their hardships, for their loss and the separation of their family. I realized that they had never stopped relying on me, and while I was absorbed in my pain, they were forgotten in theirs. But still, they kept me as the only hope for their future. With that realization, I looked around the Bernards' house, determined to find a way out of it. My time of escape would come in my senior year of high school.

I was well into my final year in high school and no one had spoken to me about college. Maybe because I was on the honor roll most semesters, my counselor assumed I had a plan in order. Some of my friends applied to the local community college, and a few others were admitted to the University of Missouri. However, the last place I wanted to live was Columbia, Missouri. I wanted to get as far away as possible from Mr. Bernard and to start a future for myself and my siblings.

Soon after, I talked with a friend who attended Washington State University. She told me the basics about the school and what life was like in Pullman, Washington. I spent the next several weeks researching different colleges, comparing tuition, programs, and the cities. Finally, I narrowed it down to between Chicago University and Washington State University. Ultimately I decided to apply to Washington State University.

When summer came, I searched for a job, hoping to save money to get me to Washington State. Walking from store to store, I applied for any position possible. Being young and inexperienced, most prospective employers never called me. Finally, after dozens of submissions, a supervisor from an Italian restaurant called me for an interview. The next day, I sat down with him and timidly described my interests, hobbies, and good grades. He smiled and told me that my training as a hostess would begin that week. I shook his hand, assured him of my readiness, and left the restaurant feeling confident.

I told a few friends about my intentions to attend Washington State University but had not talked to the Bernards about my new job or attending college. A few weeks later, while helping Mrs. Bernard in the kitchen, I felt the desire to tell her about my departure, offering her one last opportunity to be a protector and to ask why I preferred to move so far from her home. What I remember most about the discussion was Mrs. Bernard's reply. She called me selfish and claimed I was ungrateful for what her family had done for me. She reminded me she was expecting another baby and was relying on me to help her with the younger ones.

Determined to move out, I did not see a reason to continue the conversation. That summer, I took the earnings from my hostess job and bought a plane ticket to Washington, deciding to forgo my high school graduation ceremony.

With only a little over $400.00 in my purse, I caught a bus to the airport and boarded a flight to Seattle. From there, I took a bus to the small city of Pullman. Looking out the window at the Palouse Prairie and admiring the acres of golden wheat farms that surrounded the area, I thought of my past and my future. On the long bus ride of more than seven hours, I thought a good deal about my destiny. Then, a victorious feeling, similar to how I felt when I escaped my abusers in the Congo, filled my mind.

A new life awaited me.

Chapter Twenty-Six

When I arrived in Washington, I was a woman in transformation; not a caterpillar yet not a butterfly, either. Change had inevitably arrived, and a fresh phase of my life was upon me. Once settled in, I concentrated on getting a job to pay living expenses and send money to my siblings, who were living in destitute conditions. Thrilled, I took a call from a representative at Washington State University who told me I had obtained employment at their registrar's office. To add to my income from the job at the registrar's office, I found employment at a nursing home as well. Juggling two jobs and attending school full-time was a new challenge, but the fact I could satisfy my minimum needs while providing for my siblings was worth the sleepless nights.

My first winter at my new school, the snow fell often and heavily; there was no place I could think of that wasn't covered in white. The people walking and driving through the snow were resigned to traveling slowly. The arctic environment induced a sense of seclusion, and while the majority of students returned to their homes for the holidays, I had no past I could go back to and no future I could fully imagine. So I used the opportunity to pray and meditate on what my life would look like.

It was during this period that I started writing in my journal again, which was still my primary source of therapy. I pulled out a notebook and sat in my small living room, looking over what I wrote years before and reminiscing about how far I had come. This time, as I wrote, the shape of my story grew larger, and I could remain with the troubling memories longer and longer, bringing in more detail as I continued to empty my heart onto the pages. When I exerted all my emotional energy, I put my notebooks away. To release tension, I went to the university gym and ran on a treadmill for hours at a time.

I developed friendships with my classmates, but my most impactful relationship was with a couple called "Auntie and Uncle" by everybody who associated with them, but their formal names are Dr. Fred and Winnie Rurangirwa. Little did I understand at that time just how much these two people would influence my life! Almost every day, Auntie and Uncle asked me to their home for lunch or dinner. It didn't take long to figure out why many of the college students nicknamed Auntie "Mother Africa." Auntie and Uncle opened their home to all, regardless of their background or culture. Their house was steadily crowded with students and friends who enjoyed their openness and good intentions.

On one of those frosty winter nights, Auntie asked me to join them for dinner. As always, Auntie gave me a hot cup of tea and invited me to feel at home. She turned back to the kitchen, stirring about the stove, sliding various cooking pans about, and leaned to remove a dish from the oven.

She arranged three places at the table and took out a jug of orange juice.

"You never know," she announced, looking delighted.

I grinned in return.

"Are you warm?" she asked with the same welcoming smile, to which I replied, "Yes."

She then served us a delicious meal, all the while saying, "It is not much."

I ate every bite I could hold, washed everything down with several cups of orange juice, and listened as Uncle discussed the classes he taught at the university. I noticed Uncle sip his tea, his cheerful eyes set behind the thick lenses of his glasses. His cordial smile and careful handling of words reminded me of my father.

Each time I turned away to watch Auntie, she was smiling broadly but I glanced away, afraid of revealing the look of sadness that I know overtook my face.

When Uncle finished, Auntie spoke.

She chatted about the years before Uncle became a professor and veterinary researcher at WSU, and long before she came to be known as "Mother Africa" in Pullman. They grew up in Uganda, but their ancestors had moved there from Rwanda. They both spoke perfect Kinyarwanda and practiced the customs and traditions I grew up with.

"When the genocide took place in 1994, we both had family living in Rwanda. Some…" she added with tenderness in her eyes, "we never heard from again."

Auntie, recognizing the discussion was causing me to shift about in my chair, stood up, walked to the refrigerator, and removed a chocolate cake. I observed the gentle and quiet way she moved her body. Softly, she lowered herself into the seat closest to me, sliding a slice of cake in front of my folded hands. This softness, this tenderness of her bodily movements carried over into her words as she spoke about the people in her family that were killed or had disappeared. I noticed that they were looking at me directly. Auntie was silent, her eyes beaming with sincerity. Breaking the silence, she talked about the dead bodies that had washed down the river from Rwanda to Uganda. She went on about how they prayed for those affected by the Rwandan massacre.

As the conversation continued, I felt the unease in my stomach relax, and when they were both quiet once more, I talked about my parents for the first time in years. A few times I choked up and my eyes welled with tears, but I continued on, glancing at Uncle's thoughtful expression and Auntie's loving eyes. When I finished talking about my struggles during the genocide, I had told them more than any other person. It felt like an enormous weight had been lifted from my shoulders.

Late in the evening, Auntie and Uncle walked me to the doorway and embraced me tightly. "This is your home now. When you come here, you are stepping into your home," they affirmed. I smiled self-consciously and nodded. Auntie looked at Uncle, "We will help you get to know this town. It is small," she giggled, "but we will take you around." She squeezed me once more.

As I settled into bed that night, I thought about what Auntie and Uncle had done. They showed me that it was okay to talk about my past, that I didn't have to feel ashamed or embarrassed about everything that had happened to me and my family. Knowing this made me open up even more to them and changed my path forever.

Yes, indeed, thanks in large part to Auntie and Uncle, in Pullman I came out of my shell so to speak. I found myself more talkative in my classes, befriending more classmates, and attending more social events. I even joined several organizations, one of which was the African Friendship Association (AFA). After sharing my story with fellow students in AFA, I was persuaded to talk at the yearly "African Night" event on campus. I thought of my History teacher in Missouri who had asked me to speak before the class about my past. I was more or less still unenthusiastic about speaking in public about what had happened in Rwanda. However, when the night arrived, I concentrated on increasing awareness of the genocide and advocating for the victims. The next week, I was surprised to see my name printed in the local newspaper, including a short piece on my presentation.

Around this time, I also met Kerry Hasenbalg and her husband, Scott. The two possess sincere hearts, empathetic ears, and a passion to help others. Kerry immediately gravitated toward me, and I felt the same way about her. After knowing her for a short time, I found it easy to discuss my past and my present difficulties with her. Working two jobs, I could pay for the living costs and education for my siblings, yet occasionally my salary couldn't provide for all their necessities. When Kerry learned this, she and her husband volunteered to help with their school fees, as well as sometimes supporting their rent and food. Kerry and Scott worked on behalf of oppressed and vulnerable children all over the globe, and their dedication inspired me.

Over the years, they have been a continuous source of support and love. Between Auntie and Uncle and Kerry and Scott, I felt a sense of belonging. I saw these two families as my own extended family. To this day, I am grateful beyond words for Kerry and Scott's presence in my life and their continued friendship.

The suffering from the past in no way healed overnight, and I had just begun the journey. Almost every April, I am reminded of the depth of my wounds. By the second week of April in Pullman, my memories haunted me. During those times, my journal helped me integrate the world I lived in and the world I knew from my past.

When the journal failed, I reached out to my new family. Uncle, who was always considerate with his words and never had a meaningless thing to say, brought the wisdom I wanted. Auntie was a continuous source of unconditional love. When I felt down or was acting reclusive, Auntie would track me down on campus or at my apartment, always bearing home-cooked meals. Sometimes she accompanied me on long walks around her neighborhood. She would ask me how I was doing and I would tell her I was fine, but there were times she suspected I wasn't. She would place her arm around my shoulders and draw me closer. I felt she understood my pain without my having to tell her.

Even in my silence, Auntie and Uncle made one thing abundantly clear—that as long as they lived, I would be treated like their own daughter. At times, our conversations sounded precisely like that. Like parents, Auntie and Uncle warned me about driving late at night and not taking breaks from work. Other times, my conversations with Auntie drifted into territory I hadn't even experienced with friends my age, like discussing a potential romantic relationship. She believes that relationships are important and how we communicate with each other is vital.

Between Kerry's family and Auntie and Uncle, I built up faith in people again. One night, I answered a call from Kerry. She surprised me with the gift of an airline ticket and extra money to visit my siblings. Although I wanted to jump at the suggestion, I was still afraid to grapple with my gloomy history. After a few weeks of praying about it, I accepted Kerry's offer and decided it was time to go back to Africa.

Chapter Twenty-Seven

Walking through the terminal at Entebbe airport, I heard somebody shout out my name. When I saw it was my twin sister, Jeannette, I hopped up and down like an excited toddler. From a distance, I could see she was shedding tears. As the line receded, we ran into each other's arms much like we had at our reunion at the orphanage years ago. But this time, my older brother Aimable was standing behind her.

"It's my turn, Jeannette," said Aimable, sniffling and looking amused. Jeannette kept her grip firm. "Are you going to hug her all day?" he asked. With Jeannette's arms still coiled around me, Aimable joined the hug. The three of us hugged each other for so long that people leaving the airport watched and stared as they boarded buses, but we didn't mind. It had been too many years and too few hugs.

Beaming with smiles, they ushered me to a taxi that took us to a modest house where some of my siblings lived. They each took turns holding me, their faces shining with smiles. It was then that I realized we had not been under the same roof in over a decade, since the genocide. This was the most uplifting, profound night of love I had experienced in years. We prepared dinner and ate in the living room. My brothers crammed onto the sofa next to me as we talked late into the night, joking and poking fun at each other. We cleared up part of our history for the younger ones; for years, Byiringiro and Kayishema grew up with the assumption that Jeannette and Aimable were their parents. When they heard the truth, they wept. When the discussion lingered on the genocide,

Aimable became silent and Jeannette excused herself and went to sleep. All of us were still afraid of our pain—and afraid of each other's pain.

When I woke up in the morning, I remained still as a sculpture, feeling refreshed and at peace, thinking, *I am home. I made it.* I said those words in my head, and as I repeated them, I was affected emotionally. I had been gone for almost half my life, and it had been a long time since I thought of myself as being away. But now, in an instant, I was back. Being home wasn't just something I remembered, it was something I felt. There I was, surrounded by my family, finally home with the people I love more than anything in the world. In my heart, I thanked Kerry and her family for making this family reunion possible.

A couple of days later, I gathered up the strength to see Aunt Josephine. She still lived in the same house they had ordered us away from during the genocide. I thought about it for a long time and realized that my main motive to see her was to look at her face, because before the genocide she looked like my mother. Since our home had been destroyed and everything taken, my aunt was the closest I could ever come to seeing my mother's image again. Secondly, I had an unusual interest to see our preferred bush, the one near a large boulder, and the roads we walked during the genocide. I wanted to lay eyes on them from a mature view to help understand how we lived through such chaos. And lastly, I needed my aunt to know that we had made it.

It was a cloudless afternoon when we took a bus to Nyanza. The sunlight warmed my forehead as we exited the bus and walked down that same path that had been lined with piles of lifeless bodies during the genocide. A few curious neighbors were out and stopped to observe us. As we reached Aunt Josephine's gate and started for the door, I looked at Teddy's face and wondered what was on her mind, but I didn't ask.

Aunt Josephine opened the door, stared at me for a second, and welcomed us. She grabbed both sides of my face and sprinkled me with kisses. "Oh, my girl. You remembered me!" From her front doorway, I thought of where the blockade was set up, the hill where I had laid eyes on that first dead body, and the overgrown bushes where we spent weeks in hiding. I stood awkwardly as my mind flashed back to the day we were ordered out of this house, but Teddy, thank goodness, was able to carry on the conversation.

Right away, I decided Aunt Josephine no longer resembled my mother. She pulled us into one of the small rooms where Uncle Gustave sat on a chair. He waved and leaned forward to turn his radio down. Aunt Josephine served us tea, and mine sat before me as minutes dragged by in an uncomfortable silence. I concluded that they never expected to see us again and hadn't likely thought of us as being alive for some time.

Uncle Gustave broke the silence by telling us the news about Kalisa. He informed us that Kalisa had made enemies in the Hutu community and was found dead. He said they killed him with machetes and stabbed him. Teddy noticed tears forming in my eyes and patted my back.

I was unsure whether Uncle Gustave was unhappy about Kalisa's notifying the police and courts about citizens who participated in the genocide. But he soon made his feelings about the matter clear.

"Yes, Kalisa deserved what he got because some people even said he had been poisoning their cows," he said, relaxing back in his chair.

I exclaimed, "Kalisa saved our lives. If not for him, we wouldn't be here right now."

The room fell quiet again, and Aunt Josephine cleared her throat and offered us lunch. She made small talk about how nice her children were doing but never referred to my parents nor inquired about my other siblings. I politely declined her offer for lunch. We said good-bye and left. Once outside, I turned to the stretch of bushes we hid in and could not restrain the tears. Teddy took my hand as I cried and we walked up the road. It was the last time I saw Aunt Josephine and Uncle Gustave.

In the following days I made school arrangements for my younger siblings and visited with their teachers. They introduced me as their "mother." I also used the remainder of my trip to set up small businesses for my siblings.

Before my departure, Aimable, Cyiza, and Jeanette advocated to give our parents and Baby Mucyo a proper burial, which meant digging up our family's remains and having a normal burial ceremony. I told my siblings that I needed time, and after thinking about it for a couple of days, I realized that I wasn't mentally strong enough to go through such pain again. I also concluded that my siblings weren't ready despite their desire to honor our family.

"Perhaps we can just remember our parents, relatives, and Baby Mucyo the way they were before the genocide—untouched by machetes and still beautiful souls," Aimable said. We all agreed with that sentiment.

Finally, at the airport, it came time for me to say good-bye to my siblings. They hugged me about a thousand times and reminded me that they loved me.

Top: Cyiza, Myself, Aimable and my niece Keza, Byiringiro, Teta, and Kayishema, a few hours after our reunion.

Bottom: Teta, Myself, Keza, and Jeanette.

Top: Byiringiro and Aimable

Bottom: a family friend, Byiringiro, Teta, Myself, Teddy, Keza, Michael, Jeannette, Cyiza, saying good-bye at the airport.

OVER THE FOLLOWING years, I became more and more interested in global challenges. I transferred to Eastern Washington University (EWU) to study International Affairs. EWU is just outside of Spokane and a little over an hour from Pullman, which made it possible for me to visit Auntie and Uncle regularly. At EWU, most of my classes involved some degree of leadership, communication, and understanding of how governments acted together to deal with issues in strategic ways. These courses gave me an even stronger voice and assured me that my contribution was important. They also helped me understand matters in a broader light.

Occasionally the case of the Rwanda genocide came up in class. I was in a unique place to hear my classmates argue about the ethical responsibility for genocide intervention. Some of the students described the mass extermination in Rwanda as something destined to take place, how tribalism had played the principal role, and that outside intervention wouldn't have stopped the killings. Others spoke about the Belgium influence, the way they pitted one group against the other.

I recall a student stating, "The people living in their respective countries ought to be liable for all that occurs there." When he finished this statement, the image of deceased children darted through my mind. I then thought of the French soldiers, the UN officers, and my father's "identity" card, a card that came about from the Belgium colonials. That moment reaffirmed what I knew in my spirit for so many years: I had to be a voice for those who were silenced by the genocide.

A year later, I discovered another passion by volunteering for World Relief in Spokane, assisting refugees from around the world settle into their new homes and new communities. Later, I extended my services as a Bilingual Specialist at various schools in Spokane. It was in these years when I finally felt as though I was following a path that pleased me. I no longer asked God to solve the confusion from my past; instead, I asked for peace and the strength to live in the present moment. I came to accept how my emotional pain had this way of making me think I was bound to it, a way of trapping me into identifying with it, so that I couldn't tell where it began or ended. In other words, I accepted my circumstances and no longer asked "why" and "how" such horror could have happened.

I also understood that forgiveness was not something that just came to me. It had to be a conscious act, requiring intention and motivation just like a prayer. I had spent many years praying and asking God to allow me to forgive those who murdered my family and those who caused me great pain, yet I still had to accept and let go of a little bit of resentment and anger that was left in me. To lay the anger to rest meant forgiving the unforgivable. I remember it was a peaceful day and I was lying down outside on freshly mowed grass, inhaling the fragrance. I don't remember the exact month, but I remember the warm breeze. Everything appeared to slow down and I instantly felt uplifted, a sense of relief filling my mind and body. It was then when I asked God again to help me forgive those who hurt me and my family. In a way, forgiveness had two functions: one, to release myself from the struggle of pain; and two, to release those who wronged me. That day, while soaking in the sun and the tranquility, I realized it had taken me years to release myself. I had held onto the pain of my deceased family and the pain of others as tightly as I could, but on this particular day I felt released. I was no longer trapped in my mind. I was free. The next challenge was releasing the perpetrators.

Usually, it is much easier to come to terms with tragedy or abuse when someone sincerely asks for forgiveness. Since my family's killers and my abusers may not have been brought to justice, and their whereabouts were still unknown to me, I took the opportunity to say what I would have said to them face to face:

Many nights I turned and twisted in pain; many days I worked to actively repress the horror you caused me. I did this for years. I have suffered, and my family has suffered, as millions have suffered at the hands of genocide and sexual abuse. I now know that you were used by a dark ideology. And your hearts were twisted in pain. I forgive you. I forgive you for the harm you caused. And I know this wound is healing and will continue to heal. But I pray your hearts will be whole and that love, kindness, empathy, and unity will now fill your spirits. The days gone by cannot be forgotten, but healing can take place. Go in peace, you are forgiven.

I recite those words every time the pain returns, especially every April, during the commemoration of the genocide against Tutsis.

As for my fellow genocide survivors and those who experienced abuse and trauma—there is a light at the end of the tunnel. For many years I didn't see that light, but it was always there. You will encounter good days and bad days where getting out of bed seems hopeless. Be tenacious, see that greatness is in you, and if all breaks down, be hopeful. As for me, the influence of hope kept me alive.

On this journey, you may be compelled to forgive the indefensible, and that is where you will have to make a tough choice for the sake of healing. Forgiveness has many layers: we forgive not to let someone off the hook, but to clear our own minds, to free ourselves from suffering. If you are a spiritual person, you may forgive because God calls for you to. For me, I forgave for all those reasons.

As for the thousands who have and continue to inquire about Rwanda, despite the worst killing in modern history, Rwanda has, and continues to make, progress. In a country where the entire populace was damaged by genocide, President Paul Kagame and Rwandan leaders have instituted a practice of recovery and reconciliation to rebuild the nation. Today, Rwanda is more secure and is developing economically. Mass violence is no longer common, and Rwandans are no longer classified by their ethnic background. There is no Tutsi, Hutu, or Twa, just Rwandans. Today, past victims and perpetrators are living side by side in challenging but necessary cooperation. And with sixty-four percent of women in Rwanda's parliament, Rwanda leads the world in gender equality. If the world needs a lesson to learn, study Rwanda.

EPILOGUE

It was one of those snowy months when another life-shaping event transpired: that winter I met my soul mate. Even though Spokane is larger than Pullman, the downtown section has a small-town atmosphere, and it's not surprising to frequently see familiar faces. One particular man's face seemed to continually catch my attention. When he introduced himself outside a coffee shop on one frosty night, I told him a little about myself. He said he would look out for me again and wished me well in my classes. At the time, I had decided to move to D.C or New York, where I envisioned working in a broader market and could affect more people. The last thing I was searching for was a boyfriend. But I ran into Paul for a third time and he recalled all our previous conversations, so we chatted about the possibility of having breakfast together.

"You have an exceptional memory," I said in response to him recalling details about my classes.

"So, what do you think?" he asked.

"About your memory?" I asked.

"No, about going to breakfast with me!" he replied with a grin.

I could see there was something unique about Paul. Sincerity and kindness glowed off his face.

I studied him a while longer and said, "If you can memorize my number, then you have yourself a date."

He gave a little laugh and replied, "No pen and paper! You have more confidence in my memory than I do."

I nodded, smiled, and then rattled the numbers off.

He shut his eyes, repeating the numbers to himself a few times. "Alright! Got it!"

Weeks later, he got his breakfast date. He brought me to a restaurant where his brother, Matthew, worked. The conversation went well, and after Paul dropped me off at home, he sent me a text telling me that I now had a friend for life, and he meant it. There was quite a bit of difference between us: We grew up on separate continents, with different cultures, and were from two different races. Yet, none of that bothered us. We focused on the many things we had in common and the differences just interested us more. Paul and I became regulars at the coffee shop where we met, talking late into the night about everything from politics to God.

On February 14th, Paul asked if I would join him for dinner. I agreed and enjoyed a nice evening with him. After dinner, we played some music and danced a few slow songs in his living room. Paul pressed his nose against my forehead and held my hand softly as we swayed to the music that night. There was nothing shy about the way he looked at me. He looked right through my eyes, right into me, as if he was willing to have me look right into him.

From that night on, the two of us were permanently connected. For the first time in my life, I felt a love that made me feel as free as a falling stone. It did not take us long to realize that we wanted to spend the rest of our lives together.

Because I was now as close to Paul as I could get, I let out my secrets, one by one. Most days, my painful stories came out effortlessly. The tenderness in his heart and his compassion made it feel natural to open up to him. The night I told him about the death of my parents, my words worked into him, changing him physically. He stood there, his skin drawing tighter across his face, sealing his gaze, and I sobbed in his arms. He told me how strong I was and reminded me how much love I had in me despite being hurt so deeply.

Then came the day I had dreaded for many years, the day I shared a painful secret that haunted me for years: sexual abuse—the sexual abuse only I and my abusers knew about. Unsure of how it would change our relationship, I laid it all out. While giving the details, Paul's tears flowed. Instead of saying anything, he wrapped his arms around me and pulled me tightly against his chest. With his chin pressed down on the top of my head, he whispered something that I couldn't hear. Later in the night, I asked him what he had whispered when he embraced me.

He told me that he was asking God why a child should have to suffer like I did. That night, he swore to love and protect me as long as he lived.

A few weeks later, on a late evening walk in the park, Paul told me one of the reasons compassion came so easily to him. He said it derived not only from his ability to put himself in other people's shoes, but also from the heartache he experienced in childhood. His family suffered through a chain of physical and sexual abuse that stemmed from their church. At a young age, his oldest brother was raped and beaten by a clergyman and other members of their congregation. The older brother then acted out those same horrible abuses on Paul and his siblings. In some ways, this battle brought him a deeper understanding of the same abuse I grappled with. In our mutual pain, we consoled each other and mended.

Despite these challenges, Paul is open-minded and our love is true and pure. His thoughtful eyes sparkled the first time he told me how much he loved me.

"I have to tell you what's on my mind," he said. I opened my eyes widely, gazing at him. "You are like an old friend. I feel like I've known you for years... and you know my heart so well."

He could not endure my persistent stare and glanced away now that our conversation went silent.

"I love you," he announced. "I've loved you from the day I met you. And I want to experience the rest of my life with you."

Noticing his shyness, a thin, silent smile surfaced on my lips and warmth filled my body.

"I realize that's a lot to take in, but it's the truth," he added while holding my hands.

"Well, the truth is I love you just as much," I said, raising his chin.

Months later, we were engaged. We remained in Spokane the next couple of years. I went on working at schools and started a master's program at EWU. Paul finished his degree at EWU, graduating with honors. Shortly after, I introduced Paul to Auntie and Uncle, and their conversation went the way I anticipated—so calm and unhurried I could hear the fire crackle and the creaks in the walls and floor. Like a father, Uncle took Paul to play golf, and on our way home, Paul reported most of their talk was about our relationship. Paul assured Uncle that his devotion was honest and he would respect and care for me. Paul left their home feeling close to them and swiftly developed a respect and fondness for them both.

We lived across from the Spokane River and spent our nights listening to its soothing sound. It reminded me that we are so much like a river, sometimes at odds, sometimes still, but always changing. As my heart slowly healed, I attended counseling and EMDR therapy, a treatment technique to combat PTSD and disturbing memories. Paul urged me to pursue my public speaking, and that summer we set up a fundraiser for Msaada, an organization that supports Rwanda's orphans and widows that we continue to partner with to this day.

Nights before my speech, Paul and I sat down at our table to work on the details. I looked down at my notes, then at him, and said, "All of those years, I felt trapped, as if I was in dark space. Like my voice was buried in darkness, and every word that ran off my tongue or through my head slipped into that darkness." Paul rose up, kissed my forehead, and embraced me. When I gave my speech, I opened up like I had never done before. I told the audience the truth about my experiences and I told them about my challenges to forgive. When I finished, the room was hushed. Time seemed to stand still as the eyes of the crowd were fixed on me. When they started clapping, I locked eyes with Paul, his eyes watery and soft. Offstage, he embraced me and whispered in my ears, "My love, you are no longer just a voice in the darkness."

After we graduated, we moved to Texas where I serve to this day as an adoption counselor. I dedicate my days advocating for foster and orphan children here in the United States as well as other parts of the world. While the adoption system still has its challenges, I have been able to use my unique perspective as a way to connect with potential adoptive parents and children.

However, one of the ongoing challenges has invariably been to help parents recognize what it means to adopt an orphan or a child in a Child Protective System. The kids in custody may look like ordinary children on the surface, but many feel the pain of loss and separation from their loved ones as they likely endured emotional, physical, and sexual abuse. These children don't all look the same; they come from various ethnic and social environments. Nevertheless, they all have one thing in common: they want nothing more than a forever family, a family they can claim as their own, a family that will protect and love them despite the perceived challenges they come with. They want a family that will not give up on them, harm or neglect them the way they were harmed and neglected in the past. These are the children that keep me up at night and keep me motivated.

Paul and I are married now and have a beautiful baby boy of our own. We call him a miracle baby because when we had our first ultrasound, the doctor announced, "All looks good...except..." then paused. When she said "except," my heart skipped a beat and I glanced at Paul, who froze. "Your baby has a condition called Fetal Hydrops that produces fluid buildup in the body. He has it in his head, chest, and neck."

Inside I screamed, but I managed to stay composed as we asked follow-up questions. The physician described this condition as rare and said, "If all you have is three months with your baby, then that's what you have." My mind raced and my tears fell as Paul hugged me tightly. That night, we traveled home and reflected on what the doctor said. I worked to remain calm and not stress our little boy so I prayed day and night, using spiritual muscles I had developed during the darkness of the genocide. I said the same prayers I prayed when I asked God to save my siblings. I asked for miracles, and I felt like God heard my plea. We traveled to Austin to get a second opinion. The second doctor did another ultrasound that showed the fluid had increased in all three chambers and concluded our baby had only a slight chance of survival. I wept the entire trip back to Houston, but we continued praying. The next few months, we saw a specialist for high-risk pregnancy. This time, the ultrasound revealed no fluid in any of the parts of his body. I shouted with joy at the report, while the doctor added, "I was concerned when I received your referral and your baby's report, and I don't understand how this transpired." I glanced at Paul, who shared the same cheerful smile on his face. "This is God offering us another miracle," I said.

We celebrated, but at 28 weeks, after a routine ultrasound, I was admitted to the hospital because the fluid returned, this time around his heart and other organs. After ten days in the hospital, a surgeon told me our boy had a 3-20 percent chance of living but kept me in bed and treated me with magnesium and steroids to assist his underdeveloped lungs in the event he came early. That morning I cried, but kept praying and reached out to friends and every church I have ever been a member of, begging them to pray for our guy. The following day, many tests were run. Without explanation, the fluid diminished. And on a clear morning in September, our little miracle child was born. We wept tears of joy looking at our handsome little Samuel James for the first time. From that day forward, we learned we had a fighter on our hands.

Uncle and Auntie live a short distance from us, and Uncle continued the Rwandan tradition of naming grandchildren, naming our little boy "Kaze," which means, "we welcome you."

While Paul and I continue to support vulnerable children and widows, our aspiration for Samuel and future generations is simple: love your neighbors actively and tirelessly regardless of their ethnicity, religion, or cultural background.

Top: Our graduation from Eastern Washington
University
Bottom: Paul and I with our beloved Uncle Jimmy.

Myself, Paul and Samuel at our home in Houston, TX

Acknowledgments

With great sincerity, I would like to thank God. I am thankful to be alive and realize that my journey would not be imaginable without the presence of God in my heart.

To my husband, Paul: I am eternally grateful for you. Thank you for your patience and for the countless hours you spent writing this book with me. You are the therapist I needed in this journey. Thank you for the thousands of intimate questions you asked while trying to understand my experience and how to bring this book to life. I praise God for the wisdom and insight you brought to this book and my life. You have been my shoulder to cry on, my best companion, and my closest adviser. I will always treasure you.

To Kerry and Scott Hasenbalg: First, thank you for treating me like family. Your support, affection, and generosity have changed my life for the better in so many ways. Your kindness allowed me to trust again and helped me begin a healing path. Kerry, thank you from the bottom of my heart for writing an incredible "Foreword" and for being a sister in the truest sense of the word. You and Scott have been our guardian angels!

Special thanks to my "other parents," Dr. Fred and Winnie Rurangirwa: I will never forget the day you both told me that your home was my home and assured me that I will always be treated as your daughter. As a young orphan then, those words meant the world to me. Your love and comfort over the years has made a positive difference in my life in ways I can't explain or that can be measured. Also, thank you to the Rurangirwa children, especially Linda and Jackie Rurangirwa, for your encouragement and support. Linda, your feedback and support mean a great deal to us both. We love you!

To Dr. Francis and Judy Ruvuna and your children: Thank you for your love. Lisa, we miss your beautiful laughter!

To Shalita Willis: Paul and I truly appreciate the amount of effort, time, and thought you put into our manuscript. Your sound advice and thorough attention to details has truly made our work better. Thank you for your excellent suggestions, feedback, and for your words of encouragement.

To Nathalie Ndahiro and your little angels, Zizo and Jamilah: Thank you for your love, support, and belief in me. You are a great sister!

To Rachea Allert: First, thank you for your kind heart. I appreciated your encouragement in finishing this book and for supporting me to educate the general public about the atrocities of the genocide. I treasure our friendship.

To Candice Ebai Ekwoge: Thank you for motivating me to finish this book and having faith in me. You are like a sister.

To Brittany Beth Moore: Thank you for your kind words of support and friendship. You are such a beautiful soul!

To Vestine Mukarusine: Your genocide survival story moved me to tears, and I am inspired by your kindness despite the harsh reality you experienced. We love your family.

To my dearest Mary Mukamihigo: I appreciate your faith in the Lord and countless prayers!

To Monica and George: Thank you for your friendship and your thoughtful feedback on the manuscript.

To Nathalie Green: Thank you so much for your willingness to read the manuscript and for your feedback.

To Jeff Prachyl: Paul and I appreciate your creative skills on the book cover.

To Console Nishimwe (Author of *Tested to the Limit*): Thank you for your inspiration. I love you like a sister.

To Madalyn Stone, our diligent editor: Paul and I cannot thank you enough for being patient with us while we were trying to finish this book. You improved our manuscript and we are grateful for your professional work.

To my siblings: Aimable, Jeannette, Cyiza, Michael, Teta, Teddy, Kayishema, and Byiringiro: I thank God for keeping you all alive. Thank you for providing me with continuous support and the faith to go on. If not for your unconditional love, I don't know where I would be. We share so many good memories, sorrow, and unspoken pain, but my prayer is that through this memoir, you will be able to discover the details I am still afraid to share with you. I am proud of every single one of you, and I love you all so deeply!

To my many friends and family that were not mentioned, yet who have influenced me in one way or another--I love you and treasure you!

To Grace Church, KSBJ prayer group, Celebration Church in Austin, and ACF-Austin Christian Fellowship: Your prayers and words of encouragement soothed my troubled heart during my high-risk pregnancy. Thank you for being there for us. And a special thanks to Keeley Schafer from Grace Church, who constantly checked on me.

And last but not least, thank you, my son, my sweet Samuel "Kaze" James; you are an angel, and you bring us so much joy and happiness. Every day, I thank God for your life. Thank you for fighting so hard to be here.

—Jeanne Celestine Lakin

To my lovely wife, Jeanne: Thank you for allowing me to help tell your story to the world. Your affection, loyalty, tenderness, bravery, and intelligence will always affect me and push me to be a better man. Knowing and loving you has been the greatest privilege of my life. Thank you for choosing me with all my shortcomings. I am blessed to be your husband.

To Dr. Susan Sterns and Gage Stromberg: Thank you both for your comments, observations, and assistance on the manuscript.

To Dr. Peter Shields, my mentor: Jeanne and I thank you for your reassurance and patience, for the time you put in on various readings, and the valuable feedback you contributed.

To Billy Kelly: Thank you for your comments and kindness. You are one of the most selfless humans I know. It is an honor for Jeanne and me to support your work with Msaada.

To Uncle Jimmy: Jeanne and I will never forget your love and encouragement over the years. We love you and miss you deeply.

To my family: James Paul Thomas and my little brothers, Jay, Matty, Michael, Brian, and Timmy. Thank you all for being in my corner.

—Paul Lakin